HEAVEN IS A
LONG WAY TO GO

T Joe Willey

authorHOUSE®

AuthorHouse™
1663 Liberty Drive
Bloomington, IN 47403
www.authorhouse.com
Phone: 833-262-8899

Published by AuthorHouse 09/25/2020

ISBN: 978-1-7283-7334-8 (sc)
ISBN: 978-1-7283-7333-1 (hc)
ISBN: 978-1-7283-7332-4 (e)

Library of Congress Control Number: 2020917386

CONTENTS

FOREWORD
RONALD L. NUMBERS

For over a half-century T. Joe Willey was one of my closest friends. We met in the late summer of 1965, when I moved to Berkeley to enroll in the Ph.D. program in the history of science at the University of California. Joe had already been there a year, working on a doctorate in neurophysiology. By chance we ended up living a block from each other, which facilitated our friendship. Although Joe attended the large Grand Avenue Seventh-day Adventist church in Oakland, and I chose to join the struggling Adventist church in Berkeley, we bonded over our common interest in contemporary Adventism, as well as an enthusiasm for rare books in the history of science and for Sunday volleyball games with fellow Adventists.

Needless to say, we frequently discussed the denomination's antipathy toward evolution and its embrace of so-called young-Earth creationism. One evening in the late 1960s Joe and I traveled to Stanford University to attend an illustrated lecture by an Adventist professor on the famous sequence of fossil forests in Yellowstone National Park, which most Adventists attributed to events associated with Noah's flood. The speaker persuasively showed that forests had been deposited over at least 30,000-35,000 years. When we returned to Berkeley that night, Joe and I remained in my car for hours, first agonizing over, then finally accepting, the disturbing likelihood that a young Earth conflicted with the best scientific evidence. This prompted both of us to reject the authority of the Adventist prophetess Ellen G. White, who claimed to have seen in vision that God had created life on Earth in six literal 24-hour days and pointedly rejected the notion of "infidel geologists" who supposed that God had effected the creation over "vast, indefinite periods, covering thousands or even millions of years." Before dawn we had concluded that if we were willing to slide down the slippery slope for 35,000, years, we might as well go the full 2.8 million years. Before Joe left Berkeley soon thereafter, he and I pledged that we would always remain friends even if one of us or both of us left the church.

Following the completion of our degrees at Berkeley Joe took a position in the Loma Linda University School of Medicine and I joined the history department at Andrews University in Berrien Springs, Michigan. In the spring of my first year at Andrews, I arranged for Joe to stop by and give a lecture on the theological implications of his research, which he was conducting that academic year with the Nobel laurate Sir John Eccles. While visiting me, Joe learned that I was not happy teaching at Andrews, which was then taking a sharp theological turn to the right.

On returning to Loma Linda, Joe persuaded the dean of the medical school, David Hinshaw, to hire me for a vacant position in the history of medicine and to help design a six-year B.S.-M.D. program for students just out of high school. This never materialized; so I filled my time writing a book about Ellen G. White as a health reformer. To my surprise, I discovered that she had borrowed virtually all of her ideas from other reformers, often copying their writings word for word. I shared my early findings with Joe, my friend Vern Carner, and my cousin Bruce Branson. Unfortunately, Joe casually left my manuscript lying around his office, which an associate "borrowed" and copied. Before long copies were circulating widely and church leaders were aroused. Ironically, when Robert Pierson, president of the international church, Neal C. Wilson, president of the North American Division and chairman of the Loma Linda board, and Vice President Willis Hackett, a family friend, visited Loma Linda to investigate the scandal, they insisted on meeting privately with Joe, at least once in a motel room. In early July, 1974, Wilson informed me that the board had voted to sever me from the faculty.

Soon thereafter the Loma Linda University Church, of which I was nominally a member, brought up my name as a candidate for being "disfellowshipped," Adventist speak for excommunication. Joe, who was then serving on the board of elders, inquired about the grounds for my dismissal. Adultery, he was told. My wife and I had indeed separated, but as Joe informed the board, I was the "innocent party." He thus salvaged my membership in the Adventist church. Coincidentally, Joe and his then-wife were also experiencing difficulties, which his mother-in-law blamed partially on his friendship with me. Joe informed her of our pact to remain friends forever, and soon thereafter his marriage ended.

Among the many bonds Joe and I shared was the fact that we were both sons of Adventist ministers. Mine remained conservative to the end, but Joe's father, Thomas O. Willey, grew increasingly disillusioned with the church. I discovered this firsthand while conducting research for my book on Ellen G. White, subsequently published as *Prophetess of Health*. After retiring from the ministry Tom had moved to Loma Linda, where in the evenings he worked in the university library, specializing in the collection of White documents. He proved to be very supportive of my findings, which didn't seem to surprise him in the least.

Joe left Loma Linda University in 1985 to devote his considerable energy to developing professional employer organizations (PEOs). His success in this endeavor provided him with an income that most academics would envy. Much more significant for our friendship was his late-life ambition to become a historian. He filled his "office" in Loma Linda with books and traveled the country in search of sources. To improve his writing skills he even enrolled in the Writer's Workshop at the University of Nebraska Omaha. This book is one result of his effort to reinvent himself as a historian. I often read Joe's prose and gently encouraged him. One such effort was his essay "Death and Burial," in *Ellen Harmon White: American Prophet,* ed. Terrie Dopp Aamodt, Gary Land, and Ronald L. Numbers (New York: Oxford University Press, 2014), pp. 295-304. In it he convincingly showed that the public burial of the Adventist prophet had been a ruse, apparently in the naive expectation that God would take her directly to heaven. About 2014 Joe and I collaborated on two articles examining Adventist attitudes toward dinosaurs (skeptical) and the central role played by the ex-Adventist Earl Douglass in establishing the Dinosaur National Monument on the border between Utah and Colorado. Our research in both archives and in the field resulted in "The Adventist Origins of Dinosaur National Monument: Earl Douglass and His Adventist Roots," *Spectrum* 43 (Winter 2015): 48-56; and "Baptizing Dinosaurs: How Once-Suspect Evidence of Evolution Came to Support the Biblical Narrative," *Spectrum* 43 (Winter 2015): 57-68. By this time Joe's health was failing, and he required frequent dialysis treatments.

The last time I saw Joe was at his Celebration of Life, organized by his wife, Barbara, and children in January 2018. Joe was visibly failing, but he seemed thoroughly to enjoy the event, especially when reminiscing and listening to reminiscences. He died a little over a year later. To the end, our pact of friendship remained unbroken. I miss him enormously.

Postscript: While preparing this brief essay, I received some fascinating genealogical information from an old Berkeley friend of Joe's and mine, Miguel Kelley. To my great surprise Miguel demonstrated that Joe and I were eleventh cousins! Joe's great-grandfather John Cowin, whose name appears frequently in this volume, was an eighth cousin of my great-grandfather Elias Elijah Numbers. I think Joe would have found that fitting.

Ronald L. Numbers is Hilldale Professor Emeritus of the History of Science and Medicine, University of Wisconsin-Madison.

SIXTIETH HIGH SCHOOL REUNION
CHAPTER ONE

> "But the truth is that you reach a stage, whether you are a believer or an unbeliever, when you are no longer making up your mind on a purely rational basis. It becomes a matter of life, and how individuals wish to lead it, and whether temperament or experience makes this 'deep' kind of life something which appeals to them." A. N. Wilson, *God's Funeral* (New York: W. W. Norton & Co., 1999).

My father, Thomas Odland Willey, was born on a North Dakota homestead in 1910. He never felt a greater affection for any other place. Before his homesteading grandfather settled on this land, Native Americans, buffalos, gophers, badgers, and coyotes roamed the grasslands. The area was without trees and scattered by sloughs that collected water in the spring. A variety of ducks and geese raised their families on the edges of these waters.

It was a landscape shaped and etched by glaciers, the last of which retreated about 12,000 years ago. These glaciers scraped and dug their way from Canada across North Dakota, leaving rocks; rocks of all sizes and intermittent hitchhikers (called erratic boulders). Some of the rocks were as large as a small cabin and weighed up to ten tons. The farmers picked up the smaller rocks, carried them by stone boats (heavy sleds) and deposited them at the edges of the fields. The larger, more difficult rocks were left in the fields and can still be seen with crops growing around them. As the glaciers receded, they left behind great chunks of ice which, as they melted, created water-filled potholes. Many of these potholes or sloughs have been filled in and farmed over.

The homesteaders who broke the soil to begin farming for the first time confronted many challenges. Winters were cold and harsh. Summers were hot and humid. Spring and autumn were the only bearable seasons. By late spring there were spates of mosquitos, flies, swarms of grasshoppers, and army worms. Farmers put on mosquito netting and covered their horses with blankets.

Uncluttered vistas stretched for miles under a wide, deep blue sky. The wind blew nearly constantly from Canada bearing huge fluffy cumulus clouds. If you liked solitude this was an attractive place. As the area was settled, homesteads were spread out about a mile or two apart, usually with a barn, a two-story house, several smaller buildings, a garage, chicken coop and sheep or cow shed. The buildings were often positioned back from the road with a mailbox marking the entry into the farmstead.

Road Trip to North Dakota

In June 1987 my father asked me to drive him to his 60th high school reunion in Mohall, North Dakota where he had grown up. He considered Mohall, which was about eight miles from the farm, to be his hometown. All seventeen of his class were still living and planned to attend. It was also Mohall's 75th anniversary. At the time, he lived near me in Southern California. "This is going to be my last reunion, maybe even the last time I get back to see the farm and my sister," he told me. Johnny Mach, his high school basketball coach, who would be coming, had coached the local all-star basketball team when dad played against the Harlem New York Globe Trotters in nearby Sherwood during their first tour of North Dakota in 1933.

The week before we left, I drove my pickup camper over to dad's house so that he could pack at his leisure. Every few days I'd go by to see how he was doing. He kept trying to slip in a few more things because he thought we might pass some half-remembered streams or lakes along the way. He organized his camping and fishing stuff into green Army surplus duffle bags smelling of anti-fungal agents. One bag had a wind gauge, compass, a WWII hunting knife, a Navy surplus device for measuring distances, a small tarp, a stormproof gas lantern, a baseball glove, an air mattress and pump, a 12-volt aircraft landing light, and odds and ends that supposedly made camping more comfortable and pleasurable.

Another surplus bag held fishing poles, reels, a small inflatable tube and waders, and rain gear. He was proud of the hand-held surplus sonar device that could measure the depth of a lake. When he bought this surplus device, it was advertised as a fish finder, but it never revealed any fish. After these bags were loaded, he brought out two tackle boxes stuffed with lures of various designs, colors, shapes, and sizes. Then he loaded a few books and tucked his portable coffee maker in the space under the table. God knows—he must have feared someone might sell his things at a yard sale while he was gone, or the Cold War would heat up and we'd be at war with Russia, and he'd have to live off the land. Maybe a man in his later years just needs a collection of things around him to feel secure. "You never know when you might need something," he was fond of saying.

I supposed that was true, but I protested; "This is not a fishing or sightseeing trip, nor are we stopping at National Parks along the way. We're going to a class reunion where you survived the Great American Dust Bowl—Remember?"

He waved me off by telling me about his fishing expertise and then secured his argument by saying: "Fish whimper at the mere mention of my name." We'd gone over this before, and we both knew it wasn't true. To him, fishing was more than tying a hook on a line and casting with a worm and a bobber. It needed to be done professionally, with a lure made from flashy fashions, feathers and bright colors. I listened to him talk, but near the end, I concluded that he needed someone to rule over and a strong ally to drive him to the reunion.

Two of my children, Mark and Christina, came along on the trip. As we drove, they often sat up front listening to their grandpa talk. He asked how school was going, what they were learning, and about their teachers and friends. Much of his conversation contained lighthearted banter delving into life and wisdom on growing up and family gossip. At one point I heard him ask my ten-year-old Mark if he "thought the decline of civilization was properly taught in his school." Another time, to stir things up, he said, "Society can't govern itself. What we need is a king. If the king doesn't do a good job—we drown him and get another one."

I did the driving, and he did the talking—dwelling on his earlier days, hard times, lack of rain, poor crops, cold winters, blizzards, even good times on the farm. How rapidly life zipped by, he exclaimed. He told stories about his early days as a farmer and about his two favorite workhorses, Jimmy and Topsy. We got an education about horse farming before tractors. "Topsy couldn't pull her share on the harness," he said.

"When you walk behind a plow, you had to twist the handles to maintain a straight line. It was tiring. You get to know each horse like your own arms. And nothing smells better than freshly furrowed ground with gulls following behind fighting over grubs."

When we stopped for gas, he'd get out, stretch, and start a jocund conversation with someone at a nearby pump or in the store. Within a few minutes, he'd have people talking about themselves on matters they hadn't thrashed out with their own pastor, much less an amateur psychologist or stranger like himself. At one gas station in Colorado, I heard someone ask him about the meaning of life. He'd shrugged it off; and said, "Just as I discovered the meaning, they changed it again."

The High School Reunion

After we arrived in Mohall, he metamorphosed into another person —like a butterfly that lifts its wings when it emerges from the cocoon. He had returned to his ancestral home, the grasslands, flax and wheat fields; everywhere he looked there were deep and long-abiding memories. Without prompting his thoughts, I tried to imagine how he felt trying to get back to the past. At times, I watched him looking around as if something was missing or out of place. His mother and father, for example, had died several years ago.

More than 1,300 people showed up at the reunion, doubling the population of the town. Dad's sister Genevieve, who lived in Kenmare thirty miles away, arrived in her son's red Corvette. Together they drove around town with the top down cruising like teenagers. They were clumsy getting in and out, and Genevieve jerked the car and squealed the tires shifting gears. Anyone watching them could see that old age was not as exhilarating as they thought it would be.

All of dad's classmates attended, including Clara Bohm, an old girlfriend who he had a crush on during his senior year. When Clara approached him, I saw her wink at me and heard her say, "Tom, I'd love to give you a kiss, but I'm afraid my lips might crack and fall off—I'm getting so old." Despite the danger, she placed one long-lasting smack on his cheek. He asked her if she remembered how overwrought he was when they broke up by telling her he was going to run away to Canada and work on the railroads—and "you'll never see me again." Clara looked over at me, winked again and with a big grin asked him; "Have you retired from the railroad yet?" Most notable among the male classmates were some large, suave, bald, deep-voiced farmers who would have looked good in a Shakespearean play or as bouncers at the door of a crowded tavern.

As we mingled in the gymnasium we stumbled into old timers from dad's past. He was having a ball trying to return to his younger self. As I tagged along, he'd introduce me as the "heir apparent." Dad was as happy as I had ever seen him. When he saw someone he knew, he would burst out in mirth and recognition. "Gemini crickets if it isn't" so-and-so. The weekend went by quickly, and I learned a lot about the man he used to be just by watching his reactions with his former friends and classmates. One classmate accused him of cheating and wanted his money back from playing poker when they were in high school.

On Saturday night there was a banquet in the gymnasium. The older graduates sat near the front of the stage to be honored. When dad was introduced, he stood tall, and I thought I saw him sticking out his chest. Maybe he wanted to be elected among the notable local aristocrats. He grinned from ear to ear.

Coach Mach sat next to him. When the coach shook dad's hand, I heard him lean over and say, "Tom, I have Parkinson's." His trembling was beginning to show. I saw an immediate streak of sadness enter dad's mind as the words settled in. "I'm telling you," he said to me later; "What a sad way for a great athlete to go. As a young man, he had it all! He could hit and field like any baseball player in the major leagues. I looked up to him and admired him very much. He was my idol!"

I met Skipper, who, although he had lost all his fingers to frostbite, still played on the basketball team. The teams allowed him to run with the ball for no more than five-seconds since he couldn't dribble very well. And I met Florence, whose mother pinned a decorative washcloth across her dress before going to school to keep the boys from looking at her cleavage. Then there was a boy nicknamed "Rabbit" who hopped when he ran in the foot races.

Parade Celebrating 75 Years of Progress in Mohall

On Sunday there was a parade down Main Street celebrating 75th years since the founding of Mohall. The parade was not long—it could have looped around on a side street to form an endless parade. All the pretty ladies qualified as one kind of queen or another. The classic cars in the parade carried two or three graceful ladies in ruffled white or yellow dresses waving to the crowd. Some had flowers in their hair. Dad said; "They all look like virgin swans." He didn't give away his secret for knowing these things. Signs on the sides of the cars read "Senior Class Queen," "Dairy Queen," "Wheat Queen," and "Queen of the Yellow Jackets."

Then came Lee Brothers, the John Deere dealer, driving a big green combine without the header. The heavy rubber-tread grasped the road like new tires not wanting to let go of the pavement. Further back, the Massey dealer showed off his big red harvester. Then a yellow combine made by Hollister came along. Among other floats were white and red fire engines, a rebuilt Farmall Cub tractor with new paint and decals, an ambulance flashing its lights, and an old truck bed devoted to the "Mother of the Year" with an antediluvian woman sitting on a bale of hay. The Elk Royal Canadian Band marched in the parade playing American Sousa marches. All told, the parade was a great success and displayed the pride and history of Mohall.

Dad mingled with the crowd by the curb shaking hands with the spectators and wearing a smile like a meadowlark—some he knew, most he didn't. He was in a good mood; the kind that covers up shame or any past wrongdoing. It was also one of his good-grooming days. He wore a black suit, pressed white shirt with cuff links and a red tie—the first indication that he was out of place among the wheat and flax growers. He had the look and style of a man running for governor of North Dakota. He could just as well have been the pastor of the Plymouth Congregational Church in Brooklyn, New York!

After the parade dispersed, and the garlands were scattered, it was time to return to California. Dad remained standing in the middle of Main Street like a child hanging on to his mother's apron when strangers come around. He stood there longing for adoration and belonging. Genevieve drove by and waved goodbye—still jerking the Corvette as she changed gears and headed towards home. At this point I could tell dad dreaded his own departure. This was probably going to be his last visit to the farm and neighborhood.

As we stood there, he noticed that the Piggly Wiggly grocery store and Rolofson General Merchandise had gone out of business, as had the creamery and Allen's Chevrolet and Hotel Richard. The bowling lanes were closed. He showed me where Mohall once had a brothel that was raided by the sheriff. The "modern" airport on the outskirts of town had a single hanger and three "crop duster" airplanes tied to the ramp. The tallest structures on the edge of town were the grain elevators along the railroad tracks. It looked like a town that a construction contractor started to build and then ran out of lumber and nails. Mohall, like thousands of perishing towns in the heartland of America, was showing the dust and peeling symptoms of creeping abandonment.

Finally, the surroundings relinquished their hold on dad, and we got in the camper and headed west on Highway 2 towards Williston, North Dakota. He had said his last goodbyes to the homestead, the barn, his nativity, the fields and sloughs of his youth, and finally his high school friends and acquaintances. For a few short, intense, vibrant days he had joyfully lived in his past. It was a sad departure knowing it was his last. Nothing could be done to change the nature of aging or the slaying of a vengeful past or even the ruthless pursuit of happy memories.

For miles, dad sat quietly on his side of the camper looking out the window as we passed well-groomed farmlands. It began to drizzle. It was the kind of day that discourages you from changing the world or searching for high-minded gratifications. The camper windows were rolled down—the tires splashed through puddles of water on the patchy roadway. We rode in silence, looking at the rainy countryside and the slick road. I tiptoed around my own mind thinking he was still absorbed with countless goodbyes and didn't want to be disturbed. I presumed many wondrous reunion fragments were still chirping in his memories—smiling and laughing and carrying on as joyful memories do.

But now that we were headed towards home, I wondered how a person agrees to his days being numbered. Is this how life ends—wobbling on down a wet road? Do you just vanish as you drive away from your ancestral home?

With about forty miles behind us dad abruptly broke out of his silence and exclaimed: "Pull off the road. I want to talk to you!"

He looked at me as though he'd just received a death sentence from a judge's bench. I was never one to debate him when he made a boldface demand like this. I began looking for a safe place to back onto. Maybe he just needed to relieve himself!

There was a dirt road spanning the ditch where farmers moved machinery back and forth from the field. I backed onto a level spot. Then he asked me to close the sliding window between the cab and the camper shell where my children were playing. The field across the road had just been mowed, and the wet alfalfa lay in rows giving off dark-minted smells.

The Accident That Killed His Little Brother

After I parked, he looked at me and began speaking in a voice overlapping with earnest melancholy. "I suppose," he said, "that you overheard someone talking about a family tragedy that happened to me before I went off to college." He dropped his head—there was a long pause. He seemed to be passing fragmented phrases back and forth in his mind and searching for what he might say next. I felt a sickening jolt; seemingly he was going to ask me to bear some misery he wanted to share with me.

"It happened when I was twenty-one. To this day it's still heartbreaking to talk about it. After the accident I spent two weeks in the hayloft in the barn in shame and remorse, not wanting to come back to the house." There was a long silence that I did not interrupt with a question.

Then he said, "Do you know anything about this?"

"I don't know what you're talking about?" I said. At the reunion, I never overheard anything about a family tragedy. A wet wind swirled through the open window.

"In April 1931," he began again, "George and I were down on grandpa's pasture shooting gophers with a new rifle. Around noon we headed for the house. As we came up the road, I took the rifle from George and aimed at a tin can on a fence post. During the morning we'd used up all of the 22 shells, except one. One shell! One lousy shell! It had fallen on the ground, and George saw it in the mud and cleaned it and put it in the chamber. Within a split second, after I pulled the trigger, our seven-year-old brother

Billy jumped out of the tall grass to scare us. He was waving his arms above his head. (He'd played hooky from school, and we didn't know it.) One second either side of when I pulled the trigger would have made all the difference in the world. What's the chance of that happening?

"Billy fell backwards. At first, I didn't know where he had been hit. George ran over, picked him up, and carried him into the house, the blood streaming down his back. The folks rushed him to Minot's Trinity Hospital where he passed away the next day. The bullet had hit him in the temple."

I wondered why it had taken him a lifetime to get this off his chest, and I told him so. In all these years no one in the family had talked about this tragedy in my presence or with any other family members. As far as I knew dad had been an open book on everything. He didn't answer why it had taken him so long to talk about the event — he just kept repeating that if he could live his life over again, this was the one second he would change. Tears crowded his face; misery and regret overtook him. His feelings made his body slump in the seat of the pickup.

"After I give you more details you can ask any question you have about the accident, then after we're through talking don't bring it up again." It had taken him forty miles to prepare and unpack these words before sharing his grief with me.

Just suppose dad had never told me about this accident and a relative or friend of the family stood at the Loraine gravesite looking at Billy's marker, noticing that he only lived about eight years. They would never know the awful fact that he was accidently killed by a gunshot to the head. The only justification for such cloaking of the truth would be to avoid the long-lasting grievous pain it would bring to my father and family buried nearby.

What was it that made him fill in the void of his life this way? Had dad figured he had only a few months more to live? Had he been sitting there all this time thinking about what he was going to say? He talked about Billy's death as if it happened a week ago.

This distant calamity still owned him, and he emotionally carried the heavy weight of his little brother's dead body all the way into old age. Some of the time he had his hand over his mouth like he was trying to keep the sad disclosures from spilling out too fast. Near the end of our conversation, he took out his billfold and showed me a carefully folded yellowing newspaper clipping describing the accident. He'd carried it all these years.

Memories like these have their own way of telling the truth. And at least on one occasion, he told me that if he could have another go at life he'd "want to talk to the Lord first and try to work some things out beforehand."

I sat there trying to keep his sorrow from sweeping into my thoughts. He said some things that didn't make sense; it felt like we were there by the side of the road quietly waiting for the Apocalypse and the end of time. When he finished, he held the door open briefly to his memory and I asked him a few feeble questions while not wanting to add to his remorse or misery. I could not do anything about this tragedy beyond trying to understand its impact on my father's life.

Eventually, we got back on the road. The rain stopped. The hay and grain fields were darker. Most of the puddles on the road had dried. We've never talked about it again.

Introduction to the Book

The Willey homestead was just eight miles south of the Canadian border. It is abandoned now, slowly falling into the prairie and under dead tree branches and grasses. Pots and pans are scattered about in the yard. The clothesline poles are leaning over. A few old religious books are strewn on the floor in the farmhouse, and tattered curtains blow through broken windows. Raccoons have taken up residence upstairs. Rusty machinery is scattered in the grass on the other side of the windbreak near the barn. My father is gone, too. Having desired cremation, he obviously wasn't planning to go anywhere after death.

When I contemplate this family tragedy, I imagine mice tracks on the floor of the abandoned granary east of the barn. All you can see are the dusty trails, nothing of the mice that hide in the cracks of the walls and under the floor. Time has a way of erasing harsh and awful memories, even good ones, leaving only faint traces.

The high school reunion occurred more than thirty-years ago. Since then I've had time to reflect on the wonderful times with my father—going to baseball games, family gatherings, camping with my boys and fishing in crystal clear lakes of the High Sierra, spending time next to the Pacific Ocean, summer hiking in Yosemite, and going to see dad at his home. He had a warm, witty and friendly nature. His memories were like a large, open crate that he could handily pull down from the attic of his mind.

My father retired as a Seventh-day Adventist minister following over forty-years of preaching. I did not hold this against him. During retirement he worked part-time in the evenings as an assistant librarian at Loma Linda University helping to establish the Ellen G. White heritage resource room. I'd often go by to see him there in the evenings. Before he died in 1990, we had many broad-ranging discussions on religion and the spiritual engagement and limitations that Adventism plays in the life of a believer. He knew Adventism inside and out.

I made a video of him reminiscing while looking at family photo albums. He enjoyed describing these people as if they were a plaster cast of the reign of kings and queens. I have his correspondences with his father and other members of the family who asked him questions about what he remembered of the past. He was a history major at Union College during the 30s. His mentor was Professor Everett Dick, the well-known historian of homesteading in Nebraska.

Since my dad passed away, I've gone back to the North Dakota farmstead several times, and also to the home and farm where my mother grew up near Oakdale, Nebraska. I searched for records and the shadows and footprints of these early homesteaders, including how both sides of the family became Adventists. These records were abundant, along with regional history books about local peoples and events. I found financial archives in the attic of the farmhouse representing years of the farm operation. The courthouse contained records and old newspapers, and, of course, there are still neighbors who remembered my dad and mother and their relatives. (Some of the neighbors I interviewed were in nursing homes.) Also, I've taken the family picture album apart, looking for notes and trying to put faces and descriptions to each one. I knew from what my father told me that the family was severely impacted by several tragedies, not just the shooting of Billy. You will find these stories here.

This book reaches across four generations, beginning when the first family members immigrated from England and Europe to improve their lives. The theme this book is easy to understand. You could take about any family in this country, conduct the same intense scrutiny, and observe their origins, religious convictions, joys and hardships, and find similar circumstances and experiences.

During my research I thought it was important to explore the family's religious convictions to see how their beliefs structured their lives under the difficult conditions of pioneering and homesteading. In doing so I came to see how life and religion were intertwined. It was extremely important for them to believe in the Second Coming as an escape to "better conditions" in the future. Among the most sublime and exalted scenes in the Bible, Paul writes: *"And the dead in Christ will rise first; then we who are alive, who are left, shall be caught up together with them in the clouds to meet the Lord in the air; and so we shall always be with the Lord."* (1 Thess. 4:17)

This book took on new life when I scanned old newspapers and found how others lived in the same place and time. And as this project developed, I attended a writer's conference on Whidbey Island in the Puget Sound in Washington state. During the conference we were offered an opportunity to talk intimately about our projects with another attendee. I was assigned to a journalist who wrote speeches for the Governor of Alaska and articles for a newspaper. He was attending the conference to meet a literary agent and discuss a screenplay he was working on. As we were eating lunch, he asked about my project.

I told him I was writing "something" like a family memoir across multiple generations that involved the homesteading era (after 1862) in the Great Plains. As protagonists in the story, I cited the hardships from climate, prairie fires, blizzards, and lack of rain. Another protagonist was the economic conditions, e.g. the cost of machinery, the fluctuating price of wheat and corn, the railroad tariffs and the miller's buying power over the producers. I mentioned tragedies such as an accidental shooting death or suicide. He wanted to know how people coped with all of this. And I told him that deep religious convictions gave them the necessary strength and hope. He wanted to know about their religion, and this "hope thing" I kept talking about, and how it provided the power to "stick it out" under these hardships. I began to waffle, not going into details, but he pressed me to know why I was holding back about their religion. I didn't want him to think I was dealing with pagan iconography, the red dragon, the book of Revelation, or some mythical archangel.

I told him that this little-known backwater religion was not a mainline denomination but a spin-off from the Millerite prophecy that Jesus would to come back to earth in October of 1844. When the Second Coming didn't happen, I said, and the prophetic disconfirmation was obvious, the devotees went through a Great Disappointment they spiritualized the failed prophecy and established a framework to order their lives. He then inquired, "What was the name of this religion that fluttered out of the Great Disappointment?"

I told him they became Seventh-day Adventists, led by Ellen G. White, a prophetess, and others who began observing Saturday rather than Sunday as their Sabbath. They created, I said, an elaborate understanding of Christ's ministry in a heavenly sanctuary that involved judgment to determine who would be saved when Christ returned. They also believed God had called them specifically to obey His commandments to the point of perfection and to preach the gospel to the whole world. Only then would Christ come and deliver the righteous from earthly calamities and hardships.

The journalist to whom I was speaking thought that this return of Christ to gather up the saints was a marvelous idea, but he wondered what elements in the teaching and doctrines of the church would convince people that this was true and worthy of their commitment over so many generations? It seemed to him that this idea called for an overwhelming conviction that was shatterproof.

At this point he began confusing Seventh-day Adventists with Mormons and Jehovah's Witnesses. As I explained the differences and similarities, he stopped any further conversation and advised me to demonstrate in my book how this religion concerning Christ's return could stand up against prophetic scrutiny and the hardships of homesteading and farming. "People don't know anything about this religion." He emphasized that "This is the real story embedded in your book." The reader will want to know. That insight helped guide the writing of my book.

Somehow all the homesteading individuals in this book were able to accept "the message" that they had a benevolent, Divine Overseer with a wonderful exit plan contained in the Bible and the exhortations from teachers and preachers. In this Adventist story a women prophetess appears who had remarkable visions in which she traveled back and forth to heaven.

She kept telling her followers of God's glory after each vision and then went on to describe the "soon coming of Christ and the resurrection and the cheering hope of the Christian to join with their relatives." I could not determine with confidence whether our family accepted all the above – probably there was unspoken skepticism.

In the Adventist religion the world is hopelessly corrupt and must go through an apocalyptic purging. Fundamentally this means that Adventists are a world-rejecting religious movement. My ancestors were pilgrims, living with a fantasy of the soon coming where they would escape to a cosmic utopia. There they would experience no more sorrow, suffering, or death; and no grasshoppers, mosquitoes, droughts or sweltering dust. They still did not know what you would eat in heaven or whether you could skip choir practice to go fishing — they didn't need to know everything! To them Bible prophecy enables one to foretell the future and offer a convincing argument that the world is governed by Providence. The mind with a weak crust of reasoning can create a deep emotional world. This makes it possible to believe almost anything.

Christians share many beliefs, including requirements for salvation and the imminence of the Advent. In a recent survey almost 50 percent of evangelical Christians believe Christ will return sometime within the next 40 years. (Pew Research Center 2017). But this book is not about proving or disproving these second advent beliefs or the prerequisites for cosmic travel and eternal reward. But you will see that Second Coming interpretations have enormous elasticity and persistence.

It is the psychological effects of prophetic disconfirmation of the Second Coming that will be of special interest to readers. How, in the face of repeated prophetic failures and betrayals over the past two thousand years, did four generations of homesteading families sustain a vigorous and durable hope? How did they do it? In the process I'm certain you will discover how the Adventist faith attempts to glue certain ideas together to create a form of coherence.

WHEN TIME SHALL BE NO MORE

CHAPTER TWO

"I am fully convinced that somewhere between March 21st, 1843 and March 21st, 1844, according to the Jewish mode of computation of time, Christ will come." William Miller.

Christians have kept faith with the idea that the world is coming to an end. This faith extends all the way back to the origins of Christianity. Jesus hinted more than once that His Second Coming would happen during the lifetime of His apostles. Today, many identify with the highly provocative idea that the "end of the world is nigh." Recently, I saw a bumper sticker that read, "If you hear a trumpet, grab the wheel."

In a Gallup Poll 62 percent of Americans had no doubt that Jesus will come to earth again. Another 40 percent regard the Bible as "the actual Word of God," and hold that it contains no errors and should be taken literally, word for word. Another 80 percent believed that they will appear before God on the Judgement Day, and that daily good and honest faithful living, giving offerings, and attending church regularly, will prepare the individual for this final event. [1]

Apocalyptic belief systems renew themselves in ingenious ways that enliven and diversify the end-of-time narrative. When the time comes, the living righteous and dead in Christ will be "caught up together" in the clouds. Concerning this matter, the Scriptures are persuasive: *"Surely the Lord God will do nothing, but he revealeth his secrets unto his servants the prophets."* [2] Once the believer gets to heaven the book of Revelation takes over. *"God shall wipe away all tears from their eyes, and there shall be no more death, neither sorrow, nor crying, neither shall there be any more pain, for the former things are passed away."* [3] As the righteous depart, Satan and

---

[1] Paul Boyer, *When Time Shall Be No More* (Cambridge, MA: Harvard Univ. Press, 1992), 3.

[2] Amos 3:7.

[3] Revelation 21:4.

his demons, along with the multitude of the unsaved, perish in spectacular fires, plagues, wars, and earthquakes.

Herein is a story about how persistent and adaptable true believing Christians—all related by ancestry and marriage through four generations of homesteaders—continually confronted postponements of the Second Coming of Christ while at the same time living difficult lives on the Western frontier. The origin of these families reaches back to their immigration to America in the 19th century. We will follow them through each generation as they meet the plain fact that the world did not end and yet maintain their hope for an afterlife in heaven. They have been prompted like other Christians to go to extraordinary lengths to explain what seems to be misinformation about a Second Coming. It is an awkward problem. Some may think their faith would have been gravely tested by years of waiting for the Advent of Christ to no avail or that eventually the long wait would have resulted in fatigue or even rejection of their imagined redemption.

This story is relevant, not only for people of the same faith, but for all Christians. The promises of immortality and eternal life came to them, leaping out of the Scriptures as a welcomed gift bestowed through the death of Christ on the cross. But the Bible also told them to mortify the flesh in preparation for the Second Coming. This drove some into perfectionism. Their eternal life hinged on a redeemer, in this case the Son of God who lived a sin-free life, who was miraculously resurrected after dying on a Roman cross more than two-thousand years ago. Like Christ, they believed death and the tomb would not hold them forever.

If God and future glory did not exist, they reasoned, anything would be permitted and there was no epistemic reason or justification for living as pious and faithful Christians. It was important to achieve perfection and freedom from sin so that when the Son of God returned, he would call them to life again. With a limited and unfamiliar understanding of these concepts it may be difficult to grasp the thought of eternal life, of endless days stretching into eternity. This is quite unlike an earthly sojourn. In the Scriptures man's fleeting nature is likened to the grasses of the field or a holy war against the Devil and his minions.

It all came down to believing in the Bible and the promises of God. These promises appear as prophecies which are thought by believers to rarely fail. After all, failure would impugn God's integrity. If a prophet's divinations are not fulfilled, the prophecy is not of or from God, and the prophet is false.[4] But religious groups seldom organize around a single prophecy. With multi-prophecies, the group is likely to score a higher percentage of accuracy —not unlike betting on a few horses at the same time at the racetrack. Sociologists who study loyalty to a belief find that religious groups seldom follow a rational course of action under conditions of prophetic failure or faulty beliefs. [5] After an undeniable refutation occurs, it may take years for the devoted to abandon previously held "absolutes," if at all. During this time the logical mind is only a thin crust of reason and can be broken through by believing the great day of God Almighty at the end of the world will arrive soon to obliterate the Devil.

The Prophetess Joanna Southcott

This was certainly true in the life of the charismatic Joanna Southcott (1750-1814), born of a poor farmer in East Devon, England. [6] She had little education beyond the unceasing study of the Bible. Southcott joined the Methodist movement, but after pretending to be a prophetess, she was no longer welcome. She began hearing a "still small voice" glorifying the Second Coming.

Southcott's first book, *The Strange Effects of Faith*, launched her prophetic career. During the next thirteen years, she published sixty-five books and pamphlets and gathered 100,000 followers from all walks of life.[7] Spiritual warfare between Christ and Satan was central to Southcott's writings and teachings. She referred to this conflict as *The Great Controversy*.

Southcott's interpretation of Revelation 12:1 led her to believe she was the "woman clothed with the sun" who was to bring forth a messianic child

---

[4] Deuteronomy 18:21-22.

[5] Jon R. Stone, ed., *Expecting Armageddon: Essential Reading in Failed Prophecy* (New York: Routledge, 2000). See also, Paul Boyer, *When Time Shall Be No More: Prophecy Belief in Modern American Culture* (Cambridge, MA: Harvard Univ. Press, 1992).

[6] Frances Brown, *Joanna Southcott: The Woman Clothed with the Sun* (Manchester, England: Lutterworth Press, 2002), and James K. Hopkins, *A Woman to Deliver Her People* (Austin, TX: University of Texas Press, 1982).

[7] Others place this estimate around 20,000.

named Shiloh.[8] At age sixty-four Southcott claimed she was pregnant. [9] Even though she wouldn't allow a pelvic examination, a handful of doctors pronounced her to be with child based solely on her female intuition — the truth of her anticipated motherhood rested on her word. Her followers waited with keen anticipation to welcome the birth of the infant. The expected arrival was October 1814. By November her doctors were puzzled with the delay. On Saturday, December 24, a nurse standing near Southcott's side felt a swelling the size of a baby's head along her abdomen. The swelling suddenly disappeared after a sharp kick. Three days later Southcott was dead. She had instructed her followers to keep her warm for four days with hot water bottles in case she returned. If she failed to revive, doctors were to dissect her body and release Shiloh. No sign of pregnancy or the child was discovered on autopsy. Her uterus was the size and shape of a pear.

Disciple John Wroe gracefully rose to save Southcott's prophecy. First, he reminded the devoted that the doctors had found her pregnant. Indeed, many of her other specific prophecies had come true. For example, she foresaw the financial crises in England. Returning to the messianic vision, he told the believers that Shiloh had been taken directly to heaven from the womb for further education. Wroe proclaimed that Shiloh was alive and would return sometime around 1820 after receiving instruction in heaven. When this date failed the group resorted to an indefinite period. By the end of the 19th century, the sect had largely disappeared aside from a few of the hard-headed faithful.

The fact that Southcott did not come back from the dead and that Shiloh's appearance also failed, caused great stress to the followers. A way had to be found to rationalize the truth and repair the tear in the prophetic fabric. The majority of believers were not yet ready to give up on a Messiah who provided a way out of poverty and death. So conveniently, the "birth of the child" was converted into a cosmic event validated by the empty womb. The failed prophecy was reinterpreted to an invisible spiritual occurrence that could no longer be tested. In the end "they believed what they needed to believe."

Strong community bonds help believers overcome prophecy failure. If the devoted are fully engaged in their beliefs, they reinforce each

---

[8]   An obscure figure mentioned in Genesis 49:10, also in Revelation.

[9]   Medically called pseudocyesis.

other during disconfirmations. But the cognitive dissonance can be unsettling in the face of failures. They attempt to "assuage present and future anxiety created by a disconfirmation." [10] Detractors fully expected the Southcottians to abandon their messianic designs because of such a blatant failure. But persistent religious beliefs answer recondite psychic needs for any group wrapped in "truth." These inscrutable impulses bear witness to the continuing affection of their hopes and beliefs about eternal life. Members resolve dissonance by obscuring or warping the falsifiable, accentuating valid truths, and renewing their efforts to unite the group.

The Millerite Movement & Second Coming

Following the War of 1812 in America, the Methodists, Baptists, and varieties of Presbyterians, along with other sects, added a plethora of religious enchantments and enthusiasms and apocalyptic expectations. This was also a time of Westward expansion, driven in part by a world-wide economic depression, along with the beginning of industrialization and other indications that the world was unraveling at the spiritual seams. Many people began pondering the battle of Armageddon and the end of the world prophesied in Daniel and Revelation.

By the 1840's there was a sudden commotion over the compelling odds that Jesus Christ was coming to the earth accompanied by a spectacular fire that would cleanse the earth. This was all predicted by a literal reading of the doomsday prophecies found in the Scriptures.

During this "great religious awakening," as it was called, some people were attracted to strong emotionalism and ecstatic demonstrations. It wasn't unusual to hear about miraculous interventions similar to stories in the Bible. Almost every day some kind of spiritual manifestation occurred: a healing, a vision, an angelic visitation, or other signs of Providence. [11] Some supernatural manifestations were so novel they were beyond credibility even for a believer in such possible spiritual manifestations. Everywhere, and on all sides, devils and demons were being "cast out." There were mysterious rappings in the walls and under tables. Mediums claimed

---

[10] Neil Weiser, "The Effects of Prophetic Disconfirmation of the Committed," in Jon R. Stone, 109.

[11] James Haskins, *The Methodists* (New York: Hippocrene Books, 1992), 81.

these noises were the candid tappings from evil angels, although some later confessed that they could crack joints in their toes or fingers to feign these sounds! [12]

During one Methodist revival meeting, a preacher's daughter stood up and testified that she had seen a deceased farmer return to life as an angel with a "garment hung lose about him of a shining silver color." It wasn't only the Methodists who reported these stirrings. A Baptist woman told how the hearth in her home opened to reveal hell and her front room was filled with the "glory of God, brighter than the sun at noonday." A Millerite prophetess in vision was struck by a ball of heavenly fire over her heart and fell to the floor. She found herself in the "presence of Jesus and of angels." [13]

Another woman, who had a vivid inner life, was afraid to close her eyes because she feared she'd wake up in hell. Joseph Smith discovered the Book of Mormon in the form of golden plates with the help of the resurrected angel Moroni, son of Mormon. There seemed to be no end to the fits, trances, and visions of the era. [14]

What emerged was a most unlikely character to set off a religious movement: a Baptist farmer by the name of William Miller (1782-1849). Born in a frontier home where his mother taught him to read, he only attended grade school for a few months between the ages of nine and fourteen. After conversion to the Baptist Church at age thirty-two, Miller began an earnest study of the Bible starting with Genesis and using Cruden's Concordance for obscure passages.

By the time he got through Daniel he was ready to preach about the end of the world. He interpreted the cleansing of the heavenly sanctuary in Daniel 8:14 (the 2300-day prophecy) to indicate the return of Jesus Christ followed by the purification of the earth by fire. Following sincere methodical calculations, he concluded that the destruction of the world would occur

---

[12] Nancy Rubin Stuart, *The Reluctant Spiritualist*, (Orlando, FL: Harcourt, 2001).

[13] Ross Goldstone, "Early Adventist and Charismatic Worship Experiences," *Trans-Australian Union Discernment*, a publication of the Seventh-day Adventist Church in Victoria, Australia, 1999.

[14] Ann Taves, *Fits, Trances, & Visions* (Princeton, NJ: Princeton Univ. Press, 1999).

sometime between 1843 and 1844. His message was simple. "Repent and prepare for Christ's literal return to earth. He is coming soon." At first, Miller's preaching only attracted uneducated farmers in small rural churches.

But then Miller met Joshua V. Himes (1805-1895), a young energetic minister in the First Christian Church in Boston. Together they launched the Millerite, or Advent, Movement that vigorously proclaimed the Second Coming of Christ. Their prophetic message, which swept through the Northeastern part of the country, was a distinctly American phenomenon. Himes established *The Midnight Cry* and *Signs of Times* publications and later became a prominent leader in the Advent Christian Church.

When Christian churches refused to let Millerite revivalists use their places of worship the Millerites turned to outdoor tents, camp meetings, and public buildings to spread their message. At every event they hung large cloth banners depicting various beasts with wings and multiple heads — unknown to biology, but vividly described in Daniel and Revelation. There were also illustrations of the "Four Horsemen of the Apocalypse" carrying sickles and balances for harvesting the wicked. A chart with a timeline was used to show when the world would suffer the seven last plagues.

These Millerite preachers knew how to preach to sensitive ears. They didn't stand motionless using words that froze on their lips, coldly plodding on like a mathematician calculating the distance to the moon. No, these revivalists came marching into the congregation with Bible in hand singing, *"You will see your Lord a-coming!"* [15] In a short time, they had the listeners believing that the great day of God was near at hand. The preacher would exclaim, "I am a thousand times more afraid of lukewarmness and cold apathy than I am of the consequences of excitements and shouting." Then he'd strike his hands together over his head and shout, *"Glory! Glory! The Lord is a-comin."* Soon the preacher had the brothers and sisters on their feet, all shouting "glory!" "Amen and Praise the Lord!"

After the audience was sufficiently aroused they addressed the awfulness of sin and wickedness on the earth, "Do you sinners want to be redeemed and spend eternity with Jesus or do you want to feel the bite of the flames from Satan around your toes and shins?" Finally, the minister

---

[15] Gerald Wheeler, *James White: Innovator and Overcomer* (Hagerstown, MD: Review & Herald Publ. Co., 2003), 27.

made the alter call, "God is asking you to come down and give your heart and soul to him and repent."

With flowing tears and repentant hearts many came forward; many who did not come forward silently confessed at least something, even if it was a small thing. Few revivalists who came later could match the "fearful themes of eternity" these ministers cited to frighten the repentant into confession or cheer them on by proclaiming the certainty that Jesus was coming in a short while to take them home to a heavenly mansion where lions and sheep played in the field together. And when the dead in Christ joined them, they could see all their loved ones again. The preaching service ended with a farewell hymn *"Behold the Glorious Dawning Bright."* The people embraced and departed expectantly.[16]

As the climactic day in 1843 or 1844 approached scoffers and hecklers disturbed the Millerites' meetings. But this only reaffirmed to the believers the truth of the message. Those that accepted the message would be saved, and those that heckled would be lost. One New York legislator introduced a bill to postpone the end of the world until 1860! A farmer wrote a different date in black ink on a chicken egg and then pushed it back into the second hen (though he never confessed to the cryptozoology) and waited until the egg was laid a time. He carried it around claiming that God had delivered a new date for the end of the world. But all this fuss didn't change anything. The October 22, 1844 date was the correct one, and the dissonance of past dates that came and went were just that. Miller's followers were convinced that Satan, the "Prince of Darkness" was likely to do anything to hinder Christ from restoring the image of God in fallen man.

Unfortunately, the Millerites learned the hard way that the millennial kingdom could not be preached into position by human effort or by pushing forward the perfectibility of mankind, or even by re-positioning Christ in the sanctuary. Many who heard Miller preach correctly doubted that their days were numbered.

As October 22 approached clusters of adherents sang and prayed together, asking for forgiveness and repaying debts. Some gave their furniture, dishes, bedding, livestock, money, and goods to the poor, as if "a man with a coin in his pocket would be left behind." Shops were closed, and business was

---

[16] James White, *Life Incidents* (Berrien Springs, MI: Andrews University Press, 2003 reprint), 107.

suspended. Swearing, stealing, drinking and other bad behaviors nearly halted. Revelation said the angels were about to release the four winds which would cause earthly destruction never seen since the Great Flood of Noah.[17]

Others were terrified, especially those who were not secure in their repentance, or were lukewarm, or who were holding back skeptically. Children were apprehensive because they had never seen anyone go to heaven or seen fire and brimstone rain down from heaven. One little girl wondered what her mother would do when Christ came because, "thunder and lightning always made my mother faint dead away." A boy remembered telling his mother that, "as long as the world was coming to an end, why not kill all the chickens and hens, and have a good feed before the time came?" His mother sent him to his room to contemplate the solemnity of the last Great Day. [18]

Finally, the Great Day approached. With their faith resting on the Word of God the Millerites gathered on Tuesday, October 22, and spent the last hours anxiously expecting to behold the coming of the Lord in the clouds of heaven and the destruction of the wicked. Near Rochester a flagpole collapsed to the ground in mid-day without any wind. Was this a sign of the end? Believers took up positions on roof tops, in cemeteries, on hill tops, and haystacks. Several hundred gathered on the glacial-scarred rocky outcrop known today as "Ascension Rock" near Miller's farm in New York. Some farmers had not bothered to plant crops or prepare for the winter. The harvest lay fallow in the field.

Imagine the believers' joy and exhilaration as they waited expectantly for the return of Christ in the early morning hours. Imagine, too, their solemn apprehension when nothing occurred. The sun went down, and as the evening wore on and shadows stretched over the landscape, they recalled the midnight arrival of the bridegroom in Jesus's parable, and their hopes were revived. But, after midnight passed many began to weep and wonder if there were too many unregenerate or un-awakened souls on the earth for Christ to keep his word. Or was it because William Miller himself had not sold his farm?

After this dramatic failure, the Millerites faced a public image catastrophe. If they admitted errors in a literal reading of the Bible wouldn't

---

[17] Revelation 7:1, KJV.
[18] Clara Sears, *Days of Delusion: A Strange Bit of History* (Boston, MA: Houghton Mifflin, 1924).

that imply that they were murky in their understanding of the rest of the Scriptures? One preacher wrote, "Our fondest hopes and expectations were blasted, and such a spirit of weeping came over us as I never experienced before. We wept, and wept, till the day dawned." [19]

One repentant farmer picked up his weeping, brokenhearted wife and carried her into their farmhouse. A few hours later she passed away, still crying. They had waited all day and night in the cemetery next to the grave of their only son who had drowned the summer before. Both were hoping to see his resurrection and together they would join with the saints in the clouds.

Following this Great Disappointment, as it came to be called, the Advent followers were disillusioned and scattered. Deep sorrow enveloped wrapped around the devotees for weeks. To make matters worse, the Millerites encountered pent-up verbal abuse from neighbors, church goers down the street, young boys on the sidewalk, and unrepentant doubters. The press mocked them mercilessly. One man who rejected the advent appeal told his wife he thought he "should tar and feather Brother Miller for getting her to think she was leaving him without going through a proper divorce first." The October 22 Great Disappointment was truly devastating.

The Great Disappointment & the Aftermath of Prophecy Failure

In November 1844 the editors of the *Advent Herald,* a publication devoted to the movement, continued to show puzzlement and a touch of irrelevancy. Maybe it was "that first love" that could never be forgotten, or maybe they were tired and didn't know what to say. The *Advent Herald* explained:

> *We were not hasty in embracing our opinions. We believe that we were honest and sincere inquirers after truth. We obeyed our Saviour's command to search the Scriptures ... While we had the literal rendering of the Scriptures to sustain us our opponents endeavored in vain to prove that the Scriptures are not to be understood literally, although every prophecy which has been fulfilled has been so in its most minute particular.* [20]

---

[19] Paul Boyer, 81.

[20] *Advent Herald,* November, 1844.

After the disappointment the leaders of the Advent movement tried hard to focus on one message, "The Coming of the Lord." But the Evangelical Adventists found it difficult to return to their previous orthodoxy. They began to evolve diverging theological positions and succumbed to what might be called a spiritual snowball fight. Latent disagreements burst into the open and over time grew venomous and acrimonious. Sociologists see this as one of the face-saving strategies in the aftermath of cognitive dissonance found in prophecy failure. [21]

Proselytizing for new believers from former Millerite followers backfired, erupting in new periodicals and argumentative preaching, conferences, and prayer-meetings. Discussions on theological briers and thorns sprang up: holy kissing, feet washing, baptizing, visions and other charismatic gifts, the millennium, the 144,000, restoration of Jerusalem, annihilation of the wicked, the Trinity, "age-to-come," immortality, the divine or human nature of Christ, Seventh-day Sabbath vs. Sunday, secret sins, fate of the dead, and probation—in effect just about every religious connection to sanctification, human nature, and salvation one can imagine.

Evidently, the organized Protestant churches that the Millerites came out of had not properly settled these issues before the 1844 disappointment. After the disappointment, each religious group or advent publication claimed the others did not "have the truth" and were therefore apostate or of Babylon Christianity. By 1855 J. P. Cowles estimated there were "some twenty-five divisions of what the one Advent body was once." Over the next decades, they continued distancing themselves from each other or became lost in a forest of derelict doctrines. [22]

The largest group to coalesce from the failed Millerites were the open-door, or First-day Adventists. Elder Himes issued a call for a conference to be held in Albany New York in 1845 for those "who still adhere to the original Advent faith." Ironically, Himes made it known that the door was shut to the small group (not invited) who now believed in a "shut door doctrine." They also did not want visionaries, dreamers, revelators, discerning spirits, tongues, or other gifts within their group. The First-day

[21] Leon Festinger, Henry W. Riecken, Stanley Schachter, *When Prophecy Fails* (Minneapolis, MN: University of Minnesota Press, 1956).
[22] George R. Knight, *Millennial Fever and the End of the World* (Mountain View, CA: Pacific Press Publ. Assn., 1993), 232.

Adventists continued Sunday keeping, among other things, and avoided controversial doctrines such as the cleansing of the sanctuary and soul-sleeping theology found in the shut-door division. They resolved not to fellowship with any who created new tests as conditions of salvation beyond the acceptance of Christ and "a looking for and loving His appearing." [23] This division organized in 1860 as the Advent Christian Church.

Another group of former Millerites continued to hold preacher Snow's tenth day of the seventh-month interpretation of Daniel, believing no one had proven Miller wrong in his time calculations. (As a matter of fact, no one had proven him right either!) Since Christ himself had not returned maybe the whole prophecy was misguided. Sociologists believe that a group that experiences a severe disappointment in prophecy usually regresses to an earlier orientation.

That was what happened to a smaller division of the Advent movement that became known as the Sabbatarians. These people began keeping Saturday as the day of worship and not Sunday. Early members argued that the door of mercy had been shut and that only the faithful Millerites who had gone through the Great Disappointment had any hope of heaven (hence the name "shut door" Adventists). Some of these also practiced foot washing with both men and women and kissing. The Advent Christian fellowship labeled them as fanatics.[24]

The two groups rapidly gathered converts. Soon after the prophecy failure, an uneducated farmer by the name of Hiram Edson had a vision (heaven was opened to him) while he was walking across a cornfield. He claimed he saw Christ and that Christ had remained in heaven; on Oct. 22, 1844 Christ had simply relocated from the holy part of the heavenly sanctuary to the Most Holy Place.

Edson and his friend O.R.L. Crozier accounted for the delay in terms of this relocation. The Second Coming was a cosmic, not earthly event. Out of this "corn field" vision grew the teaching that Christ ascended to heaven after His crucifixion to an archetype of the sanctuary of the Jewish people. Christ became the high priest in the most sacred part of that sanctuary in

---

[23] George R. Knight, 270.

[24] Malcolm Bull, Keith Lockhart, *Seeking A Sanctuary: Seventh-day Adventism and the American Dream* (Bloomington, IN: Indiana Univ. Press, 2007), 40.

heaven in 1844. And 1844 became the day of "Atonement." [25] The prophetic timing was right, but the expected event was wrong. Christ's Second Coming was still in the future and would not occur until the cleansing of the sanctuary in heaven was over. Thus, this Advent group accounted for the failed interpretation by citing an invisible matter that could not be tested. [26]

Visions and other "supernatural" communications from God influenced the Shut-door Adventists before they organized into a church in 1863. As many as five visionaries operated in the Shut-door group at one time, four of them women. Sister Clemons became a visionary, but a few weeks later another unnamed sister had a vision that showed Sister Clemons to be of the Devil. [27] Such people came and went. But one youthful visionary emerged who indisputably impacted what would become the Seventh-day Adventist Church. Her name was Ellen G. Harmon (White after her marriage to James White in August 1846). [28]

Prophetess Ellen G. White

At nine years of age, Ellen, living in Portland, Maine, was injured by a classmate who threw a rock that hit her in the face. She was knocked unconscious by the blow, and it was claimed, probably incorrectly, that she remained unconscious for three weeks. Her long-term health was affected by the accident. She suffered from dizzy spells and frequently fainted.

White experienced her first vision at age seventeen in December 1844 in the Haines home in Portland, Maine. Over her lifetime, she probably had 200 (some claim 2000) visions or "I was shown" communications, or as "the light God has given me," messages that made her known as the "Lord's messenger" and as the "Spirit of Prophecy." Early in her career she anointed and prayed over the sick and seemed to heal people. [29] When the visions discontinued around menopause, she had dreams interpreted as

---

[25] Jonathan Butler, "Second Coming" in *Ellen Harmon White*, Terrie Dopp Aamodt, Gary Land, and Ronald L. Numbers, eds. (New York: Oxford Univ. Press, 2014), 181.

[26] Note. EGW had a vision acknowledging this interpretation. See Loughborough, 128.

[27] George Knight, 256.

[28] Terrie Dopp Aamodt, Gary Land, and Ronald L. Numbers, eds., *Ellen Harmon White. American Prophet* (New York: Oxford Univ. Press, 2014).

[29] James White to Leonard Hastings, Jan 10, 1850, in Ronald L. Numbers, *Right Living.*

messages from God with authority equal to that of a vision. She became highly the respected of *The Desire of Ages, The Conflict of the Ages series, Steps to Christ,* and her main book, *The Great Controversy.* The majority of these books are considered theologically sound, despite being written as an eyewitness to the scenes in Christ's life.

Historically, the preponderance of women visionaries (prophetesses) far exceeded the number of males having visions and supernatural dialogs with angels and God, a fact the Biblical scholar Mary T. Malone attributed to women's inability to compete with males in church leadership positions. "We hear enough, however, to be assured that many women in many different parts of Christianity, still sought access to teaching, preaching and priestly roles." [30] Once the woman prophet obtains the privilege and occupation as a visionary she can exercise arbitrary power over men and consider them as inferior to herself. Marion Ann Taylor lists 180 women across two-millennia who have been extraordinary and fascinating in seeking a dominate role normally held by males in biblical interpretation. [31] Ellen White appears on Taylor's list.

By the church acknowledging Ellen White as the "Spirit of Prophecy," followers understood God to have two authorized channels of revelation: the Bible and the prophetess' Testimonies. She maintained that *"to man's unaided reason, nature's teaching cannot but be contradictory and disappointing."* [32] She explained, *"I have been shown that without Bible history, geology can prove nothing."* [33] Thus, in one fell swoop Ellen White heroically rescued "Literal Genesis," and a "Young Earth" dialog from the deep-time abyss of geological history.

> *I was then carried back to the creation and was shown that the first week, in which God performed the work of creation in six days and rested on the seventh day, was just like every other week. The great God in his days of creation and day*

---

[30]   Mary T. Malone, *Women & Christianity* (New York: Orbis Books, 2003), 113.

[31]   Marion Ann Taylor, ed., *Handbook of Women Biblical Interpreters* (Grand Rapids, MI: Baker Academic, 2012).

[32]   Ellen G. White, *Education* (Mt. View, CA: Pacific Press Publ. Assoc., 1903), 134. *Patriarchs & Prophets* (Mt. View, CA: Pacific Press Publ. Assoc., 1891), 114.

[33]   Ellen G. White, *Spiritual Gifts* (Hagerstown, MD: Review & Herald Publ. Assoc., Facsimile Reproduction of 1858 edition), vol. 3, 93.

of rest, measured off the first cycle as a sample for successive weeks till the close of time. [34]

Seventh-day Adventists continued to recognize the importance of Ellen White's role in reinforcing and through visions guiding the church during its early years and in helping to establish "present truth" (truth that pertains to the church's teaching and doctrines). Over time, the "Spirit of Prophecy" crucially advanced the Third Angel's Message through zealous missionaries, institutions, and far-reaching publications. The church's educational institutions and health message— often called the right arm of the message as it fostered world-wide medical institutions—helped grow the church. [35] Money from benevolence giving was shown to the prophetess as the way to advance the work of the church.

> *I saw that God could rain means from heaven to carry on His work, but He never would do this. It is contrary to His Plan. He has entrusted men on earth sufficient means to carry forward His work, and if all do their duty there will be no lack. But some will not heed the call for their means.* [36]

During one of her visions in February 1845, Ellen White met Jesus and asked him, *"If His Father had a form like himself. He said He had, but I could not behold it, for said He, 'If you should once behold the glory of His person, you would cease to exist.'"* [37] *God declares in Exodus, 'Thou canst not see my face, for there shall no man see me, and live.'"* [38] Moses almost got away with seeing God visibly. At the Burning Bush God revealed His holiness in a way it had never been shown before. [39] In a lengthy presentation at Battle Creek College to leaders of the Adventist church, White revealed that *"Christ himself had been*

---

[34] Ibid, 90.

[35] Howard Markel, *The Kelloggs. The Battling Brothers of Battle Creek* (New York: Pantheon Books, 2017).

[36] Ellen G. White, *Spiritual Gifts* (Hagerstown, MD: Review & Herald Publ. Assoc., Facsimile Reproduction of 1858 edition), vol. 2, 267.

[37] Arthur White, *The Early Years* (Hagerstown, MD: Review & Herald Publ. Assoc., 1985), 79.

[38] Exodus 33:20.

[39] Exodus 3:1.

appearing to her personally and privately as he had to Moses at the Burning Bush and to Paul on the Damascus Road. Well, while I was praying and was sending up my petition, there was, as has been a hundred times or more, a soft light circling in the room, and a fragrance like the fragrance of flowers, of a beautiful scent of flowers; and then the voice seemed to speak gently." [40] Unlike Ellen White, who visited heaven guided by an angel, the biblical prophets always remained on earth. "No Hebrew prophet, not even Isaiah and Ezekiel, had gone up to heaven. God had always condescended to come down to earth. " [41]

The Sabbatarians Become Seventh-day Adventists

Over the next few years, this small group of Sabbatarians formulated other doctrines. By 1849 Hiram Edson assured his fellow shut-door adherents that "the fullness of the Holy of Holies would last seven years," and Christ would soon be stepping out of the sanctuary to return to the earth, and that this would occur in late 1850. Joseph Bates, another influential shut-door Advent preacher, agreed with Edson that Christ would return soon but concluded that Christ's ministry in the sanctuary would end in 1851. Once again, the date was pushed forward. [42] But after these two failures in time-setting the group moved to an indefinite expectation for Christ's return, while always foreseeing it "within this generation."

As noted earlier, the shut-door division also believed in the sanctity of the seventh day of the week as the Sabbath for worship. They derived this idea from the Seventh-day Baptists and made the sanctuary service where the judgment takes place, and the Sabbath the centerpieces of their teachings. Soon the shut-door division attached an investigative judgment module to the cleansing of the sanctuary as a pre-Advent event. Eventually, these distinctive doctrines became a "test" for new converts. By 1856 the shut-door teachings disappeared since the years were passing and room had to be made for new converts.

---

[40] Frederick G. Hoyt, "Wrestling with Venerable Manuscripts," *Adventist Today*, June 2004, 12.

[41] Jonathan Kirsch, *A History of the End of the World* (San Francisco, CA; Harper San Francisco, 2008), 26.

[42] Julia Neuffer, "The Gathering of Israel: A Historical Study of Early Writings, pages 74-76," *General Conference of Seventh-day Adventists, Biblical Research Committee*, 1970.

Hiram Edson (1806-1882), Joseph Bates (1792-1872), James White (1821-1881) and Ellen Harmon (White) (1828-1915) [43] became early leaders of the Sabbatarian division known as the "White group". The Sabbatarians put great stock in printing periodicals and publishing books, thus following the lead of Elder Himes who had been the marketing expert for William Miller. They incorporated a publishing house in 1860, three years before the Sabbatarians organized as a church. After legally organizing they became known as the Seventh-day Adventist Church and would go on to become the preeminent "remnant" to arise out of the Millerite movement and the Great Disappointment.

Following the prophetess Ellen White's death in 1915, church leaders took her claims of seeing Jesus and visiting heaven to justify elevating her writings to verbally inspired, infallible messages from the throne of God (see chapter ten). Throughout the history of the church, teachers, Bible workers, ministers, administrators, and other believers were disfellowshipped for publicly denying or questioning White's verbal inspiration and inerrancy. However, by the 1970s she had lost some currency as a prophet when it was discovered that some of her writings had been borrowed from other religious writers.[44] (She denied plagiarism while she was alive.)

In view of the alleged literary borrowing, Arthur L. White, grandson of Ellen White told the church how his grandmother produced her writings:

> *Mrs. White guarded against reading that which might have a bearing on her initial presentation of a basic topic. In this light it is easy to understand her declaration in 1887: "I have not been in the habit of reading any doctrinal articles in the paper, that my mind should not have any understanding of anyone's ideas and views, and that not a mold of any man's theories should have any connection with that which I write."* [45]

---

[43] James White and Ellen G. Harmon were married by a justice of the peace August 30, 1846.

[44] John Dart, "Plagiarism Found in Prophet Books," *Los Angeles Times*, October 23, 1980. Warren H. Johns, "Ellen White: Prophet or Plagiarist?" *Ministry*, June 1982. Robert W. Olson, "Ellen White's Denials," *Ministry*, February 1991. Walter T. Rea, *The White Lie* (Turlock, CA: M & R Publications, 1982). T. Joe Willey, "The Great Controversy Over Plagiary: The Last Interview of Walter Rea," *Spectrum*, January 5, 2017.

[45] Arthur L. White, "Who Told Sister White," *Review & Herald*, May 21, 1959, 7.

Believers in the Spirit of Prophecy were reassured that Ellen White received divine inspiration in her writings through God-given visions and not by paraphrasing, borrowing, or serial plagiary from the works of others without attribution. Throughout her witness for God she claimed that "there is one straight chain of truth and not one heretical sentence, in that which I have written." [46]

> *As inquiries are frequently made as to my state in vision, and after I come out, I would say that when the Lord sees fit to give a vision I am taken into the presence of Jesus and angels, and I am entirely lost to earthly things.* [47]

The emergence of fundamentalism during the 1920's, changes in religious and moral consciousness, hard times during the Depression, financial upheavals, and wars around the world stimulated prophetic speculations and renewed hope for the Second Coming. As Samuel Johnson quipped: Depend on it, Sir, when a man knows he is to be hanged in a fortnight, it concentrates his mind wonderfully." The same can be said about ordinary suffering and dying while facing the challenges of living and the maintenance of subsequent hope for salvation through the Second Coming. A cultural belief (not unique to Adventists), such as a hope in an afterlife, relieves terror and provides a promise of literal immortality. Few want to die and "religion says you don't have to. Veracity and credibility aside, that is a powerful analgesic." [48] To be assured about the Millerite prophecy, God told Ellen White that Miller's 1844 date set for the Second Coming was not a failure, just the activity was misplaced.

This book relates the story of four generations of a homesteading family and how they clung to belief in religion and the Second Coming to sustain them through untimely family deaths and crop destruction by prairie fires and storms of hail and grasshoppers.

---

[46] Ellen G. White, *Selected Messages* (Takoma Park, MD: Review & Herald Publ. Assoc., 1958), II, 48.

[47] Ibid., I, 36.

[48] Stephen T. Asma, *Why We Need Religion* (New York: Oxford Univ. Press., 2018), 167.

SEEKING HEAVEN ON EARTH
CHAPTER THREE

"All religions, or so it seems, have something to say about death. People die but their shadows stay around. Or they die and wait for the Last Judgment. Or they come back in another form. The connection between notions of supernatural agents and representations about death may take different forms in different human groups, but there are always *some* connections. Why is this so? One straightforward answer is that our concepts and emotions about death are quite simply the origin of religious concepts. Mortality, it would seem, naturally produces *questions* that religion answers and *emotions* that it helps alleviate." Pascal Boyer, 2001. *Religion Explained.* (New York: Basic Books, 2001), 203.

I first met my grandfather, John A. Willey (1884-1967), when I was six years old. He had driven down from the farm to Minot, North Dakota, to retrieve me at the Great Northern Railroad station. On the way home, as we approached the farm about a mile away, he suddenly stopped. Surprised, I didn't know what was happening and he didn't say anything, but rolled down his window, opened the door, reached under the front seat, and pulled out a 30/30 Winchester rifle. He levered the first shell in the chamber, laid the barrel of the gun over the lowered window, bent over and commenced firing at a group of coyotes across the field. The coyotes jerked up, whirled around, and scattered in every direction. I could see the bullets hitting the ground in little puffs of dust. I put my hands over my ears and ducked down. America was at war with the Germans and the Japanese and my grandpa was at war with nature!

Grandpa put away the rifle under the seat and thought of all the sheep he had lost to coyotes. He began swearing: "Those dirty Dodos." That was when I first heard swearing from a relative. The memory carved a deep furrow in my mind as a dramatic way to begin life on the farm.

Innovations and Farming Evolution

I returned to the farmstead nearly every summer until 8th grade. During this time, I observed a remarkable evolution in farming and infrastructure. Horsepower was replaced by gasoline tractors; then diesel replaced gasoline engines. The tractors became more powerful pulling wider machinery. The Rural Electrification Association began planting telephone poles and delivering electricity to the farms. That transformation alone was remarkably revolutionary. The 32-volt direct current maintained by batteries in the basement for many years and charged by a windmill was replaced by alternating 110-volt power lines coming into the farm. A General Motors Frigidaire refrigerator was added to the kitchen, plus an electric oven and stove.

Life on the farm could be extreme. I remember an unfortunate cow that was unable to deliver her calf. The cow's head and shoulders were anchored to the barn and the calves' legs pulled out and tied off with a rope. Then a car was used to pull the stillborn out of the womb of the cow. It was a bloody mess! On occasions such as this my grandpa told me to go into the house. Another time a work horse that fell into a well could not get out and panicked. While the horse was thrashing about a stone bolt (used to pick up rocks in the field) was brought in and straw, dirt, and gravel were pitched into the well until the horse could climb out.

There were parts of animal skeletons scattered over the pathway to the pastures and around the sheep shed. A farmer was killed when driving on the gravel road in high gear. His tractor rolled over him when he went into the ditch, crushing him beneath the spinning wheels. It seemed like everything was close to the margin between life and death, between good and evil.

When I got older, I thought about how the homesteaders tried to harmonize divine goodness and Providence in view of such frequent and unannounced calamities and the prevalence of raw evil (theodicy). Under such circumstances I wondered how my homesteading relatives survived the challenges of daily living and death over the years. Religion was the answer; it appeared to help them through hardships and to balance their peace of mind. They saw prayer as a form of communication with the divine, though from what I observed they never heard back directly! I don't know what my grandpa would have said if he suddenly heard from the cosmos, "Yes, John, was that you who called?" They sincerely believed the Bible, prayer, and angels, and I doubt they ever publicly questioned whether their beliefs were true or not.

> *Fear thou not: for I am with thee; be not dismayed, for I am*
> *they God. I will strengthen thee; yea, I will help thee; yea, I*
> *will uphold thee with the right hand of my righteousness.* [1]

In talking about righteousness, people do not seek perfection in everything they do, and sometimes my relatives were willing to soften the religious rules for the sake of family loyalty and a good time. Even so, they did not hold that religious beliefs required truth or logical outcomes entirely. Somehow these ideas of righteous living and divine salvation provided an escape from living in a hostile world. In this they were not alone. People all around them seemed to share many of these same values.

All Christians attempt to mitigate tragedies of one form or another by reference to salvation through Providence or a supernatural intermediary predicting a utopian deliverance at the end of time. They could forestall the final reward, a celestial life with no more suffering, sin, disease, sorrow, or death by simply anticipating the Second Coming of Christ. Just before translation God would take one last look at their score cards and shuttle them to heaven or away from heaven. Now that was what people told me. It seemed to me as I got older that only the absence of reason and an over-active imagination could produce the inexplicable reward system they followed.

Coming to America

My grandpa John A. Willey, the father of my dad Tom Willey, didn't talk much about his paternal grandparents (William Willey, Sr.), other than to say his grandfather arrived in this country from Yorkshire, England, around 1848. From New York he traveled up the Hudson River, over the Erie Canal, and across Lake Michigan to Wisconsin. There the family developed a forty-acre farm in Dana County near Madison. But the truth was that William Willey, Sr. (1818-90) was never able to settle

---

[1] Isaiah 41:10. KJV.

down in one place for long, even when times were good, and lands were plentiful.[2] Kansas was his ultimate goal.

On his mother's side, Laura Larson (1857-1921) was born in Norway before coming to America. Her father Carl Larson (1833-1920) and her mother Ingeborg Frydenlund (1827-1898) arrived in New York from Norway after having buried a child at sea. One can surmise that "free land" as outlined in the Homestead Act influenced their decision to immigrate to America. There may have been other reasons for migrating. Besides Norway having limited farmlands, the population was growing, which reduced the opportunities to make a living unless one owned a fishing boat or took up an importing business.

Letters from recent migrants in America, sent back home to Norway, glowed with enthusiasm for the wonderful wide-spread farmlands and higher wages. Not only that: everyone could eat wheat bread, rice pudding, and meat in abundance, not just simple foods like the oat bread they had in Norway. The splendid conditions in America that these letters described produced excitement and buoyancy.

Back in Norway ministers and bailiffs tried to stamp out the immigration fever by telling dreadful stories of sea monsters that might be encountered during the crossing, or by warning that immigrates might be taken off the boat in Turkey and sold as slaves. They told of cruel American savages, of fatal bites by rattlesnakes, and of monstrous man-eating beasts in the New World. But these baleful stories did not frighten adventurous minds. The more motivated individuals in Norway still wanted to come to America.

Immigrant guidebooks recommended an early start in the year as it could take twelve weeks, sometimes longer over rough seas and stubborn winds, to cross the Atlantic. Regarding the dangers that might be encountered; they were advised to travel on "a good ship, with an able captain ... and careful seamen." Beyond that, "the passenger has to trust in the Lord!" [3]

After arriving in New York from Havre, France, the Larson's traveled

---

[2] There is confusion about his grandmother as apparently his father's mother, Sarah Longworthy, died in 1861 in Wisconsin. His grandfather married Mary Ann Brooks who was John's step-grandmother. (Taken from census records in Wisconsin and Iowa.)
[3] Theodore C. Blegen, ed., *Ole Rynning's True Account of America* (Freeport, NY: Books for Libraries Press. 1971).

west until they reached a Norwegian settlement in Jefferson County, fifty miles east of Madison, Wisconsin. There they joined up with Peter Larson, a relative. Introduction to a foreign country was much easier when connecting to a colony of kinfolks, but ignorance of the English language disheartened many arrivals. Over three thousand Norwegians lived in this colony in Wisconsin, and it eventually served as a fruitful field for westward travelling Adventist evangelists. Eventually, some of the converted Norwegian children would mature to become church workers, missionaries in foreign lands, teachers and leaders in the Adventist church. One of these Norwegians, Ole Andres Olsen, became president of the Wisconsin Conference and later served as president of the General Conference of Seventh-day Adventists from 1888-1897. [4]

Many Scandinavian immigrants left their native land as Lutherans, but converted to other denominations, remembering the religious formalism and persecution in their homeland. Their dissatisfaction with the religion back home was yet another reason some came to America. They were looking for a new start in pursuing a higher standard of living; they were also looking for a "New Jerusalem flowing with milk and honey."

Some Norwegians in this Wisconsin settlement converted to Methodism. And some of these kept the Jewish Sabbath (Saturday) because of the Scriptural passages about keeping the Seventh-day holy. Because Seventh-day Methodists wanted to get along with the community, they also kept Sunday as a day of worship! When the "home office" of the Methodists discovered the anomaly, they were quickly disfellowshipped, and the Seventh-day Methodists leaned toward accepting the message of the Sabbatarian Adventists. Various factions of Sabbatarian Adventists such as the "Messenger Party" wandered in and out of Wisconsin during this time.

Debate Over a Name for the Adventist Church

Migrations through the various denominations (sect adjustments) was often due to noisy disagreements over such matters as the nature of Christ, the sanctuary in heaven, original sin, probation, and the conditions

---

[4] Lawrence W. Onsager, "Pilgrims in a Strange Land," *Adventist Heritage*, Spring 1986, 33. Immigration data obtained from the federal census in 1870.

of salvation. A debate also occurred among the Sabbatarians over the proposed name for the new church. One group wanted to use the name "The Church of God," but the White party (led by James and Ellen White from Michigan) preferred "Seventh-day Adventists." The Whites thought the name Church of God was too common, "Seventh-day Adventist" reflected certain practices such as keeping the Seventh day Sabbath and expecting the soon return of Jesus. The newly formed Seventh-day Adventists also promoted and insisted upon the acceptance of the visions of Ellen White. In fact, the choice of a name could only be resolved by a vision from the prophetess:

> *I was shown in regard to the remnant people of God taking a name. Two classes were presented before me ... No name which we can take will be appropriated but that which accords with our profession and expresses our faith and marks us a peculiar people. The name Seventh-day Adventist is a standing rebuke to the Protestant world ... The name Seventh-day Adventist carries the true features of our faith in front and will convict the inquiring mind.* [5]

Two Advent preachers in Wisconsin, J.M. Stephenson and D.P. Hall from the "Messenger Party" (the first dissidents among the Sabbath-keeping Adventists and opponents of Ellen White's visions in 1854) caused particular disruption by teaching an "Age to Come" idea. Elder White passed through Wisconsin with his wife Ellen and attempted to correct this theological heresy. White had momentarily convinced the two ministers Stephenson and Hall, to give it up as outright heresy. The debating points were found in the *Review*. Of course, having a printing press and a prophet gave the White's an advantage.

The "Age to Come" teaching held that sinners would be given a second chance for salvation before the saints entered heaven at the start of the millennium. The fanatics (terms used by James and Ellen White) in Wisconsin also strongly opposed the visions of Ellen White (as noted above) and campaigned against use of the name "Seventh-day Adventist."

---

[5] Ellen G. White, "Our Denominational Name," *Testimonies*, I, 223.

There was also a "false" theory of holiness, a holiness not dependent on the Three Angel's message being advanced in Wisconsin.

Earlier, Stephenson had attempted to wrest control of the *Advent Review and Sabbath Herald* away from James White, the main publication of the Sabbatarians (located in Rochester, New York). Dissatisfied with the Whites, Stephenson and Hall returned to Wisconsin and published a competing magazine called the *"Messenger of Truth."* Several workers in the pioneer Sabbatarian faith were carried away by the heterodoxy of Stephenson and Hall. Stephenson divorced his wife and married a younger woman. Hall entered the real-estate business, failed, and went insane. Given the apostasy and faultfinding, the church was typically "portrayed as ending in a forlorn condition, friendless, penniless, and with failing health." [6]

Elder White summarized the conditions in the *Review*; "The cause in Wisconsin is almost a total wreck." Meetings were being held all over Wisconsin to find individuals who were willing to "keep all the commandments of God and the Faith of His Son" and to stay out of theological squabbles. In the end Stephenson and Hall left the Sabbatarians to organize their own version of the Church of God (Seventh-day).

Another Sabbatarian minister working in Wisconsin was Gustaf Mellberg, a Swede converted through the ministry of James White. After preaching and visiting in Wisconsin the Whites detected theological issues with Mellberg. Prompted by one of her visions, Ellen White rebuked Mellberg as being unfit to preach the gospel. Visions obviously became an important tool for addressing the divergent factions of the church. Individuals either accepted the rebuking visions or in anguish and angst withdrew from their relationship with the Whites.

Mellberg took the expected attitude about his rebuke and sought forgiveness. "We had lived in decided opposition to the *Review* and its supporters and cherished a hard spirit; but for one I have prayed and pray still that the Lord will forgive, and I hope the dear brethren will also forgive, and overlook." [7]

Perhaps the most significant figure in these Wisconsin theological disputes was Solomon Wellcome. The Wellcomes had gone through the

---

[6] Arthur White, *Ellen G. White* (Hagerstown, MD: Review & Herald Publ. Assoc., 1985), I, 315.

[7] "Gustef Melleberg's Confession," *Review & Herald*, March 31, 1859.

1844 Great Disappointment in Maine. Solomon's brother Isaac, a minister in the Advent Christian Church, wrote the first *History of the Second Advent Message.* Isaac had watched Ellen White in vision several times and considered her a "wonderful fanatic and trance medium."

Isaac's brother Solomon Wellcome, a former Methodist minister, held a theory of "instantaneous sanctification," another variation on the theme of salvation, and preached this theory in Wisconsin. The Wellcomes were a remarkable family indeed. Brother Henry contributed to an understanding of quinine as a treatment for malaria. He brought mosquito control to the Upper Nile, and then was sent to Panama to control mosquitoes and malaria while the canal was being built. He outfitted Henry Stanley with medical supplies when Stanley was sent in search of David Livingston. Meanwhile, Solomon's only son Henry was raised in a strict religious home. Witnessing the hanging of more than 30 Sioux Indians on one occassion weighed heavily on him. He studied chemistry under Dr. William Mayo at Rochester, then went to England to form the Burroughs and Wellcome Company, a large pharmaceutical firm still operating today in many countries as GlaxoSmithKline. Founder Henry (1853-1936) was knighted by the Queen of England and became a wealthy man. His pharmaceutical company developed antitoxins for tetanus, diphtheria and gas gangrene. Welcome also isolated histamine, which lead to antihistamine production, and standardized insulin and other medicines.

James White was aware that Wellcome was also evangelizing in Wisconsin. [8] He had preached the Millerite gospel earlier with Wellcome while both were living in Maine in the 1840s and In fact had baptized Wellcome.

While a proselytizing meeting was in progress, Elder White and two Michigan colleagues were praying when suddenly the room became "filled with the power of God" and Elder White fell to the floor. He ended face down and "groaning under the power of God." It wasn't long until all three of the preachers were in this same posture. Elder White later recounted this experience to his wife. [8] But apparently the Michigan delegation was not well received by the Wisconsin brethren. Elder White reported again in the *Review* that he still had misgivings about the future of Adventism

---

[8] Ross Goldstone, "Early Adventist and Charismatic Worship Experiences," *Trans-Australian Union Discernment*, a publication of the Seventh-day Adventist Church in Victoria, Australia, 1999, 6.

in Wisconsin. [9] When he got home, he continued to report that Solomon Wellcome and M. T. Steward were creating problems, and his wife went into vision and then rebuked the two for their misunderstanding of salvation and their attitudes:

> *I saw that persons who had been so enshrouded in darkness and deception that Satan had controlled not only mind but the body, would have to take a most humble place in the church of God. He will not commit the care of His flock to unwise shepherds, who would mistake and feed them poison instead of wholesome food.* [10]

After much debate and editorializing in the *Review* the "church" began to organize. One by one the *Review* carried statements from the laity and ministers confessing their wrong attitudes against organizing and their doubts about the Spirit of Prophecy. Here is a typical letter:

> *Dear Brother White: We are taught to confess our faults one to another and pray one for another that we may be healed. I wish to confess and forsake all my faults and sins...I have murmured against Brother and Sister White, and have thought them too severe, and have spoken of them in a few of my brethren in a way calculated to prejudice their minds against them. I am sorry that I have been left to do this.* [11]

The Willeys Join the Advent Church

The Willey family stumbled into the traveling Wisconsin evangelists. Their conversion began in 1859 while they were farming in Wisconsin. Their Bible-reading neighbors told them they could be resurrected after death to everlasting life and go to heaven if they believed in Jesus Christ

---

[9] "While we were preaching, a sister broke out in an opposition shout, so we waited some time for her to get through. It was with difficulty that we finished the discourse," *Review & Herald*, Nov. 13, 1860.

[10] Ellen G. White, "Fanaticism in Wisconsin," *Testimonies*, I, 229.

[11] Arthur White, *Ellen G. White: The Early Years* (Hagerstown, MD: Review & Herald Publ. Assoc., 1985), 459.

and gave them two early Adventist's pamphlets, "State of the Dead" and "Destiny of the Wicked." Was it possible, the Willey's wondered, to place their souls before God and gain everlasting life and a two-story celestial mansion without harsh winters, mosquitoes, or grasshoppers?

The Willey's were invited to an outdoor evangelistic tent meeting where the traveling evangelists promised to answer this very question. Adventist believers in Wisconsin were beginning to organize but were confused by the stain of fanaticism introduced by newly converted believers.

In various meetings the charismatic evangelist Solomon Wellcome and his acquaintance, T. M. Steward, [12] promised to reveal how biblical prophecies predicted the end of the world. Also, Mrs. Myrta Steward, the preacher's wife, claimed to have the gift of prophecy which added to the mysterious way of how God appeared to talk directly to humans without having to read the Bible. She said she could predict how long a person was going to live based on the visions she was having. Events were advertised where she would be giving a vision demonstration and making predictions to people who wanted to know when they might die. Ellen White learned of Myrta's visions and rebuked her:

> *She was presented before me in connection with a professed sister who was strongly prejudiced against my husband and myself and opposed to the visions. This has led her to love and cherish every lying report in regard to us and the visions and she has communicated this to Sister H. She has had a bitter spirit of war against me, when she had no personal knowledge of me. She was unacquainted with my labors yet has nourished the most wicked feelings and prejudice against me, and has influenced Sister H, and they have united together in their bitter remarks and speeches. [13]*

---

[12] Solomon Wellcome was the father of Sir Henry Solomon Wellcome, a co-founder of Burroughs and Wellcome Pharmaceuticals. Wellcome also founded the largest medical research charity in the world known as the Wellcome Library. Solomon Wellcome's theory was "instantaneous sanctification," and Mrs. Steward's visions countered those of Ellen G. White. See *Miracles in My Life,* J. N. Loughborough (Leaves of Autumn Books, Inc., 1987 reprint).

[13] Ellen G. White, "Wives of Ministers," *Testimonies,* I, 329.

Once the vision became public Steward confessed the errors of his wife to the editor of the *Review*: "Dear brother and sister White. I have felt prejudiced against you and said some wrong things of you. I pray you to forgive me this wrong. Finally, brethren, I think I can say in sincerity of heart, I love you, Amen. Signed T. M. Steward." [14] Mrs. Steward confessed her fanaticism several months later.

During the Wisconsin meetings Steward had spoken about ominous famines, wars and rumors of war, dark days, star showers, earthquakes, plague outbreaks, and prophecies that would portend the Second Coming. The preachers debated with each other whether sinners had a second chance during the millennium. They explained that the existence of moral and natural evil really proved that there was a God and a final reward in Heaven. It became apparent that it was better to be loyal to these matters than to be objectively correct.

After only a few meetings the Willeys heard of a far-off universe where other inhabitants lived and of going to heaven rather than staying on earth with certain death following the Second Coming. They questioned the energetic minister one night as they leaned against the pole holding up the tent, "How can we be sure this is all true?" Steward assured them it was true. "Do you remember the signs in the heavens that Jesus was coming soon? These are markers; they've all been fulfilled! Did you not notice how God spoke to my wife through visions? What more do you need?"

After James White returned to Battle Creek from Wisconsin, Ellen asserted publicly in a *Testimony* that Steward and Solomon were corrupted by Satan. And, as noted, she also scolded Steward's wife concerning her claim to having visions.

Mrs. White wrote; *"God and holy angels were displeased with your course, and you were left in your blind judgment to figure in the most unreasonable, wild fanaticism that ever-cursed Wisconsin."* [15] This public

---

[14] "Bro. T.M. Steward," *Review & Herald*, June 9, 1859.

[15] Arthur L. White. "Charismatic Experiences in Early Seventh-day Adventist History," posted on the Ellen G. White Estates, Inc. website. See Ellen G. White, *Testimonies*, I, 335. Later Steward declared that his wife's visions were delusional, the work of the enemy. Steward's daughter became one of Ellen G. White's secretaries. Adriel D. Chilson, *Trial and Triumph on a Western Frontier* (Elko, NV: Heritage Publications, 1976), 20.

rebuke caused deep sadness and bruised the feelings of Wellcome. and, after hearing this message from the prophetess, Wellcome decided to drop his affiliation with the Sabbatarian branch and moved to another faith. His brother Isaac, who influenced him to leave the Sabbatarian Adventists, had strong negative opinions about the Whites. [16] And like a good shepherd, Wellcome gathered up his newly converted "Sabbath-keeping" Adventist flock, including William Willey, Sr. and guided them into a different religious group that kept Sunday instead of Saturday.

For a while, Solomon Wellcome continued preaching his favorite themes on "sanctification" until the prophetess in the Adventist church directly rebuked him:

> *I saw that if God's people in Wisconsin would prosper, they must take a decided position in regard to these things, and thereby cut off the influence of those who are causing distraction and division by teaching sentiments contrary to the body. Such are wandering stars. They seem to emit a little light; they profess and carry along a little truth, and thus deceive the inexperienced. Satan endows them with his spirit, but God is not with them.* [17]

That did it. Solomon did not appreciate receiving a message from God through the prophetess. He left Wisconsin with his son Henry and went off to Minnesota to serve as a Methodist missionary to the Ojibway Indians. The government recognized this work for reducing strife among the neighboring tribes.

---

[16] Issac C. Wellcome wrote the first historical book in 1874 on the apocalyptic period involving the Millerite movement and viewed Ellen G. White as a "wonderful fanatic and trance medium." He also wrote that James White was "the inebriate who staggered through the street badly intoxicated and then entered the complaint that everyone in the street staggered; that the posts and the trees ran against him." Isaac C. Wellcome, *History of the Second Advent Message* (New York: Advent Christian Publication Society, 1874).

[17] Ellen White, "Northern Wisconsin," *Testimonies*, I, 327.

Seventh-day Adventist vs. Advent Christian

By 1864 a Seventh-day Adventist church had been built in the Wisconsin settlement and as revival meetings were held more Scandinavians joined the church, including the Larson family. In the meantime, the Willey's had converted to the Advent Christian Church.

Advent Christians believed in Biblical inspiration, in baptism by immersion, and in the state of the dead called mortality of the soul. At the Second Coming, the righteous would receive everlasting life while the wicked suffered complete annihilation. Advent Christians believed that the wonder of salvation was free to all who repented, turned from sin, and sustained a faith in the Lord Jesus Christ as their Savior. Advent Christian theology contained few "do's and don'ts." But it closely resembled Seventh-day Adventism without the intense fervor for the sanctuary judgment, the Sabbath, or pre-advent perfectionism. Advent Christians lacked a prophet and dismissed the notion of a supernatural voice of God in humans.

One of the boundaries that set the Seventh-day Adventists apart from the Advent Christians was the day they chose to worship the Sabbath. The Seventh-day Adventists believed they were raised up by God with a message to obey the Ten Commandments, including the seventh-day Sabbath of the Jews. Their ideas became known as The Three Angel's Message, an Adventist interpretation of Revelation 14: 6-12 to preach the gospel to the entire world prior to Christ's return. The believers veered toward an exhausting perfectionism and hearty sanctification, such urges having derived from Wesleyan Methodism. [18]

A single transgression without repentance, such as "borrowing" a watermelon from the neighbor's garden at night or "stealing an apple out of the barrel" at the grocery store, could keep an Adventist out of God's

---

[18] Everett N. Dick, *The Millerite Movement* in *Adventism in America* edited by Gary Land (Grand Rapids, MI: William B. Eerdmans Publ. Co., 1986). Jonathan Butler, *The Making of a New Order: Millerism and the Origins of Seventh-day Adventism*, in *The Disappointed: Millerism and Millenarianism in the Nineteenth Century*, edited by Ronald L. Numbers and Jonathan M. Butler (Knoxville, TN: University of Tennessee Press, 1993). George R. Knight, *Millennial Fever and the End of the World* (Boise, ID: Pacific Press, 1993). "Perfection," *Review and Herald*, April 1, 1873.

Kingdom. [19] It was that simple! God's Ten Commandments were not to be broken, even in the slightest way. Members of the two faiths for the most part get along well because both derived from the 1844 movement.

Throughout the latter half of the nineteenth century the Seventh-day Adventists were fewer in number than the Advent Christian Church, but the federal census of 1900 identified 3,175 more Seventh-day Adventists than Advent Christians. The Seventh-day Adventist's missionary zeal and the development of the pavement-pounding evangelistic Third Angel's message explained their growth. The gospel was supposed to be preached to the whole world so that unbelievers could hear the gospel. Otherwise Jesus would remain in heaven. No one took this idea apart statistically to determine if it was even possible to preach to the entire world, nor did they wonder how the tens of millions, already dead, could receive the gospel. How would the gospel enter the Muslim or Hindu worlds? What constituted as "preaching"? How long to preach to an individual before going on to the next unbeliever?

Adventists also maintained an eye-popping literalism in Biblical interpretation. No prophetic nuance had been overlooked, even the beasts found in Daniel and Revelation. These prophetic ideas provided security and foreknowledge about the end of history. By the turn of the nineteenth century it appeared, for some reason, that Christ continued to delay His coming despite abundant preaching to the contrary. Adventism spread to many nations even as Christ's return seemed to be hop-skipping backward in time, so close yet far away like a meadowlark that flies from fence post to fence post as you approach.

The Sunday-keeping Advent Christians had no explanation of why Christ had failed to appear in 1844 other than that their prophetic calculations must have been in error. They kept hoping that the Second Coming would occur at any time despite the downright disconfirmation of the prophecy in 1844. As time passed it became clear that the failed 1844 prophecy had shattered the force of the Advent Christians' earlier persuasions.

On the other hand, the Seventh-day Adventists had managed an unlikely comeback and continued to develop the theme of the Second Coming.

---

[19] "The most solemn truths ever entrusted to mortals have been given to you to proclaim to the world. The proclamation of these truths is to be our work." Ellen G. White, *Testimonies*, IX, 19.

Following the Great Disappointment, they discovered what became accepted as an explanation for the failed prophecy. Somehow Miller had misinterpreted the sanctuary cleansing events. Rather than having Christ coming from heaven to earth to cleanse the sanctuary, the new interpretation had Christ moving from The Holy to The Most Holy compartments in the heavenly temple and in 1844 entering a second phase of his heavenly ministry (the judgement). Thus the Millerites' had the right date but misplaced the occurrence of the cleansing event. Christ would return only after the final investigative ledger for the saved was completed in the Most Holy place.

While waiting for this to be completed, Seventh-day Adventists carried the burden to preach the Second Coming to the entire world. Over time, of course, Adventist theology became complex and structured with a plurality of opinions about the nature of Christ (divine vs. human), the acceptance of the Trinity, the completion of the atonement, the divine realm, our own sinfulness, salvation by works vs. grace, the investigative judgement, and the conditions for the fulfillment of prophecies in the future, etc. Many of these topics are still debated. [20]

Some of these debates created a debris field of fallen ministers who had persisted in publishing their divergent opinions and were disfellowshipped. The leadership of the Seventh-day Adventists did not willingly tolerate variances in church beliefs, especially after guidance from the prophetess. Even what some onlookers might consider slight differences could give pause. [21]

Religion Comes to the Frontier

The Adventists, of course, didn't have a monopoly on religion or evangelizing. Circuit-riding Methodists and farmer-preacher Baptists followed these same westward migrations "spreading scriptural holiness over the land" wherever isolated families or clusters of farmers could be found. [22] They

---

[20] Malcolm Bull and Keith Lockhart, *Seeking a Sanctuary: Seventh-day Adventism and the American Dream* (Bloomington, IN: Indiana Univ. Press., 2007), 83.

[21] Virginia Steinweg, *Without Fear or Favor. Life of M. L. Andreasen* (Takoma Park, MD: Review & Herald Publ. Assoc., 1979).

[22] "In all but seven states Methodist Episcopal annual conferences were organized before the state was admitted to the union." Dan W. Holter, *Flames on the Plains: A History of United Methodism in Nebraska* (Nashville, TN: Parthenon Press, 1983), 8.

all purported to have received their authority from God, and all promised a place in heaven to those who would accept the gospel. They talked about the Apocalypse from the book of Revelation and the divine plan to establish a millennial paradise. Before they traveled west these preachers were admonished, "to chuse (sic) the fittest Subject, and follow them with a holy Mixture of Seriousness and Terror, and Love and Meekness." With gaining converts for heaven on their minds, these traveling ministers "boarded" with the settlers and accepted free food and other blessings. Immersed, as they were, in the hardships of pioneer life, the people loved to hear stories about heaven and life on a celestial star in beautiful homes with streets of gold, glittering crowns, glorious singing, and views of Mount Zion. Few realities mitigated the imaginations of these spirited traveling ministers.

How could serious and reflective men look at the harsh lives of these pioneers and settlers and doubt the existence of a benevolent God? For one thing, these pioneers believed that if people grew indifferent to religion, all the bonds of society would be loosened. If there was no God, there was no law and no reward for good behavior. It was important to broadcast this wonderful plan of salvation and garner new converts for Christianity. Celestial thoughts diverted their minds from the humiliation of poor earnings and the difficulties of farming. In this regard Adventist teachings do not vary from the broad principles of Christianity.

Summer and fall camp meetings were the preferred method for gathering souls to the churches and swelling the houses of worship with converts. These camp meetings included singing, shouting, and social gatherings. Although they couldn't see the face of the Holy Spirit, many listeners believed that the Spirit moved about the audience. One lady came to the stage and told how the night before the Holy Spirit came and sat next to her bed and told her he would bring relief from her rheumatism if she would take the plunge without backpedaling and accept Jesus as her Lord. Enticing the wayward to repent became as important as raising crops and plowing a desolate barrier around a homestead to protect against prairie fires. Temperance reforms, avoidance of novels, dancing, and gambling, and careful Sabbath keeping were emphasized. Claiming divine favor for their cause, the preachers looked upon their task as a white-knuckle fist fight against spiritual apathy and materialism.

Religion in the West

When it was rumored that Indians were roaming near the campgrounds, the preachers slept with their revolvers and kept their powder dry—the unconverted Indians were considered pagans who needed evangelizing, if not by sacred words, then by guns and bullets. Perhaps bullets were even the best form of evangelism. In other words, the preaching business on the frontier always involved a bit of lawlessness.

One Sunday a Baptist minister appeared at a schoolhouse in Missouri to deliver his sermon. He walked to the front of the room, placed two revolvers beside the Bible on the pulpit, and announced to the audience: "By the grace of God and these two revolvers I am going to preach here today!" Apparently, he had been warned that some parishioners intended to tar and feather him for his antislavery views. On this particular Sabbath they postponed their punishment!

The various Christian sects, traditions, and denominations were a synthesis of religious notions emerging out of theological conflicts and varied interpretations of Scripture. Churchgoers mostly agreed on the main points. They may have thought that their religious innovations were better than the others, but they shared a common emphasis on the grace of God in Jesus Christ as the means for salvation. In an erstwhile sermon, the famous theologian Horace Bushell, a Congregational minister, asserted that "There were two courses open to the nation: the churches must bring

salvation to the frontier, or the frontier would paganize the nation." [23] In some communities out West, things could go either way. But religion kept the believers grounded and encouraged social cooperation and group survival in the "face of free-rider temptation." [24]

Generally, in these small towns, there was only one meeting place. The Baptists might meet one week and the Methodists or Lutherans the next, or they all joined in a "union" church. When together

---

[23] Ibid. 47.
[24] Stephen T. Asma, *Why We Need Religion* (New York: Oxford Univ. Press. 2018), 124.

they exchanged uneasy glances at each other, wondering how the other side could make so many mistakes in their religion when the message from the pulpit sounded so clear and Biblical.

Believers in these new American religions would probably never agree that their faith came from what Jonathan Edwards called extreme "religious affections" and not "self-deluded counterfeits." But Christianity rested on the Gospels, and all looked to the day when Gabriel's trumpet would sound. Methodists, Baptists and other religions essentially concurred with the Adventists.

Faith in the Advent return boiled down to a simple matter. When that day arrived, believers wanted to be standing on God's side and not with the Devil. The Second Coming seemed possible from what the Bible said. Disrespect for this belief could lead to an individual's own peril. And one can rightly suppose that the Willey family became preoccupied with the nearness because others around them felt likewise. The institutionalized Seventh-day Adventist church that trumpeted the Second Coming could easily be harmonized with the Christian principle practiced in other denominations. Jesus hinted to his apostles at three different times in the New Testament that He would return during their lifetime, and since that had been a long time ago, the Second Coming must not be far off, Besides, the chaos of worldly affairs and natural calamities served as markers to indicate the end of the world.

RUTHVEN HOMESTEAD
CHAPTER FOUR

"A certain class of truths that cannot become true till our faith has made them so." *In Robert D. Richardson. William James. In the Maelstrom of American Modernism. 2006. p.203.*

As settlers moved west and confronted the hardships of frontier life, few felt content enough to settle down. They often heard of better lands elsewhere. After taking out a homestead a settler might pick up and chase after the rumors. John's grandparents, William and Mary Ann (1834-1916), then living in Wisconsin, felt the bite themselves. They were impressed that there was a greater fortune to be found in the newly opened Iowa territory. In 1870 they sold the farm and headed for the "beautiful prairie lands" that were opening almost due west around the Okoboji and Spirit Lakes in northwest Iowa. Little did they know that these were mostly wetlands which had to be drained and tilled before they could be farmed. (The lakes in the area, which were of glacial origin, were known as the Great Lakes of Iowa.

Before migrating John's father Wm Warren Willey, Jr. (1857-1920) was born in Wisconsin. He was twelve years old when the family left for Iowa, but he already knew a few things that a grown man needed to know. He put his hands in his pockets, pretended to be brave, and shoved off to Iowa with his family—his imaginations fully ablaze with excitement and adventure. The last thing he did before leaving was to hide his favorite fishing reel in the hollow of a live oak tree down by the river.

Trekking to Iowa was not easy, like catching thirty-pound pike in Elbow Lake or hunting wild ducks in the nearby sloughs of Wisconsin. And whining about the hot summer across endless miles of prairie didn't make the ground roll by any faster. The distance was over 300 miles. The family traveled in a party of twenty-six immigrants[1] and took seriously

---

[1] Dwight G. McCarty, *History of Palo Alto County Iowa* (Cedar Rapids, IA: The Torch Press, 1910).

the advice they had read from Army Captain Marcy's book *The Prairie Traveler.* [2] They traveled by prairie schooners pulled by oxen. Each day's march began at sunrise—making "nooning" during the heat of the day around ample grass and water.

Later in the afternoon they hitched up again and trekked until dark. The cursed grasshoppers were everywhere, and the marshy lowlands were full of stinging mosquitoes. On average, they made sixteen miles a day. William remembered the twenty-day journey as an adventure through nearly waist-high prairie grasses, all the time expecting an Indian to jump out from behind a boulder or come galloping across the vast open plains in war paint to defy his manhood. Thus, he carried a knife and a rifle. At night the immigrants circled the wagons to protect the horses and cattle. They posted armed sentinels to guard against marauders and prairie wolves.

One man in the party had a cracked skull from a previous Indian attack. His scalp had been ripped and torn and the ragged edges sewed together. Whoever sewed him up had treated his scalp like a burlap sack—the wound had become infected around the edges and ruffled. Only strong whiskey cured his ache. Wm had trouble avoiding staring at ole Andy and thinking to himself that the Indian must have had an arctic-cold widow's heart to do something like that to this man's head. Andy had a long white beard and was a simple-minded person, the kind that could not remember names or where he had been a week ago. Some in the party thought he was on the verge of going crazy. Clearly, Andy drank too much for his own good. Sometimes he thought he saw movements that were nothing more than the shadows of hawks floating in the noon-day sun. No one trusted him as he went about discharging his rifle at any movement in the grass. Eventually the company took away his gun during the day!

The travelers enjoyed telling chilling stories around the campfire about Indians ripping off the scalp of the white man, bashing the children with clubs, and running off with the women and dogs. Some of these stories were genuine; others were embellished. Young Wm did not believe everything he heard, but the stories made him nervous and put him on edge. Counting the meteorites zipping across the sky at night took his mind off the danger. Land treaties and purchases steadily displaced the Indians

---

[2] Randolph B. Marcy, *The Prairie Traveler. A Handbook for Overland Expeditions* (*Bedford, MA:* Applewood Books, 1859).

westward across Minnesota and Iowa into the Dakotas and Montana, but both Indians and settlers had their bellyaches about each other.

Sadly, John Chivington, an ordained Methodist minister, instigated the massacre of more than 450 Indians at Sand Creek, Colorado. The soldiers mutilated the women and children and displayed their body parts on their saddles. Afterward, Chivington was called to testify before Congress and to recount his attack on an unarmed village that displayed the American flag and a white banner over Chief Black Kettle's lodge. Chivington thought all Indians should be wiped off the face of the earth, but when the mass murder was tried in court, an army judge called it "a cowardly and cold-blooded slaughter, sufficient to cover its perpetrators with indelible infamy, and the face of every American with shame and indignation." By this time Chivington had earned the sobriquet "Fighting Parson." [3] The sad reality of the westward migration was that settlers were also disruptors. The Indians steadily lost their hunting grounds, and those who survived had to change their way of life.

Because of Indian troubles, a dark cloud of anger and fear hung over the area where the Willey's were planning to farm. It was land with a bad history of violence. When the area was first settled rogue Indians swept in and massacred the people around Spirit Lake. They clubbed the infants and drowned the women. In all, thirty-eight settlers were slain, and four women were taken captive. [4] The Indians fled into Minnesota.

The Minnesota legislature ransomed two of the women by paying for their release with twelve blankets, two kegs of powder, twenty pounds of tobacco, thirty-two yards of blue squaw cloth, thirty-seven yards of calico, and a quantity of ribbon. The Indians were never apprehended. The settlers recoiled from the event, but their minds leaped with fear that the Indians might return. For a time after the massacre, the settlers in Iowa stuck together in a large cabin in an open meadow with whiskey passed around to sooth their nerves at night. They petitioned the government to establish forts for protection.

---

[3] Dan W. Holter, *Flames on the Plains: A History of United Methodism in Nebraska* (Nashville, TN: Parthenon Press, 1983), 54.

[4] *Ruthven Town and Country* (A small book published by Town and Country Study Club of Ruthven. No date or copyright.) Also, documented by A. R. Fulton in *Red Men of Iowa* (Des Moines, IA: Mills & Co. Publishers, 1882).

A few years later the Sioux Indians began another rampage in the Minnesota territory. This time they killed six-hundred settlers and made off with one hundred women and children. Understandably, these massacre tales blunted the immigrants' ambitions to journey westward. One pioneer woman recalled how her father built small boats and planned to put the women and children in the boats and push them out into the lake rushes where they could hide until the danger passed. [3] She claimed that her father had gotten the idea from the Bible where baby Moses was hidden in the rushes in the River Nile so that Pharaoh couldn't find him.

Before the Willey's arrived at their destination, more trouble arose on the Iowa frontier—this time from the white man. In 1864 Confederate soldiers wearing Union uniforms attacked farmers in Iowa and northern-aligned refugees from Missouri. Iowa Governor Kirkwood called up a voluntary brigade that drove back the invaders. After this last skirmish, the Iowan frontier settled down – just as schooner migrations began arriving.

All one now heard were the sounds of wind against the leaves in the pussy willows along the edges of the lakes and the grasses, the songs of birds, frogs, and geese, and the noises that farmers make when cultivating crops or shingling a barn. The willows that bordered the lakes were leafy, and the area around sloughs and creeks featured wild onions, plums, choke cherries, gooseberries, and wild blackberries – pleasant distractions from the summer heat. Out on the open plains, the homesteaders built sod houses. Grasses were used for the thatched roof; makeshift corrals protected cattle and horses from the sun and wind. On calm days some farmers claimed they could hear the corn growing once it reached as high as a man's knees!

After arriving at their destination in Ruthven, Iowa, William Willey, Sr., took out an eighty-acre homestead in Silver Lake Township. From the beginning, farming conditions were swampy and economically troubling. [5] No matter how strong his intention to accumulate wealth, strong objections from mother nature and other forces thwarted him. The wind blew too hard, or there was not enough rain at the right time, or the economics were

---

[5] General Land Office Patent dated April 1, 1876 and signed by Ulysses S. Grant.

not favorable. He had left Wisconsin with $1,325 in his pocket; a decade later in Iowa his net worth was $400. [6]

When agricultural prices fell, farmers could not market their crops. They earned a little money by selling eggs, chickens, and pigs, and by raising beef cattle. Then came several drought years in a row. Dark black clouds of grasshoppers descended in June 1873, and epizootic horse disease swept through the county for two fearful weeks, nearly wiping out the horse population. (More than 150 known parasites infect horses.) Also, during the '70s prairie fires menaced the region since everything was dry from lack of rain.

One year the flames overran a big peat marsh near Lost Lake and burned for two years. These prairie fires were always a source of anxiety, and when they came blazing over the land they terrified the farmers and shop owners. Smoke filled the sky and darkened the sun, and if the wind was blowing the flames raced over the land faster than a horse could run. Sparks scattered ahead. Farmers tied wet handkerchiefs around their faces and fought the fires with wet blankets and with horses plowing or dragging harrows over the ground. It was tough going. In the shorter grasses, they sometimes butchered a cow and dragged the carcass between two horses to roll over the flames. In the deep ravines where the grass was tall, the flames leaped a hundred feet or more in the air accompanied by a terrifying roar.

A year later, in 1871, John's relatives on his mother's side, together with a group of Wisconsin Seventh-day Adventists including the Peter and Carl Larson families, dreamed of free lands in Iowa and immigrated to the Lost Lake area near Ruthven, Iowa. Once in Iowa Carl Larson purchased land adjacent to Alex Ruthven's farm. (Larson was probably the first Adventist in the state.) Alex Ruthven donated land for the town to attract the railroad and consequently the town was named after his family.

Despite these difficulties in Palo Alto County, the population grew and small towns sprang up. After the railroad came through Ruthven commerce improved. Roads were staked out, and bridges were constructed over the creeks and waterways. The winter was mild in 1873. Most farmers used hay for fuel because coal sold for ten dollars a ton. Notwithstanding

---

[6] Data obtained from 1860 (Wisconsin) and 1870 (Iowa) census records. In today's dollars the $1,325 would equal $27,219, and ten years later the $400 would equal $5,544.

some success towards the end of the 1870s, many wagons went east, returning with disappointed pioneers carrying signs on the tattered burlap covers which read;

Eaten out by grasshoppers — Lost everything to fire.
Going back East to live with the wife's folks.

By 1880, after a decade of farming, William Sr. gave the farm to his son Wm and moved to nearby Emmetsburg, the county seat (founded in 1858). By now, William Sr. had no more dreams to lift him up. Eventually, the original homesteader from Wisconsin, William Willey, Sr, moved on to Kansas. By then his son Wm was twenty-three years old and a bachelor. Wm continued to be optimistic and went about farming on his father's homestead, expecting to be successful. He struggled along, living day by day on the margin. Before leaving for Kansas, his father had warned him that farming would be hard work and that he might have to give it up to do something different for a better future. In 1890, William Sr. was buried in Lansing, Kansas without a family nearby to mourn his passing. Back in Wisconsin were a wife and three sons and five daughters. He died at age seventy-two.

A core of thirteen Norwegian families organized The Ruthven Seventh-day Adventist church in August of 1876. They conducted their services in Norwegian well into the 1900s. In 1907 lightening destroyed this small church, but no one saw in this devastation anything other than a random incident. Believing the end of time was near, Adventists had been known to link such tragedies to the Wrath of God against the remnant for not carrying out their promises to God—like the Israelites in the Old Testament.[7] Adventists who took the Bible literally thought of God as standing in the doorway of a forge ready to open the furnace as He went about to purify and harden the steel in the believer's mind. Some thought disasters, like fire and lightening, were divinely approved by Him as a warning to the saints to straighten up and knuckle down.

While thinking about his future, Wm met Laura Larson, the daughter

---

[7] Two other disasters attributed to the wrath of God occurred in Battle Creek, Michigan: the burning of the Battle Creek Sanitarium on February 18, 1902, and the Review and Herald Publishing House on December 30, 1902.

of Carl Larson (1857-1921). She was born in Norway and came to America in 1863 arriving in Iowa about the same time as younger Wm in 1871. They were the same age and married after a short courtship. With greater financial responsibilities Wm decided to sell his father's farm and move into Ruthven to work as a carpenter. (Laura was already raising a small child.)

According to the 1880 federal census, Laura's son Gideon had a "Scottish father" and was born before Wm and Laura married. At times Gideon lived with his "Uncle Alex Larson" in Ruthven. Before marrying, Wm was reminded of the Biblical text against marrying an adulterous woman, including the Leviticus instructions that she "shall surely be put to death." [8] He rationalized that the death commandment only applied to the children of Israel who came out of the land of Egypt from a slave background. That seemed enough justification when measured against the love and affection he had developed for Laura, and he became a spokesperson for tolerance of women rejected by the community.

Most people inherit their religious beliefs from their mother and father. It has never been proven that a child growing up in isolation will spontaneously create a religious faith without promptings from parents or other human beings. If you are born into a Baptist family, you were likely to be a Baptist after your own family. That is why it is rare to find a child born with Baptist parents ending up as a Hindu; or the reverse. Religious values are a lot like family values. People are highly biased about their religion. It is slanted by their upbringing, and largely subjective. Being skewed from reality does not render them weak, flimsy, or dismissible. Emotions have the upper hand in beliefs.

Continuing with our story, Wm and Laura eventually left Ruthven and migrated to North Dakota in search of some farmland that had been advertised. Son John Willey was born in 1884, then a year later a sister Grace (1885-1965) and another sister Jonetta (1885-1933). All three attended school in Ruthven.

Growing up in a family where the father adhered to one faith and the mother to another allowed John Willey (Tom Willey's father) to contrast the bewildering differences as to how mankind could be saved from sin. By then both interpretations of salvation were like a cat that had gone up a tree too far and couldn't get back down! John heard his mother Laura

---

[8] Leviticus 20:10.

describe how some of her Seventh-day Adventist friends, under a spell of guilt, thought they were beyond the mercy of God. In their minds their probation had closed. Somehow his mother possessed an inner ability to know when a person needed to straighten up to be saved.

John remembered watching how his mother had reacted when his Advent Christian father chided her about her preparation for the 1844 arrival of Christ. John's father reminded her that some Millerites were so cast down by the prospect of facing the wrath of God that they had committed suicide or gone insane. He remembered his father telling of an account in a Michigan newspaper about how "converts go roaring through the streets, warning the people of the wrath to come, and pointing to recent floods as evidence that the vials are being emptied out." [9]

There are secret pains like this in families with divergent religious beliefs. As John matured, he discovered that sanctification was a sticky point with his father. Wm would say; "What I do is my own business; I don't need a Bible or a prophet to tell me how I should live my life." These discussions made a strong impression on John.

Out of it came John's belief that sometimes your father can help you more than your mother when it comes to talking about the cataclysmic end of an age. John reckoned his mother's Adventism put too much emphasis on salvation through purity, having gotten this largely from reading Ellen White, the prophetess who kept her church on edge by describing how soon God's divine grace would be withdrawn, and Satan would be allowed to exercise his intolerance against Sabbath keepers. Such believers were either going to be put to death or would have to flee to the hills to escape the wrath of the Catholics and other infidels. John's mother spread around such views like butter on hot bread, emphasizing the horrible nature of Satan and his evil angels. It scared him at times to listen to his mother describe the deplorable things that were going to happen at the end of time:

In quick succession, one angel after another will pour out vials of wrath upon the inhabitants of the earth. [10]

---

[9] Karen Armstrong, *The Battle for God* (New York: Ballantine Books, 2000), 79. F. D. Nichol, *Midnight Cry* (Washington, DC: Review & Herald Publishing, 1944). See *Review & Herald,* August 13, 1889.

[10] Ellen G. White, *Signs of the Times, January 17,* 1900, and *The Great Controversy,* 631.

After Wm and Laura married, her family, the Larson's, tried to entice Wm to become a Seventh-day Adventist. Wm held back, arguing that both churches believed in the imminent Second Coming of Christ. But there were other reasons he kept to himself. He thought the vision-based Seventh-day Adventists sprang out of the "shouting Methodist" tradition, and he remembered the stories told about visionaries being knocked to the ground by the Holy Spirit and other enthusiasms of Seventh-day Adventist preaching in Wisconsin. Also, he remembered Ellen White's rebukes to her fellow ministers who had originally convinced his father's family to join the Advent Christian sect. The memory swept over him like a chilling wind. He pondered carefully the idea of character perfection before entrance into heaven. He thought salvation was a gift through the death and resurrection of Christ.

As a teenager, John stayed with his father's faith. For one thing, keeping Sunday as the day of worship was more popular, while the Ruthven Norwegians were looked upon as foreigners and peculiar in their religious beliefs and Sabbath practices. Thinking that keeping Saturday had the needless effect of dividing Christians. John opted for a more relaxed outlook.

Nor did he like hearing from his grandfather Larson about how he bore the Mark of the Beast on his forehead by worshipping on Sunday, the first day of the week. Grandpa Larson told him that a Catholic pope and Emperor Constantine had changed Sabbath to Sunday — and that the pope was the antichrist. Sunday worship violated the fourth commandment. He didn't know if that was true or not since it happened a long time ago. Grandpa Larson said a person would not go to heaven if he worshipped on "the Pope's Day." He also told John that if he was preparing for translation to heaven and expecting to engage in all the glories and treasures of heaven, he had to regulate what he ate and stifle any inclination to self-abuse, card playing, dancing, gambling, smoking, and drinking coffee. He also must turn about and seek perfection in obedience to God's will. Grandpa had heard the prophetess speak about these things through her visions.

The truth of the matter was that John liked to fish at Lost Lake, put on the boxing gloves, and throw a few punches with his friends on Saturday afternoon. He wondered about the fuss over which day a person worshipped as long as one day in seven was kept for the Lord. Besides, everyone else in the neighborhood worshipped on Sunday. How could the majority be wrong?

Fifty years later, John noticed his grandfather and father still had a thin distaste for the Seventh-day Adventists though not because of any deep dissatisfaction with their teachings or injustice they had personally endured. It was a subtle dissatisfaction passed on from father to son about the way the minister Wellcome had been treated by the Adventist leaders. Wellcome had shepherded the Willeys into the Advent Christian faith. The chilling wind from this event was like an indistinct and blurred sound you hear from someone trying to talk under water. One could say that the Willeys' religious faith had originally grown out of turmoil over God's judgment and sanctification and that their convictions had hardened as the ponderous questions dropped away. To put it another way, the family practiced a loose form of worship. When farming conditions in Iowa were doubtful, the Willeys were good Advent Christians, but when farming was fair to good, they wandered a bit from the fold. After all they were farmers, not religious philosophers or theologians.

John and his sisters remained as Advent Christians until they migrated to North Dakota in 1902, where their mother's influence began to gather strength. H.L. Mencken, the well-known journalist from Baltimore, famously said, "but only in the sense and to the extent that we respect his theory that his wife is beautiful and his children smart," do we need to question why a person keeps one religion over another.

FREE LANDS & RAILROADS
CHAPTER FIVE

"In the dead of winter, of course, when the blizzards are raging, and we don't see any other folks for weeks at a time, she has days when she seems to go all to pieces; but I hardly reckon that as the disease–that sort of thing happens to a good many of us, let me tell you!" O. E. Rölvaag, *Giants in the Earth* (New York: Harper & Brothers Publ., 1927), 389.

Abraham Lincoln campaigned on the promise of offering government lands to homesteaders. Expecting to see this dream fulfilled, people were singing; "Uncle Sam is rich enough to give us all a farm." After Lincoln's election, Congress moved ahead with land control measures and enacted the Homestead Act of May 1862. The Act permitted people to obtain land through personal labor instead of purchasing. In September Lincoln issued the Emancipation Proclamation, and in November he signed the Pacific Railroad Act. In a single year, America was on its way to giving away land, stamping out slavery, and changing the way people and goods moved across the country.

Southerners opposed the federal land policy because it might add slave-free states to the Union. There was also a fear that the influx of European immigration, especially Catholics, was corrupting the religious founding of the nation. Since earliest times the optimistic vision of the republic had been to create universal peace and prosperity in the world and establish the kingdom of God on earth. Now America was falling apart with a raging Civil War. Lincoln considered the United States the "last best hope of earth for the advancement of liberty and democracy."

The interest in dispersing Public Domain federal lands began under Thomas Jefferson, who thought that recently acquired public land should not be sold for profit, but rather should be freely offered to the people. Selling these lands would disgust the public and breed disharmony. Jefferson's argument had hinged on the idea that small, free-holding farmers were the most precious part of the state — "the chosen people of God." Hence, the government should give away these lands to create a rural agrarian democracy. The Secretary of the Treasury, Alexander Hamilton, disagreed on grounds that Public Domain lands should be used as a source of revenue to pay back the cost of the Revolutionary War. He thought that if the land was sold at 20 cents an acre it would encourage land sales and provide the nation with revenues to retire the national debt. The treasury secretary, Albert Gallatin, agreed with Hamilton but argued that people should pay a higher price for the land. In the end Jefferson conceded that payment for the land was vital to closing on the debt and financing canals, roads, railroads, dams, and reservoirs. [1] This was all before The Homestead Act of 1862.

This quick history provides a backdrop for The Homestead Act. When first enacted, there was not a mad rush to homestead because the Civil War and its aftermath averted people's attention. Mining in Colorado, Idaho and Montana was also diverting prospective claimants. Eventually, though, land entries began to increase, reaching a zenith in 1885. With time, homesteading slowed and nearly stopped because of locust plagues, drought, fear of Native Americans, winter storms, isolation "fever", and dry farming conditions, all of which required astonishing stamina and grit. From the beginning homesteading was hard work, and it got worse when the charm wore off and some of the better dirt blew away.

The Railroads and Land Speculation

Railroads heavily impacted homesteading. In North Dakota, the Northern Pacific Railroad alone claimed ten million acres as part of its bounty holdings (nearly a third of the state). Not sure at first what to do with so much land, the Northern offered low-cost loans and directed people's attention to the likelihood that they could become wealthy landholders at a small price. Earlier, the Secretary of War in 1827 reported that it would take five hundred years to fill the West. But by 1893 the historian Fredrick Jackson Turner claimed that

---

[1] Terry W. Ahlstedt, *You Take the Low Land and I'll Take the High Land. Land Settlement in Antelope County, Nebraska 1868-1891* (A thesis at the University of Nebraska, 2004), 61.

the West was already filled and that the frontier phase had ended. This was premature.

It was said that with a small grubstake and a twenty-five dollar down payment an "honest, humble sodbuster" could start with a minimum of forty acres and build a farm from earnings generated by the harvest. What was left out Rarely mentioned was the considerable economic risk.

Along the route, railroads built several emigrant reception houses to attract farmers. In some regions they dropped off prefabricated cabins to make it easier to get started. Immigration was just beginning and the stars above in the heavens were full of joy!

The Chicago and Northwestern railroads printed a large poster in bold red letters proclaiming, **"30 Millions of Acres of the Most Productive Grain Lands in the World. You Need a Farm?"** They posted these in public view and capitalized on the psychological attraction of grass-rich lands that made people wealthy. Agents fanned out over the British Isles and Europe, recruiting ambitious and restless individuals looking for their fortunes. Sometimes entire families banded together to come to America. And thousands came. They came from all over Europe including Scandinavia, Germany, and Russia. By far the greatest number of homesteaders, however, relocated from within the United States. The trip across the ocean was difficult. Some passengers were buried at sea because of cholera, scurvy or stormy weather. Whatever the case, after the immigrants arrived, the railroads became the vital artery that brought people, goods, and products to hundreds of prairie communities and to the land offices where claims were filed.

By the turn of the twentieth century, the railroads had sold 120 million acres. Another 80 million "free" acres were taken up by homestead claims. [2] The solitude of the prairie grasslands diminished when they were overrun by homesteaders, chickens, and livestock, and when plows disturbed the native complex soil.

The idea of perpetual progress bolstered immigration to the west. America was on the move. Settlers arrived like Russian tumbleweeds pushed by powerful winds. With each gust, more weeds were dislodged and bounced across the land scattering seeds for next year's yield. So many "Crossers" passed by one settler's cabin that he wondered if anyone had

---

[2] Andro Linklater, *Measuring America* (New York: Penguin Books, 2002), 228.

stayed back home in Pennsylvania. [3] The attraction of free lands pulled labor from the east coast, and this, of course, created another problem.

Congress increased immigration quotas from foreign countries to make up the loss of workers in the east. But newspaper articles, pamphlets, and primers continued to voice an illustrious view of homesteading. The shuffling feet of settlers entranced the railroad executives, land speculators, and state bureaucrats.

But few found instant gratification in the free land, and many found themselves penniless. Feeling the sharp sting of endless toil without prosperity, homesteaders often abandoned their claims and returned east where relatives took pity on them as unfortunate losers. But many had no relatives and were forced to stick it out.

Still most considered the legendary Homestead Act a wonderful idea. Governor Saunders of Nebraska appeared before his state legislators and spoke like a Sunday-school teacher just before the missionary offering was taken, exclaiming "What a blessing this wise and humane legislation will bring to many a poor, but honest and industrious family...The very thought, to such people, that they can now have a tract of land that they can call their own has a soul-inspiring effect upon them and makes them feel thankful that their lots have been cast under a government that is so liberal to its people." [4]

Under the terms of the "free" land in the Homestead Act, a settler to build a house, dig a well, plant ten acres of crop, and remain on the claim for five years as a way of "proving up." Once the five-year milestone was achieved, the claimant talked two neighbors into signing a voucher that he or she had met the prerequisites. The last step involved going to the land office with the voucher and paying four dollars for a "patent." This patent gave full title to the homestead even if the spring wheat had failed to germinate two years in a row or the cotton had pink bollworms in greater numbers than any time since planting. Homesteading turned every man into a farmer and handyman and every woman into a boarding house

---

[3] Everett Dick, *Vanguards of the Frontier* (New York: Appleton-Century Co., 1941), 250.

[4] House Journal of the Territorial Legislature of Nebraska. 9th Session, January 7, 1864. 13.

manager with jurisdiction over the family's spiritual legacy. Do not think homesteading was an easy life.

By 1900 nearly half of America's population lived on farms. In the 1930s this number dropped to one-quarter of the 123 million Americans. Nevertheless, the farmer remained the celebrated heart of America's democratic society. For more than a century and a half Thomas Jefferson's agrarian vision lay at the core of the country's idealism. Each independent family farm became an agency for preserving American democracy. This was one of the reasons why the Homestead Act was created in the first place—to create family farms where wealth could be spread out among the republic's inhabitants and where American civilization could flourish.

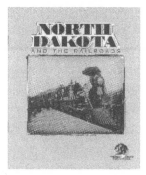

With hindsight, we see the inflated optimism. Railroad agents were so busy attracting homesteaders they failed to mention the grasshoppers or army worms that could eat every blade of grass and crop when they festered and grew outrageous in their eating habits. Nor did the agents tell farmers how hard it would be to eradicate bindweeds, quack grass, perennial sow thistle or leafy spurge and other weeds. They didn't inform the settlers that snowstorms, even blizzards, could hit before harvest, or that mosquitoes in summer could be so merciless, that horses would break loose from their wagons and make a run for it. [5]

The pestiferous insects had been entrenched in their living habits well before the homesteaders poured across the land. The settlers discovered these perils on their own after they began to work the land. They rose every morning to meet the insects head-on, chomping away at their crops. They tried to invent chicken power inside their gardens to pester the insects and poisons to stifle the weeds. Many of the first settlers dispersed like tumbleweeds, blown from the land within a few years. Profound truths, began as pygmies, emerged as giants on the earth.

Labeling the land "The Great American Desert" didn't spook the hoppers or mosquitoes. To this day these insects have the upper hand around the heartland farms of America's plains and prairies. They show up every summer ready for a free potluck provided by the neighborhood

---

[5] *Renville County History* (Renville County Old Settler's Association, 1976), 435.

church of farmers. As if these pests weren't enough, drought, high winds, prairie fires, hail, and tornadoes (called cyclones) withered or flattened the crops. During dry years the land was parched by the hot sun, topsoil blew away, and homesteaders went to bed fearing the loss of everything, including their sanity. Railroad broadsheets and the state immigration pamphlets mentioned none of these vexations. Rather than finding the proffered land of "milk and honey," settlers found dust devils and other torments besides.

Moreover, cholera sickened the hogs, sudden freezes destroyed the family garden, coyotes killed the calves and sheep, and children fell into wells or vanished in snow drifts. [6] Revival preachers traveling through the Plains cited wind, lightning, thunder, and fire in their sermons to make people contemplate righteous living. They told how to avoid hell and everlasting fires by repenting and thus protecting both their properties and their salvation. In this way, religion helped balance the troubled mind.

Salvation wasn't in the land because the Bible said man would have to work by the sweat of his brow. The preachers said that some of these troubles came from God to make sure a sinner's imagination was properly directed toward heaven. In any case, an estimated eighty percent of the early homesteaders left within twenty years of taking out a claim. And each time a settler and his family threw in the towel and moved on, the neighbors shrugged and said, "It's too bad, but ole Johannsen went to live with his wife's folks!"

William Willey, Jr. Takes Out a Homestead

In the fall of 1900, John's father William (Wm) read in the local newspaper about new land grants opening in the northwest region of North Dakota. [7] This "liberating" news turned Wm's thoughts into imaginations so grotesquely overwhelming that it shortened his breath. The newspaper said, "The requirements for land ownership are not difficult, and if things don't work out a person can sell the claim and turn the free land into money."

---

[6] Greyhound dogs were imported to chase down the coyotes. Blanche Hembree. (*Fate, Destiny, Necessity on Renville's Prairies*) Standard Book Number 533-02496, 1977.

[7] *Renville County History* (Renville County Old Settler's Association, 1976), 493.

Wm was a hard worker, sober, and not prone to revolutionary ideas or liberal politics. He lived as close as possible to the values of his upbringing so that no one could find fault in him. He enjoyed settling arguments by logical reasoning and then bringing peace and order. He was a zealous Republican with sufficient savings in the bank to speculate a little on how to obtain his felicity. Unlike some other men he never developed "girlfriends" on the side lest he jeopardize his marriage. He did not gamble and was single-minded about living and justice. What else could one say about him? He worked for his children's health and counted his blessings with gratitude, with prayer, and with devotional attention to his affairs.

Wm missed the good old days when he had farmed his father's homestead. Fearing he'd not be able to protect his young family from hunger he had quit farming in Iowa and gone into steady work as a carpenter in Ruthven. But his veiled restless spirit brooded over the lost adventure in his life. By now he was forty-five years old and still had more than a pound and a half of adventure in his soul. He was subject to mysterious influences of human subconsciousness.

Slowly the exciting newspaper article captured his mind like a candle melted by a fire and he longed to mix with the crowd that was heading west. Wm's brother-in-law Julius Larson (1863-1940), born in Ruthven, came by the carpenter shop and talked about doing the same thing. Both saw themselves as honest and humble pilgrims marching to Zion. In the Colorado gold mines Julius had gotten skunked, and so his pockets were empty. He was ready to be a little less speculative.

Telling no one, Wm went to the Ruthven train station and purchased a ticket to Minot, North Dakota, the place highlighted in the newspaper account. He was slightly perplexed by his own impulsive decision, a weakness stemming from his youth. If he was going to homestead, he must do it quickly and search out what Providence might provide. The prospects obsessed him.

When he told brother-in-law Julius what he'd done, Julius also bought a ticket, convinced now that farming was a better wealth creator than mining. Promising he would not do anything brash he said goodbye to his wife and children.

At the train station, Wm picked up an orange-colored broadside printed on cheap paper by the Hurd Land Agency from Minneapolis with the captivating title, "Free Homestead Lands in Ward County, N. Dak." Minot was the county seat and land office for the new homesteading territory. The broadside contained several extravagant testimonies from successful farmers who had made it "big" in a Danish settlement around Kenmare, North Dakota, just northwest of Minot. Anyone reading these embellished accounts became bound like a person sticking his tongue on a freezing pump handle and not being able to pull it away. As these stories swept into Wm's mind, he fancied himself joining the wealthy farmers and living in a two-story house, with a big barn full of horses and acres of wheat rustling in the wind. Based on this pamphlet there was no doubt about it; a farmer could turn a pure profit in a few years on this land. It would be a happy experience. He knew he could do it — you just wait and see!

He surmised that farming in North Dakota would resemble farming in Iowa, and he hadn't forgotten what it was like to be a farmer, despite the passing of time since he gave up his father's homestead.

Like most people who wake up the day after making a life-changing decision, Julius wasn't sure he was doing the honorable thing by pulling up stakes and moving to such an isolated place in North Dakota near the Canadian border. So, he promised Laura he'd go to Minot and take a "look-see." He might as well have been talking under his breath. By the time he reached Minot any wavering had taken flight. The alluring descriptions of the free prairie lands, plus the testimonies of others on the train, had convinced him that he was on to something. No doctor with a stethoscope was needed to tell him that he was infected with the ambition to become rich. It was obvious. Dreaming of wealth bound him to the earth like the roots of a cottonwood tree seeking water from a nearby stream.

Arriving in Minot Wm checked into the downtown Lexington Hotel. Next morning, at the crack of dawn, he walked to the land office. To his surprise, land seekers like himself were sleeping overnight on the boardwalk and in a vacant lot next to the office to hold their positions in line. [8] Some

---

[8] Ibid. 138, 543.

of these men were "just-off-the-boat" immigrants from Europe who spoke in foreign accents. Others came with money to purchase a claim outright at $1.25 per acre. A few speculators planned to file for land and sell their rights to others in a quick turnaround. Other half-hearted men hoped to acquire a patent after five years and then sell the homestead at a good price and move further west. This was not a one-sided exchange, of course. The land office officials were equally anxious to do business. They got four dollars out of every fourteen-dollar entry fee and a small percentage of the purchase price when they sold land. A huge survey map showing the location of townships with available quarter sections hung in the office. The surveyed squares were filled in as the 160-acre plots were claimed.

For the most part, immigrants and citizens filed their claims sight unseen. The claims ranged north to the Canadian border and west to Montana. As Wm took his turn filling out the paperwork, he felt the same tug of exhilaration a person gets when stepping into a circus ring just as the elephants enter. Sweat ran down his spine. Excitement engulfed him.

Even though Wm did not see his claim beforehand, he had glimpsed the vast treeless prairie from the train window in route to Minot. It had a sameness about it. Probably one quarter-section was as good as any other. Unable to restrain his ambition, Wm had already gone too far. The heavens were full of joy.

Before he left Ruthven, Julius had assured Laura he would "only put the bait in his mouth and not set the hook." He prided himself as a man with good judgment and a superior mind. Now he was hooked like everyone else on the notion of free land, easy ownership terms, and the potential for wealth. Julius took out a homestead next to Wm. He recalled hearing a newspaper journalist say that back at his office he used a kernel of wheat as a paper weight. It was that big!

Wm's claim was located in Hurley Township in Renville County, about fifty miles north of Minot. There were no roads, no towns, and no railroad. Fearing a blizzard and a difficult journey over a crude wagon trail barred by sloughs, he put off visiting the place until he returned the following spring.

Stopping off at the post office Wm sent a postcard to Laura and told her what he had done. "Get ready to build a sod house and raise a cackle of chickens; we are going to become homesteaders. I took out a claim today.

Julius and I are trying to figure out how to get to the stake and take a look at our new farm. Love Wm."

He must have thought that "It will take more persuasion than this to get Laura to abandon our home in Ruthven for a shack built out of mud and dirt and wave goodbye to her friends in the ladies' aide club." They had lived in town for nearly twenty years.

Laura had a square jaw, round face, and good child-bearing hips. She prided herself on her cooking and had the body shape to prove it. Her friends thought of her as spunky with a quick wit and a religious mindset. She openly battled demons to maintain her link with the Almighty. Around the house, she claimed that the devil made her fall behind in her baking, washing, and cleaning. The sad truth was she continued to battle every day with the devil over procrastination, seemingly wicked child behaviors, violations of the golden rule by the neighbors, and other tangible discomforts. A sudden rainstorm pelting her laundry on the clothesline could bother her also. It was easier to blame the devil than to find fault in herself or with nature. Her handsome husband thought of her as sometimes leaping before finding a landing spot. She was energetic, but she also liked to sit by the light of a smoldering fire at night and read her Bible or study her favorite missionary tracts.

How does a man communicate his high hopes for wealth and cravings for adventure when his wife has given birth to four children, likes where she lives, and enjoys deep ties to the Larson relatives? They simply had no reason to leave. The home, free of debt, was painted white with grey trim around the windows and the roof didn't leak. The crickets sounded off-key at night, but that was about it. All the neighbors were good people except one, a Methodist preacher, who seemed jealous of Laura's apparent connection to the Divine. The preacher needed many inhibitions to keep from acting on every impulse.

Wm had plenty of carpentry work in Ruthven. He believed in himself and didn't have to drum up work. The business wasn't big, but it was steady and secure. Wm had nothing to say about the need for more science or religion in his life, or for oaths against alcohol. And Ruthven, with lakes north of town, was a beautiful place to live. There was good fishing. Meadowlarks, black birds, crows, grouse and ducks nested there in the summer. Gravel roads surrounded the farms. Stores offered splendid goods and far more of everything than where they were going. Ruthven farmers were prosperous and now turning a profit—and as usual, it was about moisture and rainfall, which of course would be less where they were going. The soil was fertile and black. Corn could be grown easily, but not in northern North Dakota. Coyotes with mournful howls and reservation Indians that could not be trusted populated the new destination.

Little did Wm know that Laura also desired to shake the Ruthven dust from her feet. One of the demons she talked to Wm about upon his return was the scorn she perceived from her friends. She had a hunch that some town people still saw her as a soiled woman, a fornicator, for what she had done before marrying Wm; of course, not everyone in town could claim abstinence from sex before marriage themselves. Laura wasn't the only one that had a dark moment and a sudden sense of guilt. And in any case, she was not morally diseased.

For years, the Larson family tried to quiet the gossip, but there had been finger pointing as to who had fathered her first-born son Gideon. This came to further light after Wm and Laura immigrated to North Dakota and Gideon returned to Ruthven "to be with his father." Later when Gideon came back to the Willey homestead Wm refused to adopt him and when Wm died in 1920 he had excluded Gideon from his estate. Farmers had a saying about a man tying the knot with an unmarried woman who had a child before marriage — "the husband got a heifer with a calf." But all told, Wm did not have to persuade Laura to leave Ruthven. She was ready to go! (Sadly, Gideon grew up miserably mindful of his mother's transgression.)

In March 1902 they sold their Ruthven house and carpenter shop and prepared to break new ground in North Dakota. They traveled in a railroad box car loaded with horses, two wagons, a small amount of machinery, seed for grain, and their household effects. In Minot they transferred to the Minneapolis, St Paul SOO Line that took them to their destination in Kenmare, North Dakota. Just before they arrived, a sudden three-day blizzard had struck with the thermometer dropping below 40 degrees. Consequently, they waited a few days at the train siding for the snows to melt. After unloading the boxcar, they drove thirty-five miles east to their claim and saw their "very own land" for the first time. They really didn't own it yet, but it would be theirs if they endured five years of proving up. Only six other families lived nearby when they arrived. [9]

The snowstorm left water in the lowlands, potholes, and sloughs. That invited swarms of mosquitoes when spring arrived. They wore netting over their heads and covered the livestock with blankets. In the evening mosquitoes swirled in columns forty-feet or more in height, five-feet across, and almost as dense as a tree trunk. You could punch a hole with your fist through the swirling insects, but you'd better prepare to run and dive to the ground before doing something so foolish. It wasn't amusing to lie prostrate on your back and watch biting insects, literally looking for blood, fly overhead in a hostile swarm.

Bad as the mosquitos were, the settlers stretched the truth about them when writing to unsophisticated city folks back home. One farmer told his relatives in Illinois; "I got up this morning and found the mosquitoes had eaten my horse, laying out the bones in a manner of a horse still standing." He went on to say, "over to the side I saw two mosquitoes pitching horseshoes to see who got the harness!"

At first, the family slept on the ground under a wagon propped up with a "half-face" tent to keep out the wind. Shortly after arriving in North Dakota Wm and Laura how much loneliness would be felt and how much fortitude it would take to stick it out. They alternated between high spirits of adventure and fears that mischief could overtake them. During this first summer, Laura suffered a nameless nerve condition triggered by a vivid imagination of Indian attacks.

Before coming she'd read about the Indian massacres committed against settlers in Minnesota and Iowa. Fear of being molested and scalped haunted her sleep. Laura began drinking Motherwort tea to quiet her nerves. Seeing how a little "medication" helped his wife, Wm maintained he always felt safer after supper if he ate custard pie with extra nutmeg before going to sleep! There were no mountains, protective forests, gullies or other places to hide, just overwhelming prairie with blue sky and fluffy white cumulus clouds in the summer and low-lying grey clouds in the winter. Their nearest neighbor, Julius Larson, lived a mile away. Wisely, Wm was careful not to talk about the small band of Indians he had seen around the Souris River during his first trip to Minot.

---

[9] "Pioneers Here Recall March Storm of 1902," *Renville County Farmer*, March 12, 1933.

John Willey Stays in School at Ruthven

Son John was seventeen, four years younger than Gideon, when his father homesteaded in North Dakota. John was a very different person than Gideon; there was more personal warmth, and a greater willingness to work. He thought that electrical treatments might benefit Gideon, but he had no first-hand knowledge about such treatments, nor had he known anyone who had. But maybe it would make Gideon less despondent. He'd read about the use of electricity in treatment from a health magazine published by John Harvey Kellogg at the Battle Creek Sanitarium in Michigan.

John stayed behind in Ruthven to finish high school and play out the spring baseball season. He pitched for the towns' team with a fine curve ball. Around the middle of June, he bought a train ticket to Minot and departed Ruthven. From Minot he set out on foot, carrying his bindle-stiff, his father's claim sixty miles away. In his pocket, he carried a description of his father's homestead location and its proximity to Mohall, North Dakota. He used a compass to stay the course around the sloughs. Along the way, a stray black and white dog joined up with him. He named the dog Dibbits and they remained together until Dibbits died from eating too much rabbit— or of old age. No one knew for sure.

By winding up prairie grass and weeds into tight bundles, John made a fire and cooked fish when no hospitable farmhouse was in sight. The dog curled up around his knees to keep him warm during the night. A few times he caught buggy rides across the open plains. (In those days traveling was more by wit and grit than by road.) Sometimes he stayed at farms and met homesteaders like himself. By the time he arrived at his folk's place, he had some idea of what to expect. Fresh from high school John doubled the workforce on his father's farm.

A few weeks later he saw a huge dust devil swirling on the edges of their pasture near Uncle Julius' place. The wind was a constant source of displeasure. Before coming to North Dakota, his father had tried to talk him into enrolling in Mendota Seminary, an Advent Christian college in Mendota, Illinois, but John had decided on farming long before he contemplated the comfort and reassurance of a preacher's life.

With little protection from the elements, the men's priorities were survival and knowledge of farm practices in the northern Plains. They  built a one-room sod house out of prairie marble (sod). First, the grass was mowed. Bricks of sod were then cut from the prairie using a walking mole plow. The steel plow cut through the ground about two inches deep leaving a ribbon of sod ten inches wide that was hacked into foot-long bricks. These bricks were hauled from the field and stacked on top of each other to make the walls. Each layer alternated as the sides went up. They placed a door facing south and cut out a window in the east wall. The insides were plastered with mud and then white-washed. The roof was made of wood slats, tar papered, and more prairie marble layered over the top. The finished sod house measured fourteen feet on each side. It was cool in the summer and warm in the winter. For the time being, it provided adequate protections from mother nature.

A neighbor, who had arrived the year before, and now considered himself a seasoned settler, told Wm about the winter winds from Canada. He warned, "Make sure you're prepared to retreat from the world. A blizzard wind out here is like a battering ram. Whatever you do don't go out in the deep snow drifts and wander over the trackless prairie. You'll get lost, freeze, and die." This same neighbor also warned Wm about prairie fires and advised him to plow a generous circle around his soddy. As he was leaving, he called out, "Watch out for the prairie wolves and coyotes as they will try to lure Dibbits into the grass for a gratifying meal." By the end of the summer, the flock of twenty-four Rock Island chickens they brought with them from Iowa had vanished to the coyotes and weasels.

They dug a well sixteen-feet deep and three feet wide near the sod house and waited for water to seep into the opening. The well was covered with a wooden lid to stay the mice and gophers and barbwire around the edge to fence out the livestock. From somewhere little green frogs crawled into the well. Until the well began to produce, the men hauled water from a nearby pothole by the corner of the pasture.

They planted potatoes, carrots, and a few other garden vegetables, and prepared for winter by stacking prairie hay near the sod house for the livestock. A temporary shelter was constructed for the horses and cows, mostly to keep out the wind and snow. Everyone helped, including John's two younger sisters, Jonetta (1885-1933) and Grace (1888-1974). That first summer John also worked for other homesteaders. He broke ground behind a five-horse gang plow and he got two dollars an acre. He turned over five to eight acres in a day's work. Taking some of this money, he ordered a tennis set from Sears, Roebuck and Company. The Gates boys and the other neighbor kids came over and smoothed out a dusty tennis court where they amused themselves on an imprint of Wimbledon! [10]

Despite these preparations, they remained apprehensive about the Dakota winters. It wouldn't do any good to scream for help during a blizzard; they would discover this soon enough. The blizzard of March 1904 was the worst storm in forty years. It left so much snow that the Willey's had to dig a ten-foot stairwell to the surface of the drift in order to climb out of the house. North Dakota winters were more severe than those in Iowa. About twice a month they drove with team and bob sleigh over to Sherwood or Mohall to buy coal, kerosene, and groceries. They carried heated stones for foot warmers.

Claim shacks began to appear on the horizon. Jimmy Anderson, a bachelor, took the claim south of the Willey's. Julius Larson homesteaded the quarter to the east. Julius had graduated from Union College in Lincoln, Nebraska, and was the best-educated man in Hurley Township. For this reason, he was respected and assigned to oversee elections and chair the school district (although Julius and his wife never had any children of their own). When Julius passed away in 1940, his farm was sold for five hundred dollars, and his wife moved to Colorado to live with her sister. Julius "invented" an inside sewer system of sorts in his farmhouse, but it froze every winter and consigned him in an unmerciful battle with odors that were worse than a chicken coop.

On occasion wood claim shacks on skids were stolen by thieves taking advantage of the remoteness of North Dakota. They would come with a team and if no one was home hitch up the shack and tow it away. Once out of sight they robbed the interior and sold the lumber. One homesteader living in Grover Township hid in his shack and rode it out as the thieves

---

[10] Ibid. 493.

were making their getaway! Five miles "down the road" he opened the door and pointed the shotgun at the thieves and shouted, "Okay fellows, take it back to where you got it." [11] There was no ensuing argument, for just then he pointed the gun in the air and brought down a Mallard Duck that had flown in from the field.

The next summer Wm and son John crossed the Canadian border to buy building materials for a frame house. Construction went up quickly. Neighbors came together to form a building bee. The men hammered and sawed the timbers under Wm's supervision. When the house was completed, it looked more like a barn with swooping roof line than a house. It had the same design as John Power's stone house northeast of

RESIDENCE OF WM. WILLEY,
MOHALL, N. D.

Loraine. During construction, the women did the cooking, standing outside around hot coals or sitting on rough-hewn furniture. They filled the air with laughter, conversing about family life and gossiping about the neighbors. Such house-raisings forged strong bonds between neighbors and enabled them to share each other's joys, burdens, and sorrows. The "old" soddy was turned into a barn after the family moved into the frame house. They left the wood house drab and unpainted for many years and papered the inside with old newspapers to keep out the frost and wind. Wm next built a barn close to the house.

After proving up the homestead, the recorded patent hung in a frame on the kitchen wall. It was signed by President Theodore Roosevelt. Thusly Wm and Laura Willey came to own a quarter section in township 162N, range 084W and section 20. Soon John's father purchased the relinquished quarter from bachelor Anderson across the road. By 1907 Wm and son John were farming two quarters or 320 acres together. That was the year John got married—as they used to say, "for better or for worse."

---

[11] Ibid. 361.

SEVENTH-DAY SABBATH OBSERVANCE
CHAPTER SIX

Suppose an individual believes something with his whole heart, suppose further that he has a commitment to this belief, that he has taken irrevocable actions because of it; finally, suppose that he is presented with evidence, unequivocal and undeniable evidence, that his belief is wrong: what will happen? The individual will frequently emerge, not only unshaken, but even more convinced of the truth of his beliefs than ever before. Indeed, he may even show a new fervor about convincing and converting other people to his view. Leon Festinger, Henry W. Riecken, Stanley Schachter, *When Prophecy Fails* (Minneapolis, MN: University of Minnesota Press, 1956).

After John's parents settled in North Dakota, his mother Laura continued her faith in the Seventh-day Sabbath along with the strict dietary habits promoted by her church. His father Wm remained with the First Advent Christian church. When it came to Sabbath observance Wm nominally slowed down from work on Sunday—though he began to sympathize with his wife's Saturday Sabbath. Wm ate meat and drank coffee, which loyal Adventists were not to do. In keeping his own principles, he had signed the temperance pledge years ago while living in Ruthven.

Central Concerns of Adventism

The central concerns of the Seventh-day Adventists were salvation, the Sabbath, and the Second Coming. There were other things too. According to revelations from the "Spirit of Prophecy" eating meat "strengthens the animal passions ... and foods should be prepared without grease." And the prophetess added, "Those who profess to be fit for translation should not become butchers" [1] Pork was prohibited in Judaism and Islam, probably because pork inadequately cooked contributed to trichinosis. Poorly cooked

---

[1] Ellen G. White, *Testimonies*, II, 60, 352.

beef contributed to anthrax, giant tapeworms, and brucellosis. But eating meat will not "strengthen the animal passions." This was a phrenology concept rejected as pseudo-science.

When they took out the homestead in North Dakota, Wm had not made decided to join the Seventh-day Adventists, but he knew he must come to some kind of resolution. He'd seen and heard his wife weeping and praying over her fears that probation was closing and that her husband and children, still unconverted to the Adventist faith, might not be saved. To her a person had to be an Adventist to be taken up into heaven, but she hadn't told Wm the full story. He would have to change some mundane habits. Probably the one teaching that most concerned him was the dietary counsel to give up meat eating. Adventists were trying to avoid meat eating altogether because if you ate meat you were "liable to acute attacks of disease and to sudden death" and therefore "man shall degrade to an animal" and could not be translated. [2] Eating meat got Wm through the winter while working outside in the cold. Besides, he sold meat to the markets in town. He hunted for deer near the Mouse River and shared the meat with his neighbors.

Still, because her husband and children worshipped on Sunday, they were not ready for Christ's coming. This was serious. Laura was convinced she had the "truth" and it was horrifying to think that only she, of all the family members, would soon depart for heaven. Right now, the encampment of believers was in a preparation mode.

Then Jesus ceases His intercession in the sanctuary above. He lifts His hands and with a loud voice says, "It is done;" and all the angelic host lay off their crowns as He makes the solemn announcement: "He that is unjust, let him be unjust still: and he which is filthy, let him be filthy still: and he that is righteous, let him be righteous still: and he that is holy, let him be holy still." Every case has been decided for life or death. [3]

There was very little chance Laura would change her mind since Jesus' was in the heavenly sanctuary preparing to leave soon, and judgment was nearly completed. Her church had privileged knowledge through a prophetess, and believers had the breathtaking responsibility of preaching the everlasting gospel to all the world so that people would be ready for the

---

[2] Ibid. 61.

[3] Ellen G. White, *The Great Controversy* (chapter 39).

Second Coming of Jesus. This belief prevailed over the fact that, to this point, it had been disconfirmed. She could not be lukewarm.

Laura also faced her husband's skepticism about preaching the gospel to all the world, and about the requirement to be "without spot or blemish" before Jesus could return. *"Without holiness no man shall see the Lord."* John thought these perfection prerequisites could not be reached even with help from the Holy Spirit. But, he sighed, "It was useless to disagree with her."

Still, to gain harmony, it wasn't long until Wm began to lean toward the strong convictions of his wife. "Maybe that strange Adventist prophetess was right about some things." Wm heard that Ellen White had travelled to heaven and back in a vision and had been shown that Christ had died to make an atoning sacrifice for man's sin and "the world was coming to an end very soon with all the turmoil." Even so there was a rock in the threshing machine: the Kingdom of Heaven could not be realized by supernatural miracles but only by man's completing the responsibility to finish the work.

White told how the

> *Power of God came upon me as I never had felt it before. I was surrounded by light and was rising higher and higher from the earth. I turned to look for the Advent people in the world but could not find them—when a voice said to me 'Look again and look (sic) a little higher.' At this I raised my eyes and saw a straight and narrow path, cast up high above the world. On this the path the Advent people were traveling to the city, which was at the further end of the path. They had a bright light set up behind them at the first end of the path, which an angel told me was the Midnight Cry. This shone all along the path and gave light for their feet that they might not stumble. And if they kept their eyes fixed on Jesus, who was just before them, leading them to the city, they were safe.* [4]

From this vision it seemed that God's people were not left in the dark concerning last day events. *"The day of the Lord shall come as a thief in the night."* But other conditions were confusing. The United States would

---

[4] Ellen G. White, *Spiritual Gifts*, II, 31.

supposedly force everyone to worship on Sunday and bear the Mark of the Beast on their foreheads or in the palms of their hands. Everyone, on pain of death, would have to obey a National Sunday Law passed by Catholics and Protestants united under one banner. Thus, it appeared that America would become intolerant of religious freedom. A death decree would be the last struggle between good and evil. Probation would close and a time of trouble would ensue just before the arrival of Christ. White's authority, of course, came out of her self-proclaimed supernatural visions during which the Holy Spirit carried her back and forth from heaven to earth to deliver messages about the end of history. She warned

> *When Protestantism shall stretch her hand across the gulf to grasp the hand of the Roman power, when she shall reach over the abyss to clasp hands with spiritualism, when, under the influence of this three-fold union, our country shall repudiate every principle of its Constitution as a Protestant and republican government and shall make provision for the propagation of papal falsehoods and delusions (Sunday laws), then we may know that the time has come for the marvelous working of Satan and that the end is near.* [5]

Not everyone concurred with the prophetess. Ellen White had her outspoken critics. For instance, in the *Review* W.H. Ball raised objections to the visions.[6] Elders B.F. Snook and W.H. Brinkerhoff published a pamphlet titled *The Visions of Mrs. White Not of God*. These former evangelists now alleged that many of the things Ellen White claimed to have seen in heaven were false.[7] Their criticisms were noted by the Sunday-keeping Advent Christians, and Wm knew about them. It was not clear sailing for the prophetess.

Out where the Willey's lived on the homestead there were few religious instructions other than a pamphlet or Adventist book dropped off by a

---

[5] Ellen G. White, *Testimonies*, V, 451 (1885).

[6] "Objections to the Visions," *Review and Herald*, January 21, 1862, 62.

[7] The first tract on baptism in the Adventist church was written by B.F. Snook, *The Nature, Subjects and Design of Christian Baptism*. Adventists practice baptism by immersion.

colporteur. There were no Adventist churches or meeting houses near their homestead. Within a few years of homesteading, Methodists, Lutherans, and Catholics had built churches in nearby Mohall, North Dakota. But they all worshiped on the wrong day and didn't talk specifics about the end of the world, just general terms. These churches formed an emotional trust between its members and became truly robust foundations for the Mohall township.

All Laura had to go on for the most part was the church's weekly publication *The Advent Review and Sabbath Herald* (*Review*) that came free in the mail. It was full of end-time events, interesting letters to the editor, and reviews of the church teachings. On rare occasion, she had contact with other Adventists in the state. When possible, two or three Sabbath-keeping families would meet and read Scriptures, study the prophet's testimonies, (Red Books), and sing hymns. Occasionally an Adventist minister showed up to perform a wedding or funeral or seek offerings for missionary work or building projects.

But in the end, Laura's moral stamina was stronger than Wm's. She believed that Jesus was in heaven with the angels conducting the investigative judgment of the righteous and wicked. He was almost ready to launch the Second Coming. All of this comported with men's innate sense that they have a duty to eschew evil and do good. We reap what we sow. The teaching that God's final judgment was in full sway, and that His sanctions were eternal was mostly an Adventist view not shared by other denominations, at least not with the same intensity.

When Ellen White entered a trance people around her covered her nose and mouth. They held a mirror to her face looking for breath; they pinched her and pretended to hit her; and they shined a bright light into her eyes. But she was lost to this world, removed to a heavenly or spiritual realm. After one of her visions she told those standing around as she gained consciousness. *"I saw the great host of the lost. Oh, what a sight. The terror and agony of soul that was on those people. I looked upon them and saw here and there all among them some of our own people, some of the Seventh-day Adventists scattered here and there."* [8]

After a vision she pictured Jesus with a kind face and well-feathered

---

[8] Teresa and Arthur Beem, *It's Okay Not to be a Seventh-day Adventist* (Charleston, SC: BookSurge Publ., 2008), 81.

wings sitting at a table with a writing quill in his hand and a large bound "Book of Life" opened on top of other leather-bound books spread around his desk. A beautiful beam of light shone on his work. He was actively working on the judgment as angels traveled back and forth to earth. In this convincing illustration of the judgment provided by the church, Laura could make out the round earth with faint oceans and lands in cosmic space. This image was used often and burned into her psyche from an illustration she saw in *Our Paradise Home* (1903), a book she had obtained from a colporteur.

As a consequence of her reading, Laura practiced a strong form of legalism—good deeds, sacred obligations, and daily repentance and prayer (obedience to the law was vital to her salvation). Her faith reflected practical behavior more than deep theological beliefs. She knew about God's grace and righteousness by faith, but those ideas reduced the power of the judgement scene. The Ten Commandments, and especially the fourth commandment on Sabbath-keeping, preoccupied her. The prophetess had said;

> *Christ is waiting with longing desire for the manifestation of Himself in His church. When the character of Christ shall be perfectly reproduced in His people, then He will come to claim them as His own.* [9]

She yearned to go to heaven with her husband and all four of her children notwithstanding her pre-marital deeds involving the birth of Gideon. Back in the old country, this behavior was fairly common among young Norwegian girls, but now as she got older she loathed the very idea of children born out of wedlock

But the earlier transgression was something she could not change, and all she could do was to rely on the grace of Christ's blood—although the blood part of salvation seemed a little complicated to her. In any religion, you believe some things without complete evidence and reasoning, and sometimes even beyond the reach of human consciousness.

---

[9] Ellen G. White, *Christ Object Lessons,* 69.

Preparation for Heaven

Her folks condemned her frolicking in the hayloft with the neighbor boy. The Larson's felt that a woman who gives birth before marriage must move away and put the baby up for adoption. And it is true that during her pregnancy she was nearly hysterical, wanting to take the train West or a boat down the Mississippi. She would abandon church, family, and child. But stumbling into Wm was providential. He listened to her distress and softened her desire to run away from her kinship. To be honest, Wm considered her transgression a preparation for a healthy commitment to marriage. She knew the ropes for motherhood!

Wm first learned of Laura's pregnancy when he and Laura had taken cover in her father's barn with rain coming down in buckets. Lightning snapped all around as they stood near the doorway talking and watching the thunderous storm. Weighed down with heavy guilt, Laura confessed her moral offense and expressed her desire to run away. But Wm talked her out of it, saying "There is every place to run to but no place to hide," and "Once you eat the turkey, it won't grow feathers again. Accept your mistake and love your child just as if he had come from normal circumstances." Did he get his ideas out of a psychology or phrenology book or was this how he truly felt? It didn't sound like something most of her Christians neighbors might say under the circumstances.

Wm was attracted to her Norwegian accent, shy smile, and strange views of the future. They slowly got to know each other and eventually married. After their wedding, Wm noticed troubling glances from town people. Had he finally owned up to be the father? But this didn't bother him; he knew the truth of the matter. He'd take care of the boy as his own, and shame on the neighbor who acted innocent of any wrongdoing.

So here they were years later continuing to deal with the judgment. All along Wm was more causal about the whole idea of Biblical judgment since he believed in God's grace as the only way of dealing with sin. To him the Bible was plain: *"I do not frustrate the grace of God: for if righteousness came by the law, then Christ is dead in vain."* [10] At the time, he was more worried about the economic conditions surrounding the price of farm commodities and the work he put into raising crops against the returns. The difficulties

---

[10] Galatians 2:21.

he encountered from the grain brokers, grain elevators, railroads and Millers in Minnesota concerned him more than a religious judgment way in a future he couldn't see. A Christian should allow men and women under the guidance of the Holy Spirit to read Scripture and reach their own understanding. Wm was a cheerful and sunny individual living in his wife's world of judgement and probations and denials of freedom.

However, within a few years of homesteading Laura's Adventist convictions subtly began to prevail in the family. As the world kept industrializing, more things seemed to suggest that Christ was coming soon. No matter what was happening in the commercial world, sinners still needed to repent, believe, and be baptized. Wm's father-in-law also urged him to be baptized for the sake of harmony.

God in heaven must have heard Laura's prayers. She'd certainly cried loud enough for Him to do something. Finally, her husband's resistance weakened as he was pushed, gently but firmly, towards the Seventh-day Adventist faith. Meanwhile, Wm was feeling good. Farming showed some success. The morning air brought the odor of Timothy hay and waving wheat, which was growing higher because of the spring and summer rains. Wm added more pieces to his farm—the number of acres he farmed was enlarging, and his son John arrived to help out. Also, son Gideon, with his wife, Rachael, had moved from Ruthven and began farming a quarter west of the homestead.

Son John Becomes a Seventh-day Adventist

Son John decided to "take his stand" with the Seventh-day Adventists in July 1906 while attending a camp meeting in Stanley, North Dakota. According to the *Review* there were twelve other young people baptized during these summer meetings. [11] John was baptized by Elder P.T. Magan, who later (after taking medicine) became dean and president of the College of Medical Evangelists in California (now Loma Linda University Medical School). [12]

Three weeks later, after visiting believers in Canada, Magan came

---

[11] *Review and Herald,* July 26, 1906.

[12] College of Medical Evangelists became Loma Linda University School of Medicine in California. Notes obtained from the P.T. Magan journal in the Heritage Library at Loma Linda University. Merlin L. Neff, *For God and CME* (Mountain View, CA: Pacific Press, 1964).

through Kenmare, North Dakota. The Willey's went to hear him speak in the home of a Danish convert. On this occasion, Magan preached two sermons on the United States in prophecy. These sermons strengthened the family's faith. By the end of the summer, the entire Willey family accepted Adventism (although Giddeon not so much), and the Larson family back in Iowa rejoiced that a heavy weight was lifted from their hearts and minds. The *Review* didn't report when Wm Willey converted to Adventism; He seems to have slipped under the fence when he saw an opening in the barbed wire and simply declared himself to be an Adventist. Of course, he would have protested had he been pinned to the ground and dragged into the faith. Two daughters, Grace and Jovelle, "sort of" adopted Adventism in their youth and eventually joined the churches of their spouses.

Years later, John admitted he had gone to the Stanley summer camp meeting to make peace with his mother and explore her faith in the Soon Coming. Often, he heard her in prayer beseeching her Father in Heaven to impress her son to accept the Sabbath truth before it was too late. Perhaps he had brought this persistence on himself from talking too much about the paradoxes and contradictions in the Bible that she couldn't always explain. She'd say, "John, there is a hint of heretic propensity in your thinking, and I don't know how you expect to join me in heaven when you're such a doubter and say these things to make your mother unhappy?" He'd named one of his workhorses "Temperance," and the other "Reform," but that didn't placate his mother!

Before the camp meeting, she had coaxed him into reading back issues of the *Review*. This Adventist publication contained mission field reports, obituary notices, prophetic speculation, and religious instruction about the dead, tithing, baptism, Sabbath keeping, and other related matters. In 1906 the Review emphasized attempts by the National Reform Association to amend the Constitution to declare the United States a "Christian nation." The Association also pushed for stricter Sunday observance and this sounded like a fulfillment of prophecy. The rapid fulfillment of the prophetess's predictions of future Sunday laws be denied

President Teddy Roosevelt had been urged to share with congress his "explicit acknowledgment of the moral laws of Jesus Christ and God and His divine law as the basis and standard of all legislation." [13] And

---

[13] "Two Significant Reports," *Advent Review and Sabbath Herald*, December 21, 1905.

Congressman Heflin from Alabama sponsored a Sunday law "prohibiting labor on buildings in the District of Columbia on the Sabbath day." He lamented to the *Washington Post* that "you walk around this city on Sunday, and it is no uncommon thing to see men working on buildings as though this were a heathen land, or there was no such thing as the Sabbath." [14]

If his legislation did not pass, he said, the "wives of members of Congress will continue to hold receptions and give bridge-whist parties on Sunday." Agitation for Sunday legislation spread, although many states already had Sunday Blue Laws on the books before the turn of the nineteenth century. In January 1906 the *Review* reported that a proposal for Sunday laws had spread across the border into Canada. [15] This was close to home.

John read about sports being affected by Sunday closing laws. There would be no more Sunday baseball games in Cattaraugus County, New York. The sheriff had declared; "The order is interpreted so strictly that the mere tossing of a ball to and fro is as much a violation of the order...as if a nine-inning game and a crowded grandstand were the features on record against the defendant. The sheriff's office has received many complaints against Sunday ball this season, and Sheriff Waite has deemed it time that something be done." [16]

The *Review* reported a Massachusetts Supreme Court decision that gathering cranberries on Sunday violated a statute prohibiting any manner of labor, business, or work, except works of necessity and charity, on the Lord's Day. The Court said the law aimed to "secure the observance of the Lord's day in accordance with the views of our ancestors." [17]

Talk about Sunday laws triggered a "doomsday" fever in the Adventist

---

[14] *Advent Review and Sabbath Herald,* March 22, 1906. "If this is not going back to the Dark Ages and walking in the steps of the papacy, then I do not know the black horse and his rider in the apocalyptic vision." *Advent Review and Sabbath Herald,* May 3, 1906. Closer to home, Canada was also considering the Sunday law agitation, May 31, 1906, June 14, 1906, and June 21, 1906.

[15] A. O. Burrill, "Intolerance in Canada," *Advent Review and Sabbath Herald,* January 4, 1906.

[16] K. C. Russell, "Religious Liberty Notes," *Advent Review and Sabbath Herald,* June 14, 1906.

[17] *Advent Review and Sabbath Herald,* March 22, 1906.

mind. [18] Revelation 13 described a "beast coming up out of the earth; that had two horns like a lamb, and he spake as a dragon." Adventist theologians identified this beast as the United States. As they saw it, this beast began with the youthful energy of a lamb (Protestantism), but then turned into a cruel persecuting beast represented by the Catholics (the dark symbols of the Apocalypse. Remarkably modern events were anticipated in the Bible more than two centuries before.

By this time over a hundred Seventh-day Adventists in the United States had been arrested for working on the first day of the week. These arrests resulted in fines and costs amounting to $2,269.69, and imprisonment totaling 1,438 days, with 455 of these days served in chain gangs." [19] Upon the advice of the church, the violators refused to pay the fines and stood firm on the word of God. They explained in court that they didn't need legal representation; [20] the Bible had already instructed them to stand up to their convictions.

And when they bring you unto the synagogues, and unto magistrates, and powers, take ye no thought how or what thing ye shall answer, or what ye shall say: For the Holy Ghost shall teach you in the same hour what ye ought to say. [21]

Newspapers across America deplored these arrests as a return "to the days of Cotton Mather and the Spanish Inquisition." [22] But in Adventist eschatology two great errors, the immortality of the soul and Sunday sacredness would usher in the long-expected Adventist millennium and end of the world. Then, as suddenly as persecution had begun, the wave of arrests for working on Sunday disappeared. But for John, the prophet's

---

[18] Ellen G. White, *The Great Controversy,* 588. Even "labor unions were being used as an instrument in the hands of the Roman power to accomplish certain ends," *Advent Review and Sabbath Herald,* February 8, 1906.

[19] Richard W. Schwarz, "The Perils of Growth 1886-1905" in Gary Land. (ed.) *Adventists in America: A History* (Grand Rapids, MI: William B. Eerdmans Publ. Co. 1986), 97.

[20] Everett Dick, "The Cost of Discipleship: Seventh-day Adventists and Tennessee Sunday Laws in the 1890's," Adventist Heritage, Spring 1986, 26.

[21] Luke 12:11-12.

[22] Charles Teel, Jr., "Bridegroom or Babylon Dragon or Lamb?" *Adventist Heritage,* Spring, 1986, 25.

prediction had come true. (He ignored or did not care that Mormons, Catholics, Jews, and Negroes had suffered far greater persecution in America than the Adventists.)

Perilous Times

During the July camp meeting, John had listened to a sermon on the United States in Prophecy. This was the present keynote in Adventism evangelism. The preacher discussed how the biblical prophecies had been "fulfilled" by inventions such as the railroads, steam engines, new farm implements, clothes washers, vacuum cleaners, territorial expansion, the growth of other technologies, and fire coming down from heaven in the form of the telegraph. Great religious revivals were happening. People "were running to and fro," searching for God. The world stood on the brink of Armageddon.

The preacher went on to warn, "Just a little flaw in a rail, or in a wheel, or in a bit of machinery, just a little carelessness, and scores of people may lose their lives. We are always on the lookout for big things; but it is the little things that escape detection that cause the great mischief." [23] This was serious stuff!

The preacher told his audience that Seventh-day Adventists were the "last true church" since they alone "kept all the Ten Commandments of God and had the Spirit of Prophecy active among them." He said that once the Third Angel's Message (the sanctuary and Sabbath doctrines) became known to all the world, the Lord would come to take his remnant saints home with Him to heaven. It was the responsibility of Adventists to preach this Third Angel's message. [24] And now with the invention of the telegraph, the gospel message could be beamed to the entire world. Later, when television was invented Adventists found a new medium for spreading the gospel instantly and quickly.

Adventist preachers took most of their end-time messages from the book of Revelation, a book that had frightened John when he was young because of its dragons, mysterious candlesticks, flaming clouds, plagues,

---

[23] *Advent Review and Sabbath Herald,* March 22, 1906, 12.

[24] Revelation 12:17 KJV: "And the dragon was wroth with the woman and went to make war with the remnant of her seed, which keeps the commandments of God, and have the testimony of Jesus Christ."

a lake of fire, Jezebel, Armageddon, angels flying all over the place; God's wrath, beasts with seven eyes or ten horns, and a many other scary things. Some of these images would fit nicely into comic books!

As the preacher delivered his message, he paced back and forth across the platform with furor and excitement, wiping his brow from time to time. When he spoke about the wicked and the lake of fire John squirmed. Satan and his wicked angels were depicted as flying about tempting the saints with the least provocation. Believers were warned that Satan was going beyond ordinary sinners to focus on the Adventists who were more likely to be saved. John felt God peering down at him at that very moment, turning the pages in the Book of Life so as to take his own sins into consideration. Was he prepared for the judgment and the close of probation while the United States was on the brink of a national Sunday law? John wanted to spring out of his seat and go outside to get some fresh air. Other righteous infidels were standing around outside the tent, afraid to hear any more terror.

He kept thinking that if these last day events were recorded somewhere, what kept Satan from reading it and taking steps to throw the saints off on their predictions? Even if the "cunning deceiver" couldn't read or write, at least he could eavesdrop on humans and hear what the preacher said was going to happen. What kept Satan from foiling these plans?

There was another thing. John kept thinking, "If ministers and prophets really could see the impending events like this all laid out beforehand was the future predetermined? Where was free choice in all these prophecies, and if these predictions did not come true wouldn't that contravene the divine will?" Such doubting and self-generated skepticism annoyed John." He sometimes found himself taking the opposite position from what the preacher said. He even wondered if Satan himself might be entering his thoughts to raise his skepticism and doubts.

John's unorthodox thoughts were quickly stifled when the preacher suddenly stopped his pacing, raised his arms, and exclaimed in a loud voice; "Listen to me, brothers and sisters. I don't like to say this, but Satan is hovering right outside this tent tonight ready to devour every unrepentant sinner." John decided to not go out at this time!

"Do you want to leave here unrighteous tonight and soiled of sin? Or do you want to be ready when Jesus comes, standing spotless before the Throne of God?" Which will it be?

The preacher continued to preach about the home in heaven that was prepared for the righteous. He made Christ's soon appearance so vivid in John's mind that he could not block it out. It seemed the only missing part was the actual trumpet sounds and the appearance of a small dark cloud the size of a man's hand with Jesus and the angels coming out of the east. Sensed a mysterious power behind the preacher and his message that he could not explain. The preacher kept saying, "The final moments in earth's history will be rapid ones, and everyone will be surprised how fast the end time will come." Within religious groups, prophecy seldom takes a nose-dive. Believers will look to their ecclesial leaders for guidance to reaffirm predicted events if something goes wrong.

Toward the end of his sermon, the preacher described a vision that the prophetess had concerning the nearness of the end. Fifty years earlier an angel came down from heaven and informed Sister White that some of the people in her audience that day during the 1856 Battle Creek Conference would die before Christ comes, but others would be alive and translated to heaven without seeing death. He went on to add that many now had already passed away, but a few were still living. This can only mean that the door of probation is not completely closed. There is still time to repent. But as each person leaves the scene, the end will get closer. Pretty soon only a few will be left who were there in 1856. Now it was only a matter of a few months until the Lord would come blazing across the sky!

The preacher paused… waiting for his words to sink in. Even the people mulling outside the tent stopped talking. Then he solemnly lowered his head so he could look straight into the faces of his listeners and began reading from a book he held in his hand. He read the prophetess' exact words:

> I was shown the company present at the conference. Said the angel: Some food for worms, some subjects of the seven last plagues, some will be alive and remain upon the earth to be translated at the coming of Jesus.' Solemn words were these, spoken by the angel. [25]

After closing the book, the preacher clarified the sober words he had just read. "Sister White through her prophetic gifts, a mouthpiece for the

---

[25] Ellen White, *Testimonies to the Church*, I, 131-132.

angel, saw that some people attending this Battle Creek conference would become food for worms before the end of time. This meant they would die before Christ's return. The expression food for worms," he said, "deepens our connection to the earth when we die."

Next, he explained what would happen to those who wouldn't become food for worms. "Some people in that Battle Creek audience will be alive during the time of the last plagues but will perish during the persecution by apostate Christians. And the last group will be alive throughout the last plagues and see Jesus return to take the saints to heaven without suffering death!" [26] We are living in the glorious time of the end.

Now he had John's attention! Doubts vanished, like the footprints of wolves when the snow blows hard across the prairies. They were living at the end. The preacher pulled out a sheet of paper and read the names and ages of twenty-seven people still living who made up the original audience in 1856 that he had just described. Someone was obviously keeping a list of these people. He said, "Only about a third of the people remain alive today, the youngest is fifty-two, and the oldest is seventy-nine. Forty have already died—food for worms." In fact he said, "Clara Bonfoey died only three days after Sister White's vision." [27]

John's opposition to switching from Advent Christian to the Seventh-day Adventists finally crumbled. He resolved to keep the Saturday Sabbath and get ready for the Second Coming. As far as he was concerned, only the foolish and the dead never change their minds. Besides, you can't reason with your heart; it has its own laws.

As the preaching closed, the minister held an alter call. First, they were going to listen to a familiar hymn. He introduced a big woman, wearing a black dress that draped over her shoulders like a curtain. With a beautiful mellow voice, she began singing. the piano player roamed his fingers up and down the keyboard. Loud and rhythmic like a jazz musician, he emphasized the cords.

---

[26] This is similar to the statement by Jesus in Matthew (16:27-28) and repeated in Mark (8:38 and 9:1) and Luke (9:26-27). He said, "Verily I say unto you. There be some standing here, which shall not taste death, till they see the Son of man coming in his kingdom." This statement is troublesome for Bible fundamentalists.

[27] The last known survivor died in 1937 at age 83. His name was William C. White, son of Ellen White. His mother made the prediction. See Roger W. Coon, "Infallibility: Does the True Prophet Ever Error?" *The Journal of Adventist Education,* December 1981, 22.

You have longed for sweet peace,
And for faith to increase,
And have earnestly, fervently prayed;
But you cannot have rest,
Or be perfectly blest
Until all on the altar is laid.

Then the preacher called for the audience to sing the refrain...

Is your all on the altar of sacrifice laid?
Your heart does the Spirit control?
You can only be blest, and have peace and sweet rest,
As you yield Him your body and soul.

As people rose from their seats and walked to the altar the minister moved down to them and held his hands high in the air. At this point John Willey thought about the time he was in the Minot train station when the Great Northern Railroad was eight-hours late and the agent gave out travel vouchers to keep the travelers from leaving the station and returning to their homes.

That was how John Willey became a Seventh-day Adventist. Had he applied "Hume's Guillotine of Logic," which holds that no matter how convincingly one shows something to be true, it never follows logically that it ought to be true, he might have taken a different course. Many years later, John bemoaned the fact that the last person on the 1856 Battle Creek list died and Jesus had yet to return.

Church leaders said that prophecies could be "conditional." prophecy" And gradually he came to understand that the power of one's emotional life is total when it comes to the nature of their beliefs. John had not been outwitted by his mother and her faith, nor was he a two-faced hypocrite. Switching from his upbringing faith to a different Adventism seemed simple enough. It was the right thing to do.

Seventh-day Adventist doctrines fell within the orthodox tenets of Christianity. [28] The very idea that the Adventists could play a world-historical

---

[28] As one observer said, "they are often thought of as those who major on minors." Geoffrey J. Paxton, *The Shaking of Adventism* (Grand Rapids, MI: Baker Book House, 1977).

role in bringing about the end of the world by keeping the commandments of God and preaching the final "loud cry" was attractive to him. He decided from this camp meeting experience that Adventists would be the people to carry out the drama of the final redemption. According to the preacher, other denominations had been corrupted by Satan.

While the Adventists stressed the importance of the infallibility of the Bible, they also had the benefit of the prophetess Ellen White—although like the Mormon prophet Smith Mrs. White's writings were not accepted by "unbelievers." White's writings served as divinely inspired guidance for believers. John felt that this enabled an Adventist to face the future with confidence in a privileged relationship to God. White's writings and especially *The Great Controversy* created distinctiveness for the church and made Adventists a remnant people. This was something the Advent Christian church did not have. John could now say that "The Adventists were the only church that had it all together. It made splendid common sense!"

With Seventh-day Sabbath observance and the Three Angel's message bound together, the Adventists built a secure community and referred to themselves as God's special people (something like Mormonism—although Adventists get prickly when they are compared to the Mormons). In earlier times people often confused the two religions because both had prophets and both practiced healthful living.

On at least one occasion Adventist religious liberty leaders supported the Mormons in opposing a constitutional amendment to prohibit and suppress polygamy. The *Review* wrote "We can see no good reason for singling out the Mormon Church in this matter, when nearly all the other churches in the country are equally guilty in spirit and effort." [29] The *Review's* defense was that an individual should be allowed to practice his/her faith freely.

---

[29] When the National Reform organization proposed a constitutional anti-polygamy amendment, Seventh-day Adventists found themselves opposed on the basis that "should their proposed measure carry, it would open the flood-gates for all the evil legislation that has ever blighted the world." *Advent Review and Sabbath Herald,* November 30, 1905. See also January 25, 1906. "Practical Union of Church and State," July 19, 1906 (also November 30, 1905, December 21, 1905, and January 25, 1906).

Perfectionism

One of the hardest parts of being an Adventist was the moral imperative to stand perfectly before God without sin or blemish. According to the church's teaching, one could be within an inch or even a quarter of an inch of perfection and yet be denied everlasting life. (There was no second chance.) Some of these beliefs derived from Methodism.

Perfectionism rested on something Jesus had said; *"Be ye therefore perfect, even as your Father which is in heaven is perfect."*[30] But "perfection" was a troubling concept. How was one to know just what constituted "being perfect" or when they had obtained it? The entire goal in the life of an Adventist was to stand alongside Paul at the end of life and exclaim:

> *I have fought a good fight, I have finished my course, I have kept the faith: Henceforth there is laid up for me a crown of righteousness, which the Lord, the righteous judge shall give me at that day: and not to me only, but unto all them that also that love his appearing.* [31]

After John became an Adventist, he advanced slowly in his understanding of the teachings of the church. He came to understand that his relationship with God was like a negotiated exchange. If he kept the commandments and treated his neighbors as he wanted to be treated, he would have a good chance, in the rescue exchange, to be sanctified and worthy of salvation. These negotiations also involved suppression of his secret thoughts and the temptations he fantasized but never carried out. He couldn't explain it but when he saw a pretty woman lust came bounding up in his thoughts no matter how hard he screwed down the lid on his animalistic passions. As with other men, sexual excesses threatened. Adventism was a religion where a man or woman could work out his or her own salvation, but it required strong resistance and unceasing vigilance against temptations. [32]

---

[30] Matthew. 5:48.

[31] 2 Timothy. 4:7-8.

[32] M.L. Andreasen, *The Sanctuary Service* (Takoma Park, MD: Review & Herald Publ., 1937, 1947). Geoffrey J. Paxton, *The Shaking of Adventism* (Grand Rapids, MI:

Another blessing came to the devoted and faithful children of God through the promise of protection by ministering angels. The Bible said, *"Are they not all ministering spirits, sent forth to minister for them who shall be heirs of salvation?"*[33] When John unpacked the judgment-hour message and laid it against the reward of living an immortal life in heaven, it began to shape his emotional life. At times he still thought Satan influenced his life in Christ. Maybe it was like the time when the spirit led the Savior into the wilderness to be tested by the devil. [34] Some things were hard to comprehend.

It wasn't easy. Sometimes John felt getting to heaven was as far out of his reach as climbing a tree to get to the moon. Human nature seemed entirely incompatible with the perfection that Adventists talked and wrote about. [35] But in the keeping of his good land and his livestock, in the rhythms of planting and harvesting; and in what he called, "generous living," he found comfort. His rebellion was not against God, he reasoned, but an expression of "his human nature" inherited from Adam. Over time man in a sinful world had become weaker, severally degenerated from the original Adam seed and diminished in vital force. This made it harder to be perfect. White wrote in the *Review* that unless Christ came soon there might not be much left of humanity to save.

Enjoying Farming

Out there on the homestead, John had many happy moments, as when he stopped working in the field to take in the world around him. He'd walk into the middle of his wheat field after the grain was waist high, lie down on his back, and watch the wind ripple the grain. He felt solitude creeping in around him. Looking

---

Baker Book House, 1977). Ellen G. White, *Last Day Events* (Nampa, ID: Pacific Press Publ., 1992). This is a compilation of her writing.

[33] Hebrews. 1:14.

[34] Matthew 4:1-11.

[35] "There is not a just (righteous) person upon the earth, that doeth good, and sinneth not." Ecclesiastes 7:20.

up into the sky he could see a wide and open world. He heard sounds of meadowlarks, red-winged black birds, and sometimes the raucous call of the ring-neck pheasant. With huge white clouds over head, pasted against a rich blue sky, he imagined he was an Indian who had given over the cultivation of his farm to the women while he took up hunting for buffalo and fishing for Muskie. Here was his yearning for a simpler way of living. Maybe this came about because from time-to-time he would find an arrowhead or other Indian artifact on the ground in his fields and let these discoveries generate his vivid imaginations.

Most times during the week he fancied himself becoming prosperous, buying or renting more land, and getting a tractor. Watching the grain swaying in the wind, he calculated each head to be worth a penny or more. But first he needed a wife, and he wasn't ashamed to admit it. Like an echoing thunder roll from a cloudburst in the distance he began to think of a woman who might share his dream of prosperity and help in raising children.

THOMAS ODLAND & HIS MAGIC EYE CHAPTER SEVEN

> "And one of the verses he had memorized from early childhood was the one that whispered above the scuttling of the mice each time he opened the granary door, as though the grain spoke from the heavy cold bins: Lay not up for yourselves treasures upon earth, where moth and rust doth corrupt, and where thieves break through and steal...Take no thought for the morrow.... Consider the lilies of the field." Lois Hudson. 1984. *The Bones of Plenty* (St. Paul, MI: Minnesota Historical Soc. Press, 66.

Harboring the same ambition as the Willey's, Thomas (1845-1917) and Isabel (1850-1933) Odland homesteaded in Renville County in 1901 [1] They settled in Stafford Township (twenty miles west of Hurley Township where the Willey's lived). The Odland's had eleven children. One of the Odland daughters would marry young John Willey. Her name was Inez.

It was an unwelcome drowning that brought the two together—the kind of incident that puts your hair on end and leaves an ink spot in your memory. What was strange about the drowning incident was that in later years John and Inez mused over how they first met, telling how they discovered each other spreading out romantic word pictures like a coffee-table book. Later, the story was embellished to sound like God's hand had been in the matter. But only God knows if that was true.

Odlands Came from Norway to America

Coincidently, the Odland's were also from Iowa. Before coming to North Dakota, they lived in Badger, Iowa, some ninety miles southeast of Ruthven. Their pioneering in Iowa made homestead in North Dakota very familiar. The Odland's were of Norwegian heritage, having immigrated to America from the Odland Valley in Norway. Thomas Odland liked to tell

---

[1] *Renville County Farmer*, June 22, 1933.

folks he came to America "With a clear conscience, a clean pair of pants, and thirty-five dollars in his pocket." After fifteen years of homesteading," he said, "I lost everything, including my pants and a clear conscience." "As far as empire building," he'd laugh and exclaim, "It was a myth perpetuated by the North Dakota Commissioner of Agriculture and Labor." He never came close to prosperity, but he worked very hard.

Norwegians constituted the majority of Scandinavians who settled in the northwest part of North Dakota. Scandinavians developed their staying power through cycles of abundance and failures. They were generally literate when they came to America because Norwegian children had to read Luther's catechism before confirmation. [2] Although they were religious people who promoted their faith, they couldn't agree amongst themselves about the rough edges of their theological doctrines. At least six or seven varieties of Lutherans lived in North Dakota, each claiming to have the truth! They built small white wooden churches in the countryside or in small towns. Credit went to them for the successful introduction of prohibition laws in the North Dakota Constitution. They were also known for eating lefse and lutefisk and for being good "Republican voters."

By the time Thomas Odland homesteaded in North Dakota he was missing an eye! As a foolish lad, he had taken a bullet from his father's gun and exploded the shell against a rock by hitting it with a hammer. It was a dumb thing to do! A piece of shrapnel flew into his eye. With only one eye he couldn't always tell how far away or how big something might be. Perhaps because of this he was a cautious and gentle man.

Just before he got married, he went to the hardware store and ordered a glass eye. The back part of the artificial eye was a dark green color. When visitors came to the house, and the conversation lagged, he'd pop out his eye to scare the children and amuse the adults. Then, when he put the eye back in, he turned it around so that the green half was showing. His wife fussed over his malignant humor hoping to get him to stop scaring people with his fake green eye. Sometimes he made the eye look to the side of his face, thus looking cockeyed. He explained that this allowed him to see flies coming from the side of his face. Other times he made the eye look upwards, which he claimed helped him see mosquitos coming toward his forehead. In

---

[2] William C. Sherman, ed., *Plains Folk. North Dakota's Ethnic History* (Fargo, ND: North Dakota State University, 1988), 185.

these humorous ways he coped with his handicap "Nobody likes artificial anything," he'd say, and he often felt imprisoned by the mistake.

He also claimed his fake eye had magical properties. It "could predict the weather and a few other things." But it seemed the only thing it could divine was the cold. In freezing weather, he found it conducted heat away from his head. Under these conditions he removed the fake eye and put it in his pocket!

Rumor had it that he popped out his eye and used it as a shooter to play marbles with the boys. (The story may have been exaggerated since no one in the family saw him do it.) He kept his fake eye in a glass of water by his bed at night and claimed it watched over him along with his Guardian Angel – which, of course, no one could prove. Thomas seemed self-confident, but suspicious. He never got excited about most things and tried always to remain calm and above the storm. No one knew his private thoughts.

Drowning in the Mouse River

The tragic incident that brought John and the Odland daughter Inez together occurred on the Souris or Mouse River near the Odland's homestead, a meandering stream that came from Canada, ran through Renville County, passed through Minot and then returned to Canada. Located where the road crossed the river between Kenmare and Mohall, the town of McKinney was a favorite camping ground for horse traders, Indians, and Gypsies. No homesteaders detrained in Kenmare without stopping at McKinney to talk about farming conditions and purchase provisions.

The McKinney Mill, which operated there from 1903 until 1928, [3] was the only mill northwest of Minot, and business was brisk in the early years. A spacious picnic area near the bend of the river was where settlers gathered for church picnics, political rallies, and other events. Fourth of July celebrations, including a baseball game, began there around 1902. Officially the picnic grounds had become a public park after the land the Grinnell family donated the land in 1912. Ranchers and farmers came from miles around for the park's dedication. The bandstand was decorated in red, white and blue bunting. No one could distribute religious literature at the park lest the "agrarians" start disputing and fighting.

---

[3] Ibid. 538.

Farmers and townspeople stole time from work as often as they could to meet at the park and enjoy fishing, swimming, Chautauqua, band concerts, dancing, baseball and foot races. Here they got acquainted with other settlers. Frank Sunday, William Jennings Bryan, and Lawrence Welk's band all appeared at the park. Before the automobile extended the range of a family, this was where to come during the summer. When revival meetings in the surrounding towns brought out the cold sweat in a pioneer over the judgment and hell fire, a church picnic could remedy the situation!

One summer the House of David baseball team came from Canada and challenged a team of local all-star players. They drew a boisterous crowd. Around the backstop, rampant betting went on before the game started and when the local team won the game, some thought it may have been rigged. The Canadians led the game until the last inning when a home run by one of the Americans, hard hitting Jimmy Haugen, won the game. Afterward, the Mouse River all-stars went to Canada to play the House of David again, but this time the House of David "cleaned the American's clocks." [4]

Unfortunately, the delirious enthusiasm from winning the first game made American betting popular in Regina, Saskatchewan. Consequently, some farmers returned home having "lost their shirt" as well as seeing their team go down to defeat. Imagine the torrent of criticism inveighing against the intemperance and avarice that followed on the heels of this game! To go to Canada with the expectation of winning bigger returns, but having to come back home in disgrace kindled a veritable reformation: farmers and neighbors stopped betting for the rest of the year.

Because of flour grinding at McKinney, the Minneapolis, St. Paul SOO Railroad extended the Thief River Falls branch line to McKinney. According to poorly kept records, the Mouse River rarely, if ever, flooded, but a 1904 Mouse River flood wiped out this flood-free reputation. The railroad pulled its line to higher ground and moved west of the river to Tolley. The small settlement of McKinney thereupon began a slow decline.

---

[4] Ibid. 541.

The 1904 flood had resulted from heavier than usual winter snows and spring rains. The river valley flooded from hill to hill, with a water depth estimated at twenty-six feet above normal. Homesteaders living near the river hung their furniture from the ceiling and placed smaller articles on the counters and tabletops. They braced the doors, piled up hay barriers, and as a last resort prayed! The flood caused huge financial losses. Some settlers had to await the river crest before they could get home and stare cleaning up.

Billy McMasters Drowns

At midnight, when the flood waters began to recede, an ice jam broke loose upriver at Oxbow, Canada. During that time there were no radios or telephones to warn the people downstream. By morning the river was rising rapidly. Just when everyone thought the situation could not get any worse, something took place out on the river that terrified them. Someone yelled, "Oh, my God, Billy swim for it!" A boat making its way across the river had capsized, and two men who fell into the rushing river were trying to swim to shore or hang on to the boat. Catholics graced themselves with the sign of the cross. How could a drowning man be saved in such violently swift waters?

While Billy McMasters was helping Gene Wyatt move his household furniture across the swollen river in a small boat the bedstead got caught in some overhanging tree branches and the boat tipped over. When the boat flipped the stove crashed against Billy's head and knocked him out. The bedstead and boat floated off. Gene successfully swam to the bank of the river. Billy disappeared and never came up. No one watching anticipated there'd be a drowning right before their eyes. Many Christians wondered what the Bible really meant where it said, *"If not a Sparrow falls without God knowing, how must He care for us!"* [5]

The villagers searched downstream for Billy. They blasted shotguns into the water to dislodge his body. Someone threw in a few sticks of dynamite hoping to bring him to the surface. Then they tried dragging the bottom with a grappling hook, but the hook lodged on the flood debris. News about the drowning spread over the farmlands and people rushed to McKinney to see if they could help.

---

[5] Matthew 10:29.

John Willey Goes to the River Help

Young John Willey heard about the drowning and decided he would join the rescue efforts. He threw in a rope, packed a lunch, and hitched up his democrat buggy, and drove to the river. Certainly, he could do something. He was twenty-one years old, in the prime of life, and a good and daring swimmer. There was another thing about him: John liked a bare-knuckle fight with disasters and took squabbles like this as a struggle between good and evil, or between man and nature. After he arrived, he volunteered to enter the river and feel around the edges of the bank where Billy might be stuck. He wore long underwear with a rope around his waist. Lacking any better plan, the folks let him give it a try. Upon seeing him enter the water and struggle with the swift current, it was agreed that he should abandon the effort. Wet and shivering, John was pulled back to the bank. A friend standing nearby asked him jokingly if it bothered his Presbyterian conscience to abandon Billy so readily!

At the edge of the crowd stood an attractive unmarried woman—her name was Inez Odland (1885-1965). She was domestic, thoughtful, kind, and thoroughly Norwegian. After John came out of the water, and she saw him bent over and shaking from the cold, she walked up the hill to her family's buggy and fetched a patchwork quilt for him. (Norwegian girls were taught how to make quilts at an early age.) She brought her quilt to the men who were trying to figure out how to warm the reckless swimmer from Hurley Township. As she shyly passed the quilt through the crowd, John turned and caught a brief glimpse of her. He blinked at her beauty and felt an ancient primeval attraction. Afterward, he dreamed how of seeing her again under better circumstances. Years later, he and Inez insisted it was God, not Billy's drowning, that brought them together. (Most Christians don't believe that God drowns people so future lovers can begin a courtship. Infidels and heretics, on the other hand, have been known to say things like this in order to blame God for unexpected drownings.)

After a few days had gone by and they still had not found the body, ole Jacob Patt, the father of the McKinney Miller, suggested that they take a burlap sack of wheat, add some gravel and rocks to simulate Billy's weight, and drop it over the side of a boat where Billy had fallen into the river. They tied some binder twine around the sack, dropped it over the edge of the boat, and let it drift with the current. After the sack lodged, they followed the twine and found Billy's body.

Since there was no undertaker in McKinney or nearby, they hung Billy upside down by his ankles in a nearby barn to let him dry out. [6] Afterwards they took him to his homestead where his neighbor John Pellet and friend David Clark "laid Billy on a cooling board" (a door off the barn) and sat with his corpse during the night—as was the custom. Having been in the water three days Billy was "full of gas and every little while he would groan and make a belching noise." It made Pellet nervous. "Where," he asked, "Is the intelligent architect of the universe, and why does he not suppress these ghost-like horrific noises?"

Clark remembered this experience for the rest of his life. One might suppose that the reasoning behind this cooling board custom was that it gave St. Peter time to prepare an address in heaven to receive the ready-to-arrive soul of a drowned man. But the real reason behind the custom turned out to be the concern that a corpse should be observed overnight to avoid premature burial. People who drowned under the ice in a lake had been known to recover several hours after coming to the surface. This preoccupation with premature burial seems to have begun around the middle of the eighteenth century when the distinguished Dr. Jacques-Benigne Winslow published his book, *The Uncertainty of the Signs of Death*. Dr. Winslow claimed to have been placed alive in a coffin on two separate occasions.[7] Surely the good doctor must have been delusional or without ordinary common sense. Clearly, something was wrong with his account.

Terrifying images came from England about coffins pulled out of cemeteries, emptied, and used again; and finding that one out of twenty-five coffins had scratch marks on the underside of the lids! None showed yet that the corpse had left for parts unknown. When a cemetery was relocated in Paris, the number of skeletons found face down in the coffins convinced medical and lay people that were happening prematurely. [8]

There was another story that just before marriage a young lady fell into a hysterical paralysis over the anxiety of having sex for the first time. A

---

[6] Ibid. 544.

[7] Roy Porter, *Flesh in the Age of Reason* (New York: W. W. Norton & Co., 2003), 215.

[8] Robert Wilkins, *Death: A History of Man's Obsessions and Fears* (New York: Barnes & Noble Books, 1990), 25.

mirror held near her mouth for thirty minutes showed no detectable sign of life. After she was buried, her relatives thought she might have been buried alive. They gossiped that she was dutifully "buried for the sake of hygiene in a hot climate."

The thought of having sex for the first time might have been fearfully real for a virgin without the additional fear of a premature burial. She could have waited a few weeks, if necessary, to see if sex was as bad as she anticipated, but that is just an elevated view of virginity. Some people even left explicit instructions in their wills that their hearts be cut out to avoid the possibility of a premature burial. About this time an inventor proposed tying a string to the dearly departed's wrist and connecting it to a bell above ground. This would give a person at least one last chance to save themselves! Perhaps this is the origin of the expressions "saved by the bell" and "dead ringer" came from.

Billy had been under water three days, and *rigor mortis* had already taken hold. He could have been formally committed to the grave straight away. There was no chance of premature burial. Resurrection by human means was hopeless. Death had overtaken Billy's mundane life and the portal to life eternal for his soul had opened. "His soul was ready to leave his body, once out of the water." Incoherent traditions fade slowly, but there was absolutely no reason to sit up all night to make sure Billy was gone. Maybe it just boiled down to the fact that some Protestant theology taught that the soul remained in contact with the body for a short time after death. Billy's soul simply wasn't ready to leave until he'd been given some "observation time." This was often stated as the reason why a corpse remained at home under the watchful eye of a relative or friend for at least one night before burial.

The Next Time John and Inez Saw Each Other

John and Inez next stumbled into each other during an auspicious Fourth of July celebration at the Mouse River Park. "Weren't you the one with the quilt?" he asked. Inez's reply caught John off guard: "Weren't you the muskrat they pulled out of the river after you had been feeling around in the mud for Billy! When do I get my quilt back?" He felt a sudden pang of guilt for keeping the quilt. With this humorous exchange they were off to a promising start. John had been hoping to run into the "noblest work of God" at the park and he was there to collect some possible social data for a wife (there weren't many such opportunities in this neck of the woods).

At first, they gabbed about Billy's drowning, but something powerful drew them together as kids chased each other around their feet playing tag and stirring up the dust. Afterward, when John got back to the farm, he told his father that he felt pleasures coming from antediluvian attractions between a man and woman. After they married, John teased Inez by saying he was drawn to her "because of her lavender scent" rather than some ineffable force. But of course, like most things involving a man and woman, there was more to it than smells.

They had both talked about their common roots in Iowa, having arrived in North Dakota with nearly the same hopes and dreams and never doubting that Providence had guided them there and that they were in God's gentle care. They were at the age when young people search for distant conjugal shores. John poured out his heart about his future dreams. Overflowing with enthusiasm and goodness, he said, "There is a great bounty to be collected, and the land and farming brings all of us to the promise."

With so much word embroidery Inez felt John might suffocate under his sublime sentences. Perhaps he was only lonely and making a subtle pitch to attract a helper in the kitchen, an egg gatherer, and a helpmate around the farm? She, on the other hand, was charmed by his convictions and attracted to the twinkle in his eye. He clearly intended to take over his father's farm and make something of his life. All of these impressions broke down her frosty resistance. He was fascinating, and handsome besides. Additionally, John made her laugh with his repertoire of humorous stories, some of which were surely embellished. Still she trusted him. Had he stopped talking and looked at her for a while, he would have seen that he already had her approval. Inez was a year younger than John, and her dreams were wound tight like the hair in her braid; and a little more snugly for another reason. A year before, she had nearly married a dashing swagger who offered a pocketful of gold coins but was dubbed a skunk by her father and brothers.

Inez' parents were pious people who raised their children to fear God and keep His Commandments. John fit in well with her family, even if they came from different religious persuasions. He didn't cuss, smoke, drink, or gamble like some other young men she had known. For that matter, he didn't drink coffee or tea. The cast of his mind seemed to lean towards religious propositions and building a successful farm. He did like to box for the sport of seeing a stalwart man wobble a few times with a sharp blow to the jaw, go down, and struggle to get back up on his feet. In other words, John, like most people, had opposing natures.

Inez met a few of his friends at the park. They all applauded John's charms, wit, open-mindedness, and ability to get along with others. But more important, she found in him someone who was fresh, eager, a good tease, and felicitous. John was a decent looking almost handsome man, part Norwegian and part English.

Weeks later John drove twenty miles to the Odland's farm near Norma, North Dakota, and thus began their courting. On his first visit, Inez insisted that he get acquainted with her family. "This would be an important step in our courtship," was the way she put it. She was afraid that her father might oppose John as he had done with others before. Her father prided himself in figuring out a suitor's interior life before the fellow had time to talk about himself or explain whether he was a Democrat, a Republican, a Progressive, or a non-voter. Even though Thomas and Isabel Odland had seven daughters they weren't giving any of them up easily.

During their first date, the Lutheran church sponsored an auction box social Sunday night at the schoolhouse. John studied the numbered garlanded boxes lying on the table. Each young woman in the church made a box lunch which concealed the creator by using elaborate decorations. With clues from her brothers, John figured out which one belonged to Inez, and he outbid the competition for that box. Maybe God was already tipping his hand. John could have made a mistake and bid on the wrong box and ended up eating supper with another woman and gone in a completely different direction.

After winning Inez's' box in the auction she wanted to know what part of the box made him bid so aggressively. "After all," she asked, "would you have gone hungry if you had to eat with another girl?" "Don't worry about that now," he said, "We have an apple and a sandwich to share, and I want every bite to count, including the seeds." They had a good time, and afterward John slept overnight in the hayloft of the Odland barn. A religious conversation was not their main objective though John was curious about what Lutherans believed. Every aspect of the box social event was a hit, and John intended to do more to get to know Inez.

Back when Billy drowned, Inez's father had been stood on the riverbank. He was also there when John appeared and bravely volunteered to enter the swirling waters. This made an impression. It was troubling that he had qualms about Englishmen, and despite John's bravery he decided to withhold his judgment. When John told Inez's father that his mother was full-blooded Norwegian, born in Norway, Thomas abandoned all doubts and accepted John as a legitimate suitor for his daughter, "essentially an honest, upright, and a fine man."

John and Inez Marry

When John asked Thomas if he could marry his daughter Inez, Thomas proposed to use his magic eye to assist him in making the decision! "How would that work?" asked John. "Well, here's what we'll do," said Thomas. "I'll spin the eye on the table and when it stops and looks at you, you'll have my blessing." Otherwise, the answer is no. Inez standing over in the corner wasn't worried because regardless of how the eye ended up looking, she was going to marry John. You could say that this is the way a lot of magic works.

John and Inez married on October 1907 at her parent's home with the Rev. Bobrick officiating. Years later Inez told how she and John outwitted their friend's planned chivaree on their wedding night. It was a simple strategy. They parted after they were married and went their separate ways to their own homes. Back then there were no marriage licenses, honeymoon suites, or attractions to draw a couple away for a week. Often, they ended up spending the first night with one of the parents or a relative, although this was not always the best arrangement for the first occasion. During the night, the newlyweds would be awakened by whirling chaos from a noisy crowd beating pots and pans with wooden spoons, whistles, and firecrackers.

John went home and returned the next day to retrieve his new bride in simple splendor. Seeing him coming down the road, Inez ran out the door and threw her arms around him and made him promise to take her everywhere he went from then on. They celebrated their fiftieth wedding anniversary in Loraine in 1957 attended by 250 relatives, neighbors, and friends. By then they had fifteen grandchildren, more than enough to replace themselves. [9]

They set up homemaking in the Willey's farmhouse, moving upstairs and taking one room to themselves. John's sister Jonetta was the same age as Inez and became a close sister-in-law. But Inez' sisters lived twenty miles away, so she didn't see her siblings much after she married. Twenty miles in those days, as John used to say, "Might just as well have been to the moon and back." They went to visit her family less often as the years rolled by. "One reason," John said, "was to avoid getting the advice he didn't solicit."

"I hear the trend of pioneers,
Of nations yet to be,
The first low wash of waves where soon
Shall roll a human sea." [10]

[9] *Renville County Farmer,* June 1957.
[10] *Bismarck Tribune,* November 14, 1915.

LIFE ON THE FARM
CHAPTER EIGHT

> "Wheat was the sole source and meaning of our lives...We were never its masters, but too frequently its victims...It was rarely long outside a conversation." Eric Sevareid, quoted in Robinson, *History of North Dakota* (Lincoln, NE: Univ. of Nebraska Press, 1966).

When he married in 1906, John held a Sabbath faith that did not match his wife's Lutheran practice. As a compromise, she began keeping John's Sabbath. But asking a Scandinavian- Lutheran to give up Sunday keeping altogether was like asking a bee to find another hive. At first, she could not abandon her own customs and traditions. Furthermore, she liked attending church, hearing a rip-roaring sermon, and feeling good afterwards.

Regarding religion, neither John nor Inez saw atheism as an option – it reflected a sickness of the mind. Of the two, John was more likely to see the theological world in contours and toy with deep metaphysical meanings, but neither doubted the existence of God.

Despite a lack of fellowship with active believers, Inez appreciated Adventism's well-marked boundaries on how the Sabbath was supposed to be kept, and also other distinctive beliefs regarding forgiveness and reconciliation, the denial of everlasting hell, the explanation of how life began at creation, and the value of prayer. Of course, Adventists were not to think that salvation could be had by trusting in themselves. God's reward of eternal life came only to those who worked hard at being obedient to the will of God and who treated others fairly. Basically, this homesteader couple saw obedience to the law as the pathway to salvation. They were to strive for perfection in the image of God. Justification by grace alone was not widely accepted by Adventists, despite some serious debates by church fathers in 1888.

Adventists were quite aloof, those referred to as outsiders. There was almost a cultivated social exclusiveness. True, the end of time had been delayed many years since 1844 and there were scoffers everywhere, but that only indicated that the end was near. And Sunday, on which others worshipped, was just another day for secular work.

> *Six days thou shalt labour, and do all thy work: But the seventh day is the sabbath of the Lord thy God: in it thou shalt not do any work, thou, nor thy son, nor they daughter, nor thy manservant, nor thy maidservant, nor thine ox, nor thine ass, nor any of thy cattle, nor thy stranger that is within thy gates: that thy manservant and thy maidservant may rest as well as thou.* [1]

John used a straight reading of his Bible, the King James Version, to convince Inez that Saturday was set aside by God to commemorate the six-day creation and liberation from Egypt's Pharaoh. And speaking of creation, Adventists teach that man was created in God's image and even that the body was God's temple. From this, an emphasis on health reform followed naturally.

What Was Inez Like?

Inez Willey (1885-1965) was a short, plainly dressed woman with blond hair. She rarely wore pants. Her hair turned grey, then white as she aged. She dressed in soft cotton dresses that reached below her knees. Reading glasses hung around her neck. The dresses were never brightly colored, and the patterns seemed muted. Working around the farm she buttoned her loose-fitted dresses down the front and even in summer always wore a slip. Her clothes, summer and winter, were always the same except on Sabbaths when she wore a black dress with a white hat and gloves. She pleased the Lord by avoiding a lot of color or adornments. Her heart was weak, perhaps from a childhood disease or genetics, and her six children wore her down and frazzled her. As for the birthing experience, she would tell you how naïve you were about real pain.

Agrarian wives played a central part in the family system. A good wife was an asset to the farm; she provided the basic necessities for subsistence.

---

[1] Deuteronomy 5:13-14

Divorce was hardly a respectable alternative. But isolation of farm women made them vulnerable to a husband's rage. [2]

Inez didn't talk much about her childhood, maybe because it was filled with work rather than leisure or adventure. Physically she was buxom and because of her modesty she never went swimming. She had sturdy ankles and muscular forearms. As she got older her arms became flabby and her arms shook so violently that it was nearly impossible for her to eat without assistance. She had natural curly hair pulled tight against her forehead and parted down the middle. During the day she rolled her hair in a bun on the back of her head. Her chin was firm. She wore no makeup, even into town, and eschewed jewelry, lipstick, and eye shadow. Sex was private and nothing like sex education existed for her children. What girls knew likely came from siblings and peers rather than through their mother. Of course, the other teachers were farm animals, although Inez discouraged her two girls from observing the sexuality of animals.

Inez had a mind that took in what was going on around her. She was what you might call a busy body. If you tried to hide something from her, and she thought you were guilty of malfeasance or malice, she would look you straight in the face, with powerful penetration, and demand the truth. She wanted things to be plain and simple. Around a group of her friends she was self-assured and amused by small things like pretty tea cups and saucers, or a roll of uncirculated Canadian pennies. The older she got, the more she thought young people were frivolous and had too many things given to them. She did not want as many children as she was capable of having. There was always the risk of infectious disease (diphtheria, typhoid, cholera, and diarrhea) and children could be killed or severely injured around the farm. Having come from a large family herself, she saw the hardships on her mother and the financial difficulties of larger families.

Inez was vice president of the Hurley Hustlers Homemakers in Loraine. In the summers when the gypsies came through town driving

---

[2] Deborah Fink, *Agrarian Women. Wives and Mothers in Rural Nebraska* (Chapel Hill, NC: Univ. North Carolina Press, 1991), 62.

their horses and colorful painted covered wagons, she helped shoo them away. Rather than buying clothes the gypsies "shopped" for their clothing on neighborhood clothes lines.

Certain things were not said in her presence, such as the word "bull" for a male cow. A bull was called a "gentleman cow." She said things like "the gentleman cow did this and the mother cow did that." When the chickens in the yard reproduced, she saw little tact or ceremony by the male bird. The rooster simply grabbed the hen by the back of the head with his beak, climbed on her back, and completed the act in less than fifteen seconds. Afterwards the hen fluffed her feathers, wiggled her rump, and walked away. As noted earlier she sought to confine chicken reproduction to places where the children couldn't see it. [3]

On Friday afternoons in the summer, she took her once-a-week bath outside on the kitchen porch. In winter she bathed in the kitchen. She drove everyone away, expecting her desire for privacy to be honored.

Chores Around the Farm

She could perform many chores around the farm. For instance, at the beginning of every summer she used a net on a long pole to capture the bright green frogs in the soft water cistern under the porch. She tossed her wiggling captives into a tall steel container burning with kerosene in the driveway. The sounds of sizzling frogs emanating from the steel drum didn't seem to bother her. She prepared chickens for the table by catching the chicken and holding it by its hind legs. Then she laid the head of the chicken over a block of wood and severed it from its body with an ax. The headless chicken then bounced around the yard with its neck squirting blood. After the chicken calmed down she dipped it in boiling water and then plucked its feathers. Her son Tom told her once that she should blindfold the chickens before chopping off their heads. Then they wouldn't know who the executioner was!

Many farm families raised chickens and sometimes turkeys for eggs as well as meat. They provided these fowls with oyster shells and feed. Some eggs were allowed to incubate to produce chicks in the spring under a

---

[3] In this reticence Inez would have agreed with the Shaker belief that it was sinful to watch animals copulate.

sitting hen. Extra eggs were taken to town to barter with the owner of the grocery store for groceries or cloth from which to make a dress or a shirt. It was a fair and equitable exchange.

Life on the farm seemed to oscillate between good and evil, between calm weather and storms, and between keeping the livestock alive and the small children from being snatched by the great coyote reaper, or drowning in a slough, or falling into a well. It seemed there was always something threatening or foreboding.

Inez, like others around her, accepted pain, sweat, and suffering as a necessary punishment for original sin. She was willing to wait until she got to heaven to get answers to the perplexing question of why evil happens to good persons without discrimination.

Understanding of Sex

When John and Inez first married, a neighbor lady of strong moral judgement came to give advice. She suggested that Inez and John retire to separate rooms and pray one hour every evening that no strong or unkind words would pass between them. Inez took this to be a subtle form of sexual advice. But with so many common tastes, habits, and pursuits, they sustained a happy marriage. They had worship each morning before chores while sitting together at the kitchen table.

Inez wouldn't want her Adventist friends to know everything about her, since, as the vice-president of the local lady's club, she enjoyed tea each week with her neighbors. Like coffee, tea was a lifestyle issue for an Adventist, though not an unpardonable sin. Smoking, drinking, and gambling were held with greater distain and could bring swift disfellowship from the church if discovered.

Adventists were supposed to practice vegetarianism, which was difficult on the farm. The prophetess taught that a person acquired the traits or propensities of the animals that they ate. If you ate frogs you could jump higher! And the prophetess inveighed masturbation which, she taught, sapped the vital force of an individual.[4] Loss of vital force in turn caused

---

[4] Conference workers in Wisconsin and Illinois noticed a similarity in wording between Ellen White's health statements and the common health reform literature of the day, and so they asked Review editor Uriah Smith for clarification. Ellen White

numerous diseases and destroyed self-respect and nobleness of character. The practice could make individuals immoral. Women, who were weaker in this regard, were more prone to loss of vitality from masturbation. Additional side effects included "dwarfed forms, crippled limbs, misshapen heads, and deformities of every description." It could even "cause dropsy, headaches, loss of memory and sight, great weakness in the back and loins, affections of the spine, and cause the head to decay inwardly." [5] Such early nineteenth-century ideas had been promoted b Sylvester Graham (1794-1857) who advocated vegetarian diets and invented the Graham Cracker. [6]

It was nearly thirty years after her health vision that White herself overcame the temptation of the "flesh pots." By the beginning of the twentieth century most Adventists were either vegetarians or not talking about what they ate. [7] Dancing was considered as bad as attending a movie. Swearing was out, too. Talking "fresh" or talking back to your parents was unacceptable. Children were to honor and obey their parents. Following the advice found in Proverbs many Adventist parents did not spare the rod.

Such moral standards came from other Christian denominations, some reaching all the way back to the Puritans. Orthodox evangelists reminded their followers that; *"Not everyone who says to Me 'Lord, Lord' shall enter the kingdom of heaven, but he who does the will of my Father in heaven."* [8] But believers knew they were living within the boundaries of moral restraint.

---

responded by saying, "My reply was that I had not, neither should I read them till I had fully written out my view, lest it should be said that I had received my light upon the subject of health from physicians, and not from the Lord." *Advent Review and Sabbath Herald,* October 7, 1876. Also see, Ronald L. Numbers, *Prophetess of Health: A Study of Ellen G. White* and Walter T. Rea, *The White Lie.*

[5] Ellen G. White, *An Appeal to Mothers Relative to the Great Cause of the Physical, Mental and Moral Ruin of Many of the Children of Our Time* (Battle Creek, MI: Steam Press Seventh-day Adventist Publ. Assoc., 1864).

[6] Ronald L. Numbers, *Prophetess of Health: Ellen G. White and the Origins of Seventh-day Adventist Health Reform* (Knoxville, TN: The University of Tennessee Press, 1992).

[7] Ibid. *xxii.*

[8] Mathew 7:21.

Inez Was Strict

Inez liked Adventist convictions about being faithful, doing good, acting kindly, and avoiding dishonesty. But she was not narrow minded. Always cheerful, she enjoyed a good laugh. Her husband and sons delighted in "pulling her leg." When she learned that Tom had been caught stealing, she filled both of his pockets with sand and sewed them shut. After wearing the sand in his pockets for a week, he chaffed about irritations and clearly had learned his lesson.

There was one significant religious idea in Adventism that was hard for Inez to swallow. Lutherans believed (and still do) that the righteous go to heaven after they die. Adventists believe that the body and soul remain in the grave until Christ's second coming. Inez couldn't abide the idea: the grave was a dark and wet place. Why not at least allow the soul after death to join with other souls in heaven?

Like other religious groups, Lutherans built churches before they built hospitals on the Plains. When they did construct hospitals, a nurse training program was included. [9] Medicine was primitive: there were few doctors, surgery was limited, and drugs were largely ineffective or even mordant. The settlers coped with the ever-present danger of injury and, like today, many diseases, cancers, and the like were hard to treat. Prayers and songs created feelings of comfort and consolation and got people past the bad or dangerous times.

The Railroads Continued to Sell Homesteading

At the beginning of the twentieth-century railroad primers propped up homesteading in North Dakota and the Great Plains by marketing economic optimism to potential settlers. "For the farmer who loved his family and his home, December, January, February and March were the pleasantest of the year." On the other hand, the days were short—daylight lasted only a few hours—and the winter temperature could drop to a minus -40°. Despite what the railroads said, the winters were hardly "the pleasantest of the year."

Blizzards often isolated farm families for weeks. Snow reached as

---

[9] Lutherans built seven hospitals in the Dakotas between 1899 and 1923.

high as the roof of the house. To get water to the livestock, holes were cut through the ice. Cleaning the barn of cow and horse manure, tossing straw bedding around the animals, and feeding the livestock consumed considerable time each day. Often farmers tied a rope between the house and the barn to assure safe passage during a storm.

There was also raw winter beauty on the farm. On cold nights, the sky could be so clear, and the stars so numerous that settlers felt like they were walking into the Milky Way or into the dancing northern lights or the Aurora Borealis, glowing with strange blotches of colors. Even with cold crisp air the human eye could see only a few light years away. Heaven escaped the naked eye! Some thought you had to go to the other side of the earth to see it.

Once a shy young girl named Philomena Musil got lost in a January blizzard and wasn't found until eighteen hours later in a deserted settler's shack. She was shivering in the corner with her coat wrapped around her legs. Both hands and feet were frozen, and parts had to be amputated. She ended up with only a thumb on her right hand.

If a homesteader and his family didn't plan adequately for the long winter months they could run out of coal, flour, sugar, kerosene and other provisions. In March 1904, a blizzard struck with such force near the Willey farm that all seventeen children and the teacher in a one-room school froze to death before they were discovered. It was the worst storm in forty years.

The railroad also glamorized spring in its pamphlets. "Spring breaks suddenly into bird-song and blossom, and summer basks in golden sunlight above the growing crops." But, as it turned out, spring wasn't so great either. As the snows thawed, mud resulted, which meant the livestock had to be kept in the barns. Water troughs still iced over at night.

Farmers had to break young work horses to accept a harness for the field work that would ensue when the fields dried out. They dispirited the horses and trained them to pull with other horses. Newspapers reported farmers being trampled to death while doing this. Other perils arose with farm animals in the spring. Sixteen-year-old Ralph Fyiken, living near the Willey farm, was attacked by a sow and died a few hours later. (Apparently, Ralph had been playing with the sow's young pigs and she became overly protective.) [10]

Summer conditions could be hazardous. Near the end of summer, prairie fires, generally caused by lightning, occurred. Over in the next township Mrs. Conkey, a blind and invalid woman was in the path of a raging prairie fire that swept down from Canada. The fire jumped fireguards as fast as the men could plow them. Before the fire was extinguished, several horses died and a young farmer lost his life. Later, someone told Mrs. Conkey what had happened. Knowing nothing of the danger that was sweeping towards her, she had sat quietly in her front room wondering what the noise outside was about. [11]

During this same fire a neighbor had staked two milking cows in the taller grass about half a mile from his farmhouse. When the fire came, he didn't have time to retrieve them. With pails of water he, his wife, and two daughters fought the flames that ascended the outside of their farmhouse and barn. He climbed on the roof and doused the flames there too, and then, when the fire was out, he went down the road hoping to find his cows. They were standing with their hair burnt off and blinded, oozing strips of flesh hanging from their shoulders and sides. Seeing this terrible sight, he wept; having no choice, he walked back to the barn, got an ax, returned, and clubbed them to death. Afterwards, his wife coaxed him back to the house.

Even without causing a fire, lightning from thunderstorms could leave a black scorched mark down the length of a farmer's body, burning off his clothes, and parting his hair. Lightning frightened the horses when it hit with a booming blast. The scared animals might take off and destroy machinery and fencing.

Fred Harris, a hired man who worked one summer on the Sawyer quarter, was with a team of horses when a bolt of lightning hit a nearby slough. [12] He fell to his knees and promised the Lord then and there that he would destroy the hooch in the machine shed and give up drinking

---

[10] *Renville County Farmer*, June 20, 1933.

[11] *Renville County History* (Renville County Old Settler's Association, 1976), 191.

[12] Each quarter section was designated by the names of the folks who first filed on that claim.

altogether— if God would just save him and the team from lightning. (During a Nazarene revival meeting in Mohall the week before, Harris had nearly signed the temperance pledge.) Then another lightning strike missed him, and this put the finishing strokes on his convictions. Suddenly he became convinced that protection results from doing the will of God.

Mailmen and preachers also worried about lightning. In an adjacent town a minister bringing in hay was standing in the hayrack when a bolt knocked him over. He slid unconscious to the ground, but he survived. Maybe mailmen were next!

Fierce winds could be a problem, too. Nearly every summer cattle were lifted off the ground by tornados and bashed or killed. Hailstorms damaged crops and battered younger cows and sheep to death.

Julius Larson, living just east of the Willey homestead, lost twenty young turkeys to a hailstorm. Another year, with no more than five minutes' warning, the Willey barn blew to pieces when a tornado touched down in a windstorm. Falling timber crushed all the livestock inside. John and the boys gathered what was left of the shattered wood and rebuilt the barn. A few chickens sitting on eggs in the haymow had scattered out as the roof came off. The family found one hen with no feathers, but otherwise unharmed.

In the fall of 1931 Tom loaded a boxcar with beef cattle raised on the farm. He rode the train with the cattle to Winnipeg, Canada, where he was to negotiate the sale and collect the money. While there, he happened upon a fellow from Michigan who was attending the sale of beef. Ben Wright had attended Emanuel Missionary College in Berrien Springs, Michigan, an Adventist institution of higher learning. When they fell into a discussion, Tom learned about an apostacy in the church spearheaded by A. F. Ballenger (1861-1921). After searching the Scriptures and finding no biblical support for the Investigative Judgement, Ballenger had abandoned the teaching and began promoting a concept of universal forgiveness. The young student from Michigan related how he had agreed with Ballenger and left the church.

Many saints lose their faith in God because of relentless materialism. Skepticism and doubts can grow over time. After years of education and indoctrination, one doesn't easily abandon Adventism. Many Adventists who never attend church remain who might be known as DNA Adventists. Mormons that quit the church are known as "jack Mormons." Others follow Pascal's wager that a rational person might as well live as though God exists and seek to believe in God. If God does not exist, such a person suffers only a finite loss (pleasures of various kinds), whereas if God does exist, people receive infinite gains (eternity in heaven).

The thought of Christ's coming has enormous holding power. But the prophecy failed over time and this unsettled people. The fear of losing out on heaven triggered profound depression, self-hatred, and melancholy.

The believer begins to doubt the Second Coming when learning about the vastness of the astronomical universe and the long geological history of the earth. Increasingly aware of these difficulties, they slowly abandon the spiritual dimensions of going home to a heaven that has been talked about for centuries. Then other beliefs erode: the existence of angels, the literal "truth" of the Bible, and belief in the prophetess Ellen White. With repeated onslaughts of disease, financial anxiety, unhappy marriages, or miserable combinations of these, the universe becomes ever more godless. People may come to see "suffering as not so much innocent as pointless." [13] But the God question never goes away; it just becomes hazy and mystical.

---

[13] A.N. Wilson, *God's Funeral* (New York: W.W. Norton & Co., 1999), 4.

HARVEST & THRESHING
CHAPTER NINE

"Now the God of peace, that brought again from the dead our Lord Jesus, that great Shepherd of the sheep, through the blood of the everlasting covenant, make you perfect in every good work to do his will, working in you that which is well pleasing in his sight, through Jesus Christ: to whom be glory for ever and ever." Hebrews 13:20.

There were good times on the farm, including occasions to come together with neighbors and others. Weddings were held in settler's homes, or outside in good weather, or at a church. Raising a new granary or barn could bring people together, not only to work, but also to dance, play music, sing, sample homemade candy, make ice cream, and tell survival stories. If help was needed during calving, haying, ditching, harvesting, or seeding, neighbors came together to assist each other. On the slightest provocation they assembled for pies, dramatic readings, music, box socials, and card parties—even in the harsh winters. People drove many miles with horses to attend these parties and dances. Often, they would go together by wagon to Kenmare for lignite coal or wood, helping each other with the loading and unloading. Coming home over the crossing at the Mouse River they would tie a chain over the rear wheel to act as a brake on the steep grade.

The Willey's were friends with the Mitchells, Andersons, Tuors, Bohms, Gates, Noilings, Lees and Eldreds, all nearby neighbors and, for the most part, original homesteaders. Doc Fitzmaurice, who also filed a claim in Hurley Township, drove a well-matched team known as the fastest in the district. Fitzmaurice had style: he dressed in leather and chaps, looking part cowboy and part Indian. When he was injured, the "boys rendered him service" and helped him recover. In response, he invited them to a "deer feed." The "deer proved to be exceptionally good because they had the nationally known Greek chef Harry Polius touch it up with a bit of garlic."

If a person died in the winter, and a grave couldn't be dug, the body was wrapped in burlap and stored by the side of the house or on the porch. Tar paper kept out the moisture.

Speaking of winter, the team of another neighbor, Jack Ketcham, ran away and embedded themselves in a snowbank. A neighbor helped extricate the team, but was himself trampled by the horses. Taken to Doc Fitzmaurice, he remained unconscious for several hours. Later he bought treats for the doctor from Nelson's Confectionary store in Loraine.

During the homesteading era, a handshake was stronger than an attorney's contract. Parties didn't have to look for a piece of paper in a cluttered bureau drawer to see what had been agreed upon. They trusted and depended on each other's word. They had no other choice but to be honest, ready to help each other and abide their commitments. People bought groceries at the market and left the bags up front while they shopped in other stores. No one made off with them.

If someone got lost in a snowstorm, the men hitched up their sleighs, wrapped bear skin cutter rugs around themselves, and went searching together. Family crises were shared by the community. Genteel farmers waved to each other in the fields or when passing on the road. If time allowed, they'd stop and talk politics and gripe about commodity prices or crafty grain brokers or the high cost of freighting on the railroads. This lifestyle promoted strong family affections and a powerful identity with the land, the seasons, and the community. People were close to each other because they were close to the earth. Land was good for more than growing crops; it served also as a community bonding agent. For this reason and others, even during "the worst of times" people were reluctant to leave their homesteads.

When phones were introduced, they were hung on a wall in the kitchen. The Willey's ring was a short, then a long, then a short. When you answered you could often detect "rubbering" on the line. A neighbor would butt in and offer a suggestion or expand the gossip.

Harvesting the Crops

The busy threshing times (September and October) were especially colorful and filled with excitement and joy. There was "rejoicing as they brought in the sheaves." Men greased the threshing machines and replaced parts that had worn out in the previous season. Neighbors joined together to thresh each other's grain. Crews began before sunrise and worked into the night. As many as twelve bundle teams included a pair of horses, two spike pitchers, two field pitchers, a fireman, an engineer, a separator man, a tank man, and a straw boss. Bundles of wheat were brought in from the field with a hay rake, and then the spike pitchers cut the twine and thrust the bundles into the threshing machine. The shelled grain that came out the other side of the threshing machine was collected in gunny sacks. The straw was blown into a pile and properly stacked. A heavy rubber belt ran between the steam engine's flywheel and the threshing machine. Work around the belts and pulleys was noisy and dangerous. The grease nuts around the bearings were checked twice a day lest the bearings freeze up.

A cook car often arrived in the field near the threshing machine. The men washed their hands in big tubs and sat around makeshift tables, eating and poking fun at each other. The providers fed the harvest crew three big meals a day and two smaller lunches in the mid-morning and mid-afternoon breaks. The typical fare included bread and pasta along with potatoes, beans, peas, chicken or beef, and watermelon. The smaller lunches featured sandwiches, pastries, cookies, and milk or lemonade. The women cooked alongside their daughters and neighbors' wives. They brought vegetables from the garden and could slaughter a young steer or behead some chickens. Flies were a constant annoyance. Children armed with flyswatters chased them.

John Willey's neighbor, Sid Elder, owned the biggest smoke blower (steam engine) in the township, a two-cylinder Nickols and Shepherd steamer with a 44-inch J. I. Case thresher. The steamer moved slowly, shaking the ground and belching smoke and steam. It powered the threshing machine with a long belt. Children would forever remember the great steam-blowing monster, hissing, growling, and belching smoke as it crawled around the fields.

The Sabbath

Since the beginning of the SDA church, a faithful member observes the Sabbath from Friday sunset to Saturday sunset. Church leaders warn members to respect the sacredness of the Sabbath as a celebration of God's creation. Cooking, cleaning, taking baths, washing the car, filling the gas tank, and other Sabbath preparations all happened by late afternoon Friday. Threshing in John's fields that was not completed by Friday afternoon stopped and then resumed Sunday morning. The neighbors seemed not to wonder why John was so scrupulous in his practices. John invited his friends to attend worship with him, but they preferred to fish on the Mouse River or simply take the day off.

Early Power was Horses

Maintaining the horses and livestock took considerable time. Afterall, horses were the main source of power used for farming until tractors replaced them. (One of the first tractors in the county was a Waterloo, the forerunner of John Deere.)

It took eight to twelve horses to farm a quarter section. The ground was broken up by four horses pulling a harrow or disc that followed the plow. Once the ground was prepared, the farmer seeded the wheat, barley, flax or oats using a "drill" pulled by four horses. Rain, thunderstorms, hail, and gusty winds left the earth with a pleasant odor referred to as "the smell of happiness."

Cured prairie grass, or Timothy hay and oats, provided food for the horses. During field work horses were fed two or three times a day (it took more than a ton of hay and 180 pounds of oats to keep a thousand-pound horse fed for six months). A highly prized Percheron or Clydesdale draft horse could weigh twenty-six-hundred pounds and cost as much as six hundred dollars and these larger horses required more hay and grain. (A modern economist estimated that today it would take ninety-two million horses to farm North Dakota.) When mechanical farming arrived, it changed the homesteader's life forever and completely.

John and Inez Move Across the Road

Not long after John and Inez were married, they took over the Jimmy Anderson quarter across the road from the Willey's original homestead. Jimmy had been born into a wealthy farming family in Copenhagen, Denmark. He crossed the ocean with the dream of a new life in a free country. Before leaving home, his father gave him a Stradivarius violin at which he became proficient and in demand for dances and weddings. (Unfortunately, this violin was destroyed when his house burned to the ground in Mohall.)

Jimmy bragged to John that he busked his way to America by playing the violin on the ship. His future wife, who also came from Denmark, had arrived at the New York City dock the day after President Lincoln's assassination. After homesteading Jimmy sold his quarter to John's father and continued west to a homestead in Montana. Then he returned to Mohall. Wm Willey paid $2,500 for the quarter, a tidy sum in those days. Jimmy's water well produced only enough water for a single man and a few turnips and potatoes; hardly enough to water a cow. [1]

After taking over the Anderson quarter, John planted wheat, flax, Timothy Grass, and barley, but left some land for pasture. There were no trees, so all the buildings stood bare to the sun and wind until John grew a shelter of cottonwoods and alders to the west and north of the house to create a wind break.

Inez recalled her first visit to the Anderson place: "The Anderson shack had a leaky roof and smelled like a pig pen." So Inez and John retreated across the road and stayed with John's parents through the first winter of their marriage Four years later, after John and Inez "proved up their marriage" by giving birth to their first child, George, Wm and Laura sold the Anderson quarter to John and Inez for one dollar. By then they had

---

[1] *Renville County History*, 1976 (p. 467).

constructed a house, garage, granary, outhouse, and a barn. They has also deepened and expanded the well near the barn.

For buildings on the Anderson quarter lumber was shipped by rail from the Potlatch Mill in Lewiston, Idaho. With the help of a "building bee" of neighbors, the construction of the house only took a few days. The house turned out to be a three-room single floor plan with tar paper tacked to the bare boards on the outside next to the siding and newspaper glued to the inside walls for insulation. They collected rainwater from the roof and stored it in a concrete cistern dug near the kitchen porch. Rainwater was softer than well water and was used for washing hair and bathing in the kitchen. There were two hand pumps at the kitchen sink, one for the hard water well and the other for soft water from the cistern. The house had been constructed over the hard water well near a corner of the kitchen to protect it from freezing in the winter. The other well was by the side of the barn for the livestock and had a larger pump.

An Indian Came by Every Week for a Pie

Each summer Inez laid up canned foods, and stored vegetables such as carrots, potatoes and beets in a root cellar dug out under the kitchen floor, where it could be reached by stairs through a trap door inside the kitchen. Three years later, after the children began to arrive, they added a second floor on the west end of the house and constructed two bedrooms upstairs with a hallway in between. The house was not insulated or constructed like a modern house. In fact, if you walk into the homestead today you wonder how they kept the place warm in the winter. Sometimes the rooms upstairs were -10 degrees. After John's parents passed away in 1920 John and Inez inherited the original Willey quarter across the road. The house remained vacant for several years until son George married and took over the original Willey homestead with his new wife, Thora.

One of Inez' favorite stories about her earlier years in North Dakota was in telling about how she baked a pie every week and left it outside on the kitchen windowsill next to the road coming into the farmyard. A Chippewa Indian, with dirt under his fingernails and smoking a cigarette, would come by and pluck the pie from the window, hardly making a sound. Seeing him coming down the road she fearfully hid upstairs, holding a loaded shotgun.

Although she didn't know much about the Indian, she was convinced that the pie was her insurance or bribe against harm from any Indians roaming in the neighborhood. The Indian also gave her a stone mortar and pestle to grind wheat for the pie crust. He'd promised her that his chief would watch over her and protect her children, chickens and the farm animals.

Inez discovered later that the Chippewa was from a reservation and had a pass to travel around the territory. He spent his summers camping, hunting and fishing near the Souris (Mouse) River and enjoyed a weekly pie as a treat from a Norwegian newlywed who had been spoofed into believing that wild Indians might come and burn her house down while her husband was out in the field working.

John kept honeybees out back of the house and for a hobby he raised pigeons, the kind with fancy flaring feathers around their feet. Out by the west side of the house he planted a large garden where he grew cucumbers, muskmelons, sweet corn, potatoes, radishes, beets, carrots, cabbage, peas, and beans. It was watered by hand when necessary. In the winter he made ice cream from straight cream. He attributed his sweet tooth, and why he preferred pancakes with syrup three times a day, to his English heritage. Inez allowed for his weaknesses and let him poach pretty much what he wanted to eat. At the top of his list was chocolate, when he could afford it.

Rural Living was Better Than Urban

Society's celebration of farming (Jeffersonian agrarianism) permeated the Willey household. John believed that rural life was better than urban life, despite never having lived in a big city. Nevertheless, he could grumble about the way farmers were treated in the marketplace. "We don't have any voice to change things or to protect the farmer's way of life," he said, "We are left to fight our own battles." Other things beyond his control also frustrated him.

One day a severe hailstorm destroyed the neighbor's wheat field but somehow skipped around his own field without causing any damage. Being a religious man, he attributed this to his faithful tithe paying. He boasted about this to his friends. The following year when his own field was destroyed by high winds and heavy rain, he concluded that God was telling him something about humility, and so he stopped expecting special favors and talking about Providence.

John was savvy about working with horses. He knew the characteristics of different breeds, what made them skittish, and how hard to work them. When buying a horse, he followed a phrenological profile his father taught him about judging the shape of a horse's head to determine the best features. He kept veterinary supplies in the barn including de-worming pills, horse liniment, salves, winter green, and other remedies for treating livestock and sheep. When the children came along, he used these same potions to treat their strained muscles, upset stomachs, boils, and other childhood ailments! Taking a less caustic approach, Inez depended on Dr. John Harvey Kellogg's common-sense book, *"Practical Guide to Health,"* to answer her family's medical questions and guide her in treating family illnesses. [2]

The Birth of the Family

John confessed to Inez that he enjoyed playing the piano and mandolin in the Loraine community hall during their dances. The people spread rice over the floor to make the dancing easier. Although John saw no spiritual harm in the dances, the minister at Minot reminded him that "one casual temptation led to a stronger one."

After George (1909) was born, John and Inez had five other children, totaling four boys and two daughters. Son George arrived after a heavy rain and no midwife could reach Inez during the birthing. Hence, John's sister Jonetta and his mother Laura became the midwives. Lutefisk could pretty much dull a person's senses, but, as Inez explained later, "My pain was beyond lutefisk or whiskey." Hearing this, John wondered how she knew about whiskey, having been raised under the banner of temperance in the Lutheran church.

A little more than a year later, before the next child came due, John took Inez across the Mouse River to her parent's homestead in Norma. Disposed to privacy, she made all men leave, including John. The house became empty

---

[2] John Harvey Kellogg was a famous physician head of the Battle Creek Sanitarium. He was an Adventist until he was disfellowshipped for problems in managing church leadership, for failing to recognize the church's prophet, and for writing a pantheistic book titled *The Living Temple.*

except for her mother and a midwife who arrived from down the road, and the two younger Odland children sleeping upstairs. Her mother held Inez's shoulders against the bed during delivery. Throughout her childbearing, Inez avoided all references to sex. Perhaps she thought it might affect her moral judgment, but probably it stemmed from custom or life in a conservative family.

The second male child came into the world with a loud squawk, and so Inez told her friends that Tom was named after the Norwegian god of thunder! Thomas Odland Willey (1910-1990) will become the central figure in this story.

Growing up around his mother's folks gave Tom an appreciation for Norwegian culture and language, and he learned enough Norwegian to engage in modest commercial and social exchanges. He could ask for sweets, or whisper "sweet Norwegian nothings" in the ears of the girls. When he tried to learn some swear words, his mother refused to let him. After Inez' father Thomas Odland passed away Tom inherited his grandfather's glass eye, which he carried in his pocket for good luck! Everyone seems to be born with a little superstition about luck, whether it be four-leaf clovers, rabbit's feet, glass eyes, or many other good-luck charms.

Four more children were born to John and Inez: two middle sisters, Genevieve (1912-1995) and Marjorie (1916-1955), and two younger brothers, William (or Billy) (1923-1931) and John, Jr. (1925-1984). The girls were pretty and charming. When they got older, they caught the attention of boys. Marjorie, particularly, was "daddy's little girl." She had curly hair like her mother and played on the girls' basketball team in Mohall. As Genevieve, the older daughter, matured she developed a reputation as a good cook, which remained with her for life.

The Willey brood was spread across seventeen years. On a North Dakota homestead such birth planning was called "spawned-workers" strategy. A homestead without children did not have a future. John and Inez raised their children to be mild-tempered, truthful, dependable, strong in devotion and spirit, and highly moral.

Nearly twenty years after son George was born father John went to the county courthouse in Mohall and filled out birth certificates for the whole lot. In the process he got some birthday dates mixed up, but the names were correct.

The Farm Grew on John as Much as He Grew the Farm

Farming truly appealed to John. It was his life, and he wanted his sons to share in the same blessings. Growing up, the boys pitched hay with their father and rode on the machinery in the field. Before his sons arrived, of course, John had worked alone with the horses. (Believe it or not, after he purchased his first tractor, he still preferred horses for many tasks and kept horses in the barn to do light work.) But, after the two older boys reached manhood the farm became easier to manage. With the help of the additional labor, John added to his land and eventually farmed a full section, or 640 acres. And another full section was added when tractors appeared. George lived across the road and would remain on the farm until he retired. Tom and Marjorie went off to college in the 30s, the desperate years.

For several years, when rainfall was good, the farm prospered. The price of wheat went as high as two dollars and eighty cents a bushel and came in from the field at fifteen bushels or higher per acre. Debt free most of the time, John even put away money for hard times. But not in banks, which John didn't trust. For one thing, the Loraine State Bank had been robbed twice and depositors lost money on their uninsured funds. When the bank closed during the depression it financially crippled John's neighbor, Robert Mitchell, the owner. Excessive loan expansion and poor judgement resulted in farm mortgage debt reaching nearly twenty-four percent of the full value of all the land in North Dakota.[3]

Leasing land for drilling oil began sometime around 1931 in Mohall. In the process, oil companies discovered gas, but no oil. Representatives from Standard Oil discussed a lease with John, but it was mostly talk. Standard Oil Company of California drilled a well, but for technical reasons, abandoned the well. Later the oil companies showed up again to

---

[3] Blanche Hembree. *Fate, Destiny, Necessity on Renville's Prairies* (Self-published, 1977), 97.

lease the mineral rights of the farms when oil was discovered west of the Willey farm in Williston, North Dakota.

Prior to the depression, farmers began using credit to purchase cars and machinery. Banker Mitchell believed the invasion of the automobile on borrowed money would wreck the country. [4] He had experience in banking and saw that debt usually came home to roost on a farmer's head. Such talk resonated with John because time was short, nations were in turmoil, there were crises in politics, industry, finance and morals, and he thought the "antichrist" of Revelation might be money instead of the Catholic Pope. As John observed farms around him start to deteriorate, he sensed an impending calamity and feared that money, as well as the Pope, would surely be at the center of it.

---

[4] *Renville County Farmer,* July 9, 1931.

WHAT HAPPENS IF THE PROPHET DIES BEFORE THE SECOND COMING?
CHAPTER TEN

"It is the distinction of our days that the American Church has enjoyed the teachings of two prophetess…Our two later prophetesses, Mrs. Eddy, founder of the Christian Science Church, and Mrs. Ellen G. White, leader and teacher of the SDAs, lived and died in comfort and honor, surrounded by their admiring followers. Many of Mrs. Eddy's disciples believed she would never die, and Mrs. White hoped to be one of those who would be taken up alive to meet the Lord in the air." Arthur L. White, *The Later Elmshaven Years* (Takoma Park, MD: Review & Herald Publ. Assoc., 1982), VI, 443. *New York Independent,* August 23, 1915.

The charismatic prophetess, Ellen White, cofounded (along with her husband) the Seventh-day Adventist Church. Although she lived a long time, she suffered poor health. Her formal education did not extend beyond the third grade. Some clerics, traveling brethren, and others with whom she worked, found her overly zealous and blind to the fact that the delay of Jesus' coming was making people weary of her repeated warnings. Second Coming fatigue was setting in.

Importance of White's Testimonies

Her letters and "*Testimonies*" to church members, which often pointed out their faults and errors, were important, but not always accepted. Aware of her enormous influence, the brethren who guided the SDA church emphasized that "Brother and Sister White were called of God to an important sphere of labor in the great work of the third angel's message to instruct, to warn, and to reprove; and we hereby unitedly pledge to them our sympathies and our prayers in the discharge of their arduous duties." [1]

At the heart of this approval was the understanding that the writings and teachings of Ellen White greatly benefited the Advent evangelicals: with a prophetess of God at their side, church leaders and ministers became remarkably effective in stirring revival embers into flame. The church continued to grow, not least because of having a living prophet and her published works and exhortations.

But there were critics such as D. M. Canright (1840-1919), a one-time successful minister and evangelist for the SDA Church. James White baptized Canright and invited him to debate the Sabbath question with "outside" ministers when the opportunity presented itself. But In 1873 during a summer vacation with James and Ellen White in Black Hawk Colorado, Canright and his wife Lucretia had a falling out with Whites. As a result they received a lengthy twenty-five-page *Testimony* from Ellen White, which began.

> *For some months I have felt that it was time to write to you something which the Lord was pleased to show me in regard to you several years ago. I was shown that you were both deficient in essential qualification and that if these are not obtained your usefulness and the salvation of your own souls will be endangered.* [2]

No one welcomed a rebuke like this from the prophetess. After leaving the church, Canright became a Baptist minister and wrote *Seventh-day Adventism Renounced* (1889). He later expressed his loss of confidence in Ellen White by publishing *The Life of Mrs. E. G. White* (1919). Both books were reprinted several times. [3]

White sometimes wrote her *Testimonies* in church while other

---

[1] Arthur L. White, *The Progressive Years 1862-1876* (Hagerstown, MD: Review & Herald Publ. Assoc., 1986), 230.

[2] Ellen G. White, "To a Young Minister and his Wife," *Testimonies,* III, 304.

[3] Carrie Johnson, *I Was Canright's Secretary* (Takoma Park, MD: Review & Herald Publ. Assoc., 1971). See also Nancy Page's description how Arthur L. White influenced her grandmother to write *I was Canright's Secretary, Proclamation Spring,* 2018, 5.

ministers were preaching! After a service she once stood before her audience and explained;

> *I arose and spoke one hour to individuals. I had testimony for reproving individual wrongs. We had an interesting, exciting time. Brother Fisher was encouraged and comforted. He had been passing through a terrible struggle, giving up tobacco, intoxicating drinks, and hurtful indulgences. He was very poor and high, proud spirited. He had made a great effort to overcome...Some felt exceedingly bad because I brought out these cases before others. I was sorry to see this spirit. The testimony was more especially to impress upon those particularly in fault through the sin of hasty speaking, jesting, joking, and laughing. All this was wrong and detrimental to their growth in grace.* [4]

Many members felt that God spoke through the voice of the prophetess. She and her husband could be sharply critical or direct because of their privileged status as divinely appointed expounders of sacred truth. The extensive messages came in the form of *Testimonies to the Church,* often beginning with "I was shown" and intended for all to read. To explain why White put out such a constant stream of messages, some scholars chalked it up to hypergraphia, an intense and continual need to write.

To her son Edson, she wrote this about the *Testimonies:* "Some felt exceedingly tried, especially Sister Doude. She came to me in the morning, accompanied by her husband. She was crying and said to me, 'You have killed me, you have killed clean off. You have killed me.' Said I, that is just what I hoped the message I bore would do...Brother Doude accused me of violating Scripture by not telling the fault between them and me alone. We told him this scripture did not touch the case. There was no trespass here against me. That the case before us was one of them that had been mentioned by the apostles; those who sin, reprove before all, that others may fear." [5]

---

[4] Arthur L. White, *The Progressive Years 1862-1876* (Hagerstown, MD: Review & Herald Publ. Assoc., 1986), 228.

[5] Ellen G. White, Letter to Edison, Letter 6, 1868.

The Ellen G. White Estate claimed that the "Spirit of Prophecy" included more than 2,000 visions and approximately 50,000 pages in letters, pamphlets, and books. After her husband died in 1881, White employed faithful assistants and secretaries to continue her publishing work and literary output. Her claim that Christ had appeared in her house on several occasions added to the weight of her authority and her divine role in unfolding the great work of Christ, the cross and assurance of salvation.

White never came to terms with human degradation and depravity. She believed that unless Christ appeared soon humans might become so degraded that there would be no one left to save. *"Degeneration had created confused species which God did not create, which were the result of amalgamation were destroyed by the flood."* She warned her followers against interracial marriages after Lincoln emancipated the slaves in 1864. Near the end of her life she claimed that there would be no "colored line in heaven" — the blacks *"will be as white as Christ himself. Let us thank God that we can be members of the royal family."* [6] She told her people that *"Satan's power upon the human family increases. If the Lord should not soon come and destroy his power, the earth would soon be depopulated."* [7] She sought perfection in the members of the church, but, as noted earlier, scholars soon discovered that some of the prophet's writings had been "borrowed" from other authors.

Unequivocal evidence of this did little to disconfirm her as an agent of God. [8] Even today she is highly revered.[9]

---

[6] Ellen G. White, "The Flood," *Spiritual Gifts* (Battle Creek, MI: Review & Heald Publ. Assoc., 1864), III, 76. See T. Joe Willey, "Ellen White's Ingratiating Amalgamation Statements," *Adventist Today,* Spring 2018, 26.

[7] Ellen G. White, *Testimonies,* 19:162.

[8] Malcolm Bull and Keith Lockhart, *Seeking a Sanctuary: Seventh-day Adventism and the American Dream* (Bloomington, IN: Indiana Univ. Press., 2007), 34. Walter T. Rea, *The White Lie* (Turlock, CA: M & R Publications, 1982). T. Joe Willey, "The Great Controversy Over Plagiary: The Last Interview of Walter Rea," *Spectrum,* January 5, 2017.

[9] See Jerry Moon, "The Role of Ellen White in the Development of Adventist Doctrines," www.andrews.edu/~jmoon/Documents/GSEM_534/Class_outline/07.pdf, 2006.

God was speaking through clay. In these letters which I write,
in the testimonies I bear, I am presenting to you that which
the Lord has presented to me. I do not write one article in
the paper expressing merely my own ideas. They are what
God has opened before me in vision the precious rays of light
shining from the throne. [10]

Ellen's husband James was intensely religious and a born entrepreneur. With keen ability as a financial and theological manager, editor, and publisher,[11] he immediately took on significant leadership roles despite his minimal schooling and ministerial experience. [12] During the course of his life, he edited several church publications, preached widely, raised money, oversaw the publishing of his wife's books, and established an organized structure for the church as a denomination. Ellen White confirmed by visions that her husband was a special agent of God.

Despite her "direct connection to the throne of God," Ellen White grew old. In 1915 W. C. White, her youngest son described how his aging mother had fallen near her study and incurred an intracapsular fracture of the left femur. (Meanwhile her secretary and literary assistants rushed to prepare the final chapters of *Prophets and Kings*.)

Following the accident, the staff drew up plans for the expected funeral and prepared biographical press releases. Two years before at the 1913 General Conference session in Takoma Park, Maryland, her son William had answered the question, "Did Sister White expect to die before the Second Coming?" He replied that:

The Lord has not told her how long she will live. He has not
told her in a positive way that she is to die; but she expects to
rest in the grave a little time before the Lord comes. [13]

---

[10] Visions of Mrs. E. G. White, *Testimonies*, 31:63.

[11] Isaac C. Wellcome, *History of Second Advent Message and Mission, Doctrine, and People* (Yarmouth, ME, 1874), 406.

[12] Arthur L. White, *The Progressive Years 1862-1876* (Hagerstown, MD: Review & Herald Publ. Assoc., 1986), 313.

[13] *General Conference Bulletin*, 1913, 219.

Before she passed away, three nurses cared for her: May Walling, Carrie Hangerford, and her traveling companion, nurse, and faithful secretary, Sara McEnterfer. When there was little hope of recovery, Ellen said in a faint whisper, "I know in whom I have believed." [14] She passed away at 3:40 in the afternoon on Friday, July 16, 1915, at eighty-seven years of age.

For the funeral in Battle Creek (one of three services) the church headquarters in Takoma Park sent out more than a thousand invitations. The mayor and city commissioners received special invitations. Carefully prepared news releases were given to editors and reporters in Battle Creek "to prevent the publication of a lot of derogatory matter." [15] Evangelist S. N. Haskell (1833-1922), who once had proposed marriage to the widowed Ellen, gave the life sketch at the funeral.

After the services in the Tabernacle Church a carriage took her body to the Oak Hill Cemetery. More than a hundred automobiles and carriages, and nine city street cars chartered by the Church, followed the procession to the grave site. The services there were brief. The *Review* reported that, "The remains of our dear sister were tenderly and silently lowered into the grave to rest beside the body of her husband, James White." [16] What actually happened in the burials of both James and Ellen White would remain undisclosed for over fifty years.

Delayed Burial of James White

Thirty-four years earlier, following the death of her husband James White, his coffin had been secretly removed after gravesite services, and placed in a cemetery vault. [17]

Before the funeral, the leading brethren came to Ellen White and urged her to appeal to God to raise her husband from the dead which, of

---

[14] Arthur L. White, *Ellen G. White, The Later Elmshaven Years* (Washington DC: Review and Herald Publ. Assoc., 1982), 431. See also "I am a Christian, I know in whom I have believed," in *The Lonely Years,* 173.

[15] Letter from W. C. White to Edson White, July 10, 1915.

[16] *Review & Herald,* August 3, 1915, and *The Battle Creek Enquirer,* July 25, 1915. "The casket was then lowered in the grave beside that of her husband."

[17] The funeral was delayed for Elder W. C. White and wife Mary to cross the continent by train and the arrival of James White's brother John from Ohio. Elder W. C. White arrived on Friday August 12, 1881.

course, would have given additional evidence of God's power in her life and stifled all critics once and for all. "Do not let them bury him," they invoked, "but pray to the Lord, that He may bring him to life again." After reflecting on the request, Ellen White said "no." She would not invoke her powers to raise her husband from the dead. "He had done his work... Would I have him suffer all this over again? No, no. I would in no case call him from his restful sleep to a life of toil and pain. He will rest until the morning of the resurrection," which she posited was not far off. [18]

During the public funeral Ellen White stood in the front of the church with one hand on the casket and told the audience, "I cried to God to spare him to me—not to take him away and leave me to labor alone." [19] Maybe she had put in a request for his resurrection after all!

The Michigan Tribune reported; "The funeral possession was one of the largest ever witnessed in this city. Ninety-four carriages and a large concourse on foot followed the remains to the cemetery, where, surrounded by flowers and evergreens, was laid to rest "all that was mortal of Elder James White." [20]

The bereaved did not know what happened afterwards. A diary turned up by the armchair historian Mark Bovee tells how James White's casket in fact had been removed from the grave. The diary of William H. Hall casts doubt on the burial interment at the time of the funeral on August 13th, for the August 23rd entry says that "Tonight, I went to J. E. White [and] we went to Oak Hill and we moved the remains of Eld. White from the vault to the grave. We opened the casket and took a last look until the morn of the resurrection. Rest in peace war worn soldier, sleep on." [21] James White was then taken to the White plot and finally buried.

---

[18] *Manuscript Release*, VII, 419 (The White Estates Archives). Also see Ellen White letter 396-06 written to "Sister Belden" on December 25, 1906. Arthur L. White, *Ellen G. White, The Retirement Years* (Hagerstown, MD: Review & Herald Publ. Assoc., 1990), 164. During her public comments at the funeral, she told the audience, "I cried to God to spare him to me—not to take him away and leave me to labor alone."

[19] Arthur L. White. Ellen G. White, *The Lonely Years* (Hagerstown, MD: Review & Herald Publ. Assoc., 1984), 175.

[20] *The Michigan Tribune*, August 20, 1881.

[21] James White Library, Andrews University, Berrien Springs, MI, Box 11, Fld. 9, Mark Bovee (Collection 146). Center for Adventist Research. Letter from Mark L. Bovee to Mrs. V. E. Robinson, April 29, 1973.

Why feign the burial of James White after the mourners had departed on August 13th? Had son Edson and his compatriot Hall hoped that James White might have been resurrected while stored in the vault? We can provide a possible answer after we review the fact that Ellen White's casket, like her husband's, was also removed from the grave after the mourners departed and delayed for burial.

Ellen White's Burial Was Also Delayed

After the gravesite services Ellen White's coffin was spirited out of the grave and stored outside in the cemetery vault. under lock and key. (For years the Ellen G. White Estate and the church maintained that Ellen White was buried immediately following the grave site services. But this was not true.)

Psychologists and psychiatrists predict that a strong expectation of the soon coming under continuing anxiety can lead believers to explore and create other redemptive alternatives or even update fundamental beliefs in different ways. On this topic, without revealing what provoked his motivation for writing in the *Review,* J. O. Corliss (one of the "traveling brethren" living in Battle Creek), asked a question related to the Second Coming; *"Is death the second coming of Christ?"* [22] In other words, once a loyal follower of the Lord is buried does such a person bypass the second coming itself and go directly to heaven? Ellen White claimed to have met Elijah and Moses in heaven. She wrote in *Desire of Ages* that, "Moses passed under the dominion of death, but he was not to remain in the tomb. Christ Himself called him forth to life. Satan the tempter had claimed the body of Moses because of his sin; but Christ the Saviour brought him forth from the grave." [23] That sounds like Christ can resurrect an important leader before the Second Coming.

Most remarkably, as Mark Bovee's research showed, and as son Edson confirmed, both husband and wife had delayed burials. The clandestine removal of the caskets puzzled grandson Arthur White, the director of the Ellen G. White Estate in Takoma Park. He did not know what to make

---

[22] "Death Not the Second Coming of Christ," *Review and Herald,* September 6, 1881.
[23] Ellen White, *Desire of Ages,* 421.

of it [24] and had been "unable to track down any other information that would support the claim. I have never heard it mentioned in the family." [25]

And he could not accept the historical facts. He explained to Bovee, "You write of the fact that Ellen White was not placed in the grave until about three weeks after her funeral. I appreciate the data you have sent to us on this. The whole thing was rather incredible to me, but I think there is ample evidence to support what seem to be the facts (the facts being what the *Review* said at the time of the grave side services). Thank you for going to the trouble/to investigate the matter thoroughly there." [26] And thus, only a few people came to know about the interruption of the burials of James and Ellen White. [27]

> *A man with a conviction is a hard man to change. Tell him you disagree, and he turns away. Show him facts or figures and he questions your sources. Appeal to logic and he fails to see your point.* [28]

The ghost in the delayed interments finally stepped out to reveal itself through the beliefs of the two living sons of this pioneer pair. The two sons knew what their mother had written about the faithful dead who had

---

[24] Arthur L. White's biography of his grandmother covers her funeral in *The Later Elmshaven Years* published in 1982 and makes no mention of Edson's 1915 letter or his knowledge about this delayed burial event, not even a footnote.

[25] "Seventh-day Adventists have accepted on the basis of those who were present at the funeral and the reports which appeared in the *Review and Herald* and the news media that Ellen White in her casket was lowered into the grave in the White plot at Battle Creek cemetery on the Sabbath of the funeral, and thus having been laid to rest had not been disturbed." Arthur L. White Memorandum, November 4, 1974.

[26] Letter from Arthur L. White to Mark Bovee, April 1, 1976.

[27] Patricia Guest Pryor, *The Controversial Christian Prophetess Ellen G. White* (Maitland, FL: Xulon Pres, 2014), 52. T. Joe Willey, "An Adventist Historical Puzzle. The Delayed Burials of James and Ellen White," *Adventist Today*, Vol. 19-1 (2011), 10. T. Joe Willey, "Death and Burial," in *Ellen Harmon White: American Prophet*, Terrie Dopp Aamodt, Gary Land, and Ronald Numbers, eds. (New York: Oxford Univ. Press, 2014), 295.

[28] Leon Festinger, Henry W. Riecken, and Stanley Schachter, "Unfulfilled Prophecies and Disappointed Messiahs," in Jon R. Stone, *Expecting Armageddon* (New York: Routledge, 2000), 31.

been resurrected with Christ and taken to heaven during His ascension. No one but the two brothers and two independent observers knew about the delayed burials of their parents. The original intent was probably to test if it was possible that their parents might be favored by God in the same manner as faithful witnesses taken to heaven at Christ's ascension. They must have thought that their parents were of the same quality as the faithful who were raised from the dead with Christ and, of course, it would have been a wonderful testimony had they been resurrected. Ellen White had written about miraculous resurrections during the time of Christ in *The Great Controversy*.

> *Those favored, resurrected saints came forth glorified (with Christ during his ascension). They were a few chosen and holy ones who had lived in every age from creation, even down to the days of Christ. And while the chief priests and Pharisees were seeking to cover up the resurrection of Christ, God chose to bring up a company from their graves to testify that Jesus had risen, and to declare his glory.* [29]

Evidently, in both cases the brothers must have hoped that something like this might happen with their parents. They removed the caskets from the grave where they could be observed and waited a certain amount of time before lifting the cover of the caskets to determine if their parents had taken early flight to heaven. Disappointed when they found the caskets still occupied, they sealed them, returned their parents to the grave, and buried them properly. Then the two brothers kept the family secret to themselves.

After Ellen White's death, her articles were reprinted or published as books or in church periodicals. Church officials continued to discuss the death of Ellen G. White and the heirloom of her writings for the remnant. World War I and the death of the prophet became a possible fulfillment of Bible prophecy. Maybe the end was very close, and such speculation prompted the church to sponsor a Bible conference.

---

[29] Ellen G. White, "The Resurrection of Christ," *The Great Controversy*, 70.

1919 Bible Conference Under Objections

Delegates to Bible Conference, Washington, D. C., July, 1919

The conference was a series of round-table discussions held at the church headquarters in Takoma Park, Washington. [30] Attendance at the conference was by invitation only. Sixty-five of the most trusted leaders, educators, historians, and editors in the church came together to discuss theological issues that kept arising in teaching the doctrines of the church, issues driven in part by higher-biblical criticism, evolution and biblical hermeneutics dealing with the inspiration and infallibility of Ellen White's prophetic writings. The discussions focused on how to teach Biblical truths in the classrooms of Adventist schools and colleges and even in the pulpit.

Concerns mounted that church members just like John Willey and his children might become "terribly upset if they should discover that both the Bible and Ellen White were fallible." At the end of the conference, the 1200 pages of transcripts were "squirreled-away" until accidently discovered seventy-five years later in 1974.

A.G. Daniells, president of the General Conference, expressed concerns about the need for the manifestation of the supernatural in presenting the gift of prophecy. In particular, he worried about "physical and outward demonstrations." He brought up the story about Ellen White carrying a heavy Bible (18 lbs.) on an outstretched hand for thirty-minutes. "I do not know whether that was ever done or not. I am not sure. I did not see it. I do not count that sort of thing as a very great proof." Perhaps something had "crawled into the story." [31]

During the Conference, one outspoken Bible teacher expressed the need for transparency of their discussions:

> *Can we hold something in the back of our head that we are*
> *absolutely sure about, and that most of the brethren stand*

---

[30] Ibid. 42.

[31] Ibid. 154.

with us on? Can we hold those things back and be true to ourselves? And furthermore, are we safe in doing it? Is it well to let our people in general go on holding to the verbal inspiration of the Testimonies? When we do that, aren't we preparing for a crisis that will be very serious some day? It seems to me that the best thing for us to do is to cautiously and very carefully educate our people to see just where we really should stand to be consistent Protestants; to be consistent with the Testimonies themselves, and to be consistent with what we know we must do; as intelligent men, as we have decided in these meetings. [32]

Discussions like this vexed the conservatives in the church. Some teachers were said to be using textbooks in the classroom by "infidel authors." They were warned about being heterodox in their teaching. (These discussions occurred exactly when the Adventist academic colleges were considering accreditation.) On the other hand, the conference attendees did reach an agreement: they were firmly united on all the fundamentals of church teachings and doctrines. Later, A.G. Daniells opposed the publication of any new Ellen White materials.[33] The suspicions of several, including J. S. Washburn and Claude Holmes, were aroused by certain positions taken during the conference and they saw "This Bible Institute" as one of the "most terrible things that has happened in the history of the denomination." [34]

Self-styled Ellen White expert Claude Holmes and others who believed that Daniells and W.W. Prescott were seeking to do away with the Spirit of Prophecy found assurances of this conspiracy in the 1919 Bible Conference. Soon Daniells was removed as president of the General Conference. [35]

What emerged was a conservative reaction to the liberalism and modernity of other denominations. Adventism turned sharply in the direction of fundamentalism. Because the Conference emphasized the unity of doctrines and teachings of the church, Adventists insisted on the inerrancy and verbal inspiration of the Bible. This augmented the authority

---

[32] J. N. Anderson, "1919 Bible Conference," (SDA Archives).

[33] Paul McGrew, "Without a Living Prophet," *Ministry,* December 2000, 11.

[34] Neither Washburn or Holmes were present at the Bible Conference.

[35] Paul McGrew, "Without a Living Prophet," *Ministry,* December 2000, 13.

of the prophetess regarding the virgin birth, substitutionary atonement, the bodily resurrection, the reality of miracles, the Second Advent, and the doctrine of creation. Evolution and the long history of earth geology lost out entirely. The Bible and the writings of White were literally and completely trustworthy. [36]

Spasm of Fanaticism: A New Prophetess

During her lifetime Mrs. White had been careful to safeguard her preeminent prophetic position and to push aside any new "prophet" who challenged her authority. Anna Garmire, Anna Phillips, Martha Steward, and Mrs. Mackin were such people.

Mrs. White did not name a successor, not even her own son Willie White. She advised the church brethren that because Jesus was coming soon it would not be necessary to replace her, especially since the denomination had enough *Testimonies*, letters, sermons, books, and messages from "the Messenger of the Lord" to manage until the end of time.

Willie White reported that more than a dozen would-be prophets came forward after the burial of his mother. One of these came in contact indirectly with John and Inez Willey living on the farm in North Dakota. News and description of this new prophetess was brought to them by Matthew Larson, a cousin of John.

Matthew Larson had attended Battle Creek College and studied theology under Uriah Smith, the sometime editor of the *Review*. As a young man he had gotten a reprimanding *Testimony* from the prophetess for his wrangling and argumentative style. He would serve thirty years as an Adventist minister in various conferences—at one time he worked under the presidency of H.M.J. Richards in Arkansas. (This Richards was the father of H.M.S. Richards who later directed the Voice of Prophecy radio programs in Glendale, California.)

Whenever the denomination needed a debater against the Mormons, they called on Larson. Invitations to debate came from the Texas, Oklahoma, Kansas, and Iowa conferences. At the time he visited John Willey, Larson was exposing exposing what he thought to be a serious

---

[36] Mollerus Couperus, "The Bible Conference of 1919: Introduction," *Spectrum* 10:1 (May 1979), 23-57.

mutiny: "Satan is using his agents in a scheming, lying, deceitful manner in the operations of the Kansas Sanitarium." Meanwhile he fought the claim of C. S. Longacre, a lawyer in the church, that Margaret W. Rowen was a false prophetess and vigorously affirmed her authority.

Matthew came to visit his cousin in North Dakota and told John that his fate, and his family's, would be sealed by a decision he was about to make. Speaking like a true evangelical, Larson announced the arrival of the "sealing time" White had predicted: Adventists were encouraged to sell everything and give the money to the church to finish the work. This was serious talk to a farmer who along with his family believed that Jesus would be returning soon, but who had invested his life, sweat, and tears in developing his farm.

Larson hoped, specifically, that John and Inez would sell their farm and venture with him in the promulgation of Rowen, the new prophetess. Larson kept the pressure up by arguing that since the Lord would come soon, owning anything would be worthless.

By soon he meant that the end would come in 1925. According to the new prophetess, probation would close February 6, 1924 and Jesus will return a year later on February 6, 1925. Inez wanted more information about Rowen.

Margaret Rowen experienced her first vision of coming world events while in the presence of some women in Los Angeles. During her vision, her body was rigid, and her eyes were open and staring upward. She was oblivious to everything around her. Her "inhalation of air was limited to an extreme minimum," as had been the case with Ellen White. Matthew said the "news swept through the Southern California churches like wildfire. God had chosen another prophetess." Still, some noted her inexperience in the church and recalled the Scriptures that warned of false prophets in sheep's clothing. After comparing her teachings with the Bible and Ellen White. After a preliminary review of her prophecies, the conference brethren decided that Rowen could not present her beliefs before church members or at camp meetings.

B.E. Fullmer, a graduate of the College of Medical Evangelists in Loma Linda, California, began his own investigation of Rowen and noted her self-sacrificing spirit and her highly moral character. Her teaching, he concluded, were in harmony with the Bible and the Spirit of Prophecy. Soon Rowen's visions were soon published in a 32-page pamphlet titled *A Stirling Message for this Time* and prefaced with some words of Larson: "May the readers of this little tract rejoice to know that God has in these last days again chosen a mouthpiece through whom He speaks to his people." Her visions continued, and a few misled SDAs channeled their tithes and offerings to the treasury of Rowen.

Matthew told John and Inez that he personally knew Fullmer because, before Fullmer had taken medicine, he had converted and baptized him. Mrs. Fullmer had been associated with Matthew as a Bible worker and organist in his tent meetings. Eventually, Fullmer became Rowen's editor and financial support. His endorsement of Rowen emboldened Matthew.

Rowen claimed to have a letter from Ellen White appointing her as the next prophet. She indicated that a copy of the letter could be found at the home of Ellen White in Elmshaven, dated August 10, 1911. W. C. White did not believe such a letter existed and refused to check the archives. But eventually he discovered such a letter! The closing paragraph of the letter stated, "I saw that many of the leaders refused to accept the messenger. [White had a dim view of church leadership at the end of her life.] I saw that the one sent of God was one of limited education, small in stature, and would sign the messages as Margaret W. Rowan." At the bottom of the letter was Ellen G. White's signature.

Although W. C. White regarded the letter as a forgery, he did not know how it got into the files and spent several weeks trying to explain it. The truth is that Fullmer had deposited the forgery during a visit to the White Estates when the vault was open and unattended. (Rowen had convinced Fullmer that he needed to "return" the letter to the file.) Of course, Matthew Larson knew nothing of this when he was promoting the prophetess to John and Inez.

Matthew made no headway with John and Inez regarding Rowen's exaggerated assertions. After a time, Matthew said goodbye and headed for his brother's homestead down the road.

Ellen White had had believed that lukewarm church members were holding back the Second Coming and that a dramatic revival was called for, a revival originated by laypersons, not from church leaders. Hence she had unwittingly set up the conditions for the arrival of a competing prophet. When Rowen preached on reform, she specified reform among the laity. Consequently, church members awaited new, invigorating messages from the Lord through a new messenger:

> *But I saw that God would keep his promises in Israel and would have a people—a remnant unspotted from the world. To accomplish this I saw it was necessary to call for a reform in the church of God. I saw that the spirit of God moved upon a few to seek for a purification of heart … I then saw that just a little way in the future after my labors were finished, that God would call one to give the cry to the church of god, 'Repent. Repent. Lift up the standard. Purify yourselves for the coming of your King.' I saw these earnest praying ones annoyed by their brethren.* [37]

Over the next five or six years the church brethren accumulated enough evidence to further discredit the new prophetess. In November 1919 the church disfellowshipped both Rowen and Fullmer, which Matthew felt was not fair since no proper church trial had been convened. He defended Rowen in a tract published by the movement.

After this, the Rowen Movement attacked the church and formed a spinoff church called the Los Angeles SDA Reform Church. This small group alleged that the original Adventist church had departed from its founding fathers and had repudiated the Spirit of Prophecy. An aggressive campaign commenced through publication of *The Advocate,* edited by Fullmer and Matthew, and believers began selling their goods, homes and property in preparation for Christ's return.

Robert Reidt (a Rowen follower) spread the doomsday message in New York City through the publicity of the *New York Times.* The newspaper reported that a cloud would descend from heaven, take 144,000 in the air, and transport them to San Diego, California.

Then on February 5, 1925, like other newspapers, The *Bismarck Tribune* carried the headline, **End of the World Not Here But May**

---

[37] Martin Gardner, *From Wandering Jew to William F. Buckley Jr.* (Amherst, NY: Prometheus Books, 2000), 41.

Come Yet. Cloud Which Was Expected at Midnight Did Not Come. The report went on: "Reidt and his flock of 18 followers who have lived through the hectic night as ever may be their lot, were still confident today that the 'promised signs' of the advent return of Christ is still not far off. Just when he would not say, although he had declared that the end of the world would take only seven days." When John read the newspaper to Inez a few days later she said, "See, I told you Rowen was a phony prophet."

Rowen's reputation as a prophetess virtually ended on February 6th, 1925. By then only a few companies of followers remained. On February 6th they stood on their lawns as the expected advent neared. But February 6th came and went. Rowen disappeared for a time and upon reappearing reassured her believers that Jesus had left heaven, but that the journey to earth was taking longer than anticipated.

Karl Frederick Danzeisen, another believer, shot and killed himself and severely wounded his wife. There were threats on Rowen's life. One newspaper carrried an advertisement requesting "all debtors to call and pay their bills before midnight as we don't want to be compelled to chase all over hell collecting accounts." [38]

To those who had sacrificed everything, the despair was palpable. Fullmer repudiated Rowen and her teachings and threatened to go the *L.A. Times* to reveal that she had taken money out of the movement's accounts. With this threat on the horizon, Rowen and two colleagues lured Fullmer to a travel motel for a medical house call and then tried to kill him by hitting him over the head with a pipe and injecting him with morphine and strychnine. The police arrested the two accomplice's and eventually Margaret Rowen herself. She had fled to the ocean to drown herself, but the waves kept pushing her back to shore!

Rowen Went to San Quentin Prison

At a trial held in Judge Charles B. McCoy's court in Los Angeles, Rowen, Mary Wage and Dr. Jacob P. Balmer were found guilty and sent to San Quentin penitentiary for a year. Dr. Fullmer died April 4th, 1926. After prison, Rowen moved to Florida and was not heard from again.

---

[38] Larry White and Margaret W. Rowen, "Prophetess of Reform and Doom," *Adventist Heritage*, Summer 1979, 38.

The next would-be prophet to emerge was Mrs. Irene V. Sandal, an ardent follower of Rowen. Sandal was voted out of the Central SDA church by its members after writing a book entitled *The Good Shepard Calleth His Sheep* in which she memorialized Margaret Rowen (who was still in prison).

Although the predicted Second Coming on February 1925 was completely falsified, such failures are not new. Prophets have predicted the end of the world countless times, reaching all the way back to the New Testament. As Richard Kyle summarizes, "They are batting a perfect zero, but apocalyptic thinking has withstood many disconfirmations and is still going strong." [39]

Ellen White was cleverer. She used a ballpark estimation for the advent of Christ. It was just over the horizon, a date not set, but imminent. She also served important psychic needs. Her writings offered an opportunity to see God's plan unfold in history and provide evidence for God's oversight of the world. The prophecies came across as a logical inference of events already fulfilled. The Adventist world was governed by Providence. The Bible was divinely inspired, inerrant and infallible. Some leaders and teachers, of course, knew that this was not exactly true.

---

[39] Richard Kyle, *The Last Days are Here Again* (Grand Rapids, MI: Baker Books, 1998), 187.

CONFRONTING THE DELAY
OF CHRIST'S RETURN
CHAPTER ELEVEN

"The Seventh-day Adventist brethren, alone among the divines of the country, have something to say officially about the depression, and what they have to say is singularly clear and simple. They laugh at all the current diagnoses…and reject every projected cure as vain and preposterous. It is not Hoover who must be blamed, they say, nor is it the tariff war, nor is it the French or the Japanese, nor is it overproduction, nor is it the foreign bond swindle, nor is it the war debts, nor is it sun spots or witchcraft or marital and spiritual infidelity or any of the other things that have been accused. It is simply the fact that the world is coming to an end." H. L. Mencken, *Adventist Heritage*, January 1974, 47.

Immediately following World War 1 *The Wallaces' Farmer*,[1] a magazine highly regarded by the farmers for its advice, warned its readers that: "Now would be a good time to reduce your debts. Prosperity is likely to continue for two or three years after the war ends but then it could be followed by a depression." Signs of future upheavals abounded. The Spanish flu of 1918-1919 took the lives of an estimated forty million world-wide. In the United States twenty-five million people contracted it, and an estimated 675,000 died. More solders died of this pandemic than were killed in battle. To Adventists this disease constituted yet another sign of the end.

Economic Conditions During WW1 Were Good Years

During the war farmers increased wheat acreage by nearly forty percent and output by almost fifty percent, and this produced chronic overproduction during the 1920s. Edgar Cayce, known as "The Sleeping Prophet," claimed a depression was coming and dated it to the year 1929. President Coolidge

---

[1] A farmer's advisor magazine published in Des Moines, Iowa,

apparently saw the same thing while he was in office. First Lady Grace Coolidge said succinctly, "Pappa says there's a depression coming."

The Wallace family, which published *The Farmer*, maintained a strong religious focus that John agreed with. For instance, in a Thanksgiving editorial *The Farmer* reported: "Dare we assume that the great Ruler plunges half the world into war, that the other half may profit by the manufacture of war materials and the growing of foodstuffs? Who are we, and what have we done, that material blessings should be showered upon us so lavishly?" [2]

Out on the Dakota Plains the war had indeed brought security and stable profits to farm families, sometimes in bursts of short duration. Economic issues made interesting talk with the neighbors, but John didn't think that conversations could solve the political dilemmas. In the meantime, the Willey family maintained fidelity to the Bible and spoke of God's blessings. World War 1 shaped the events of their age. It seemed that the completion of the judgment and the prompt triumphal return of Christ were at hand, provided mankind didn't destroy the earth first and launch Armageddon before the Second Coming. But "end times" are quite adaptable.

As noted earlier, John and Inez had four sons and two daughters. As a father, John began gathering up his savings. He wanted to buy another quarter and enlarge his holdings so that he could give each son a quarter section of land. You could say he was putting off the end times in his planning for the future, but he kept these plans to himself. Inez liked to joke with the neighbor ladies that her husband was "a poor fish but he was the nearest thing she ever got to the big one that got away."

For the most part, the war years were market years, and so John was able to sell wheat at a reasonable profit and lay "some shekels" aside. That didn't necessarily make him a rich man, for a farmer never knows when a bad year is just around the corner. A liability waiting in the wings was always ready to take away any accumulated wealth. Perturbing economic irregularities were the life of a farmer. But while people in the cities had trouble feeding and taking care of themselves, farmers could sustain themselves by growing their own vegetables and butchering their own meat. [3]

---

[2] *Wallaces' Farmer*, November 24, 1916.

[3] *Renville County History*, 470.

Living on the Farm Was Distinct from Urban Life

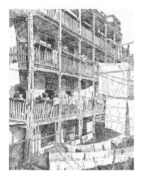 As for urban living, John had seen the powerful photojournalism book, *"How the Other Half Lives,"* by the Danish immigrant Jacob Riis. The photographs exposed the slums of New York City and inspired reforms of the squalid working-class housing and improvements in public health. Such photographs convinced John that living as he did on his homestead was preferable to living in a highly congested city.

When society adopted new fashions and other cultural shifts, North Dakota farmers lagged behind by about ten years. They got their news from many different sources including religious magazines, agriculture newsprint, word of mouth around the machine shops, and the postman.

When the tractor age began, Congress passed the Federal Farm Loan Act of 1916. Every town that had a well and a sheriff could establish a farmland banking institution offering forty-year loans at six-percent interest. This tempted economic fate because droughts and dust storms came and went on the prairies and tractors carried mortgage and maintenance costs no matter the production or price of wheat. As far as North Dakota was concerned, the depression hit in 1919 when grasshoppers hatched in the spring to consume and doom the upcoming harvest.

Bread lines in the large cities of the east seemed a long way off, but thousands of men riding on top of the railroad boxcars through the Dakotas suggested trouble for the country. When farmers left the farms for California, Washington, and Oregon, very few returned.

Conservative Republicans in rural areas lashed out against young ladies in the cities who smoked, put on lipstick, wore short skirts, bobbed their hair, and rode in automobiles with men who used strong language, smoked cigars, and drank booze. The young people of the Jazz Age appeared to be changing the values of Americans. Conservative farm people like John and Inez saw this as the end of American civilization. Low-cut gowns and rolled hose on the legs were born of the Devil and the wicked angels that pushed young people in the wrong direction. Times were changing.

Indeed, and very fast. Seismic, cultural shock waves were striking.

Worst of all, the sons and daughters of settlers drifted away to the cities to participate in the corruption. By now farm families accounted for only nine percent of national income. They pled with the government to intervene and spread some of American's wealth to them.

Modern Times Matched by Ignorance

The Federal Bureau of Soils gave bad advice by declaring that land resources could never be exhausted or used up. False information like this often triggered financial depressions. The wind could blow fertile topsoil away. As a young man John had seen what could happen to soils. Complete crop failures persisted in North Dakota throughout the decade before the Great Depression.

During this time John kept looking for ways and means to save money. He became more self-sufficient and self-reliant [4] and, for a short time, he owned the Allen car dealership in Loraine. The family raised food in the garden and produced eggs and milk on the farm. Meat came from chickens and mutton and like others around them, they bartered for supplies at the store and creamery.

John and three others managed the Grange Elevator in Loraine. Each fall he organized the Hurley Township into a cooperative to purchase a boxcar of Jonathan apples from Wenatchee, Washington. After distribution to the other farmers, John stored his own apples in the root cellar below the kitchen.

Because of poor roads and isolation in the northern part of the state, the farm families felt independent and encouraged personal toughness in their children. From an early age, farm children looked after a few livestock or raised gardens. In this way they made pocket money and learned to manage things for themselves. Youngsters were isolated by distance from peers of their own age. Many could not go to high school because they lived too far from school and their parents could not afford housing in town. But George and Tom boarded in Mohall in the winter while attending high school.

---

[4] John also kept his money out of the Loraine State Bank nearby because it was robbed and there was no insurance for farmers who lost deposited money. See *Renville County History*, 494.

Home Remedies

In everyday life, when the spirit moved her, Inez measured out two drops of croton oil and squeezed it into the bean soup she made for the family. She claimed this stirred the bowels. Or so said her mother and John Harvey Kellogg at the Battle Creek Sanitarium. Kellogg was always concerned about bowel intoxication and preoccupied himself with the prevention of constipation. John wished for fair warning: croton oil in his bean soup gave him the "runs." In fact, one afternoon after lunch, he went to the outhouse followed by a puppy and while "sitting on the throne" he outgassed so violently that the dog ran to the house where it found safety under the porch!

These were small vexations compared to everything else, including the lack of adequate medical care and hospitalization. Language could also be a problem because immigrant homesteaders who could not speak English mistrusted what they could not understand. But the problems notwithstanding, North Dakota became the largest producer of wheat and flax in the nation after the war. This was remarkable, but also consequential for the economies of farming.

The Good Times

Like other farmers during the good times, the Willey's bought their first car and radio and other conveniences. The Fuller Brush company with a force of saleswomen (Fullerettes) came to the farm periodically to give out free samples and peddle their brushes and cosmetics.

Mechanization was sweeping through the land and altering the methods of farming. *The Farmer* advised that "you are going to have to abandon horses and convert to gasoline tractors as soon as possible." John realized that by doing so he could cultivate more income acreage and reduce the amount of land devoted to hay making (except for the milk cows and his experiment with raising sheep for diversification). But since converting to tractor power would be an expensive venture at first, he considered purchasing or renting more acreage to justify the expense. Therefore, he bought the Sawyer quarter just north of the original Willey homestead, hoping for higher annual production and higher grain receipts.

With his strong fathering instincts, he began planning for keeping his sons on the farm to carry the work and eventually their own families into the future. Sometimes, on moonlit winter nights, when the wind died down and the storm clouds cleared, he'd bundle up and walk down the road alone to the section line. There he would entertain his hopes and dreams without interruption. There was a beautiful simplicity in the snow-covered fields, a simplicity that John wanted for his own life and family.

Helping the Neighbor Lars Neilson from Norway

John's neighbor Lars Neilson (1859-1921) had emigrated from Norway when he was twenty-years old and taken out a quarter section of land to homestead near the Willey farm. Neilson was a speculative farmer, but the quarter he chose had two large sloughs on the eastern side that reduced the productive acreage by almost half of the tillable land. Farming this quarter had always been precarious and uncertain for Neilson.

Neilson should have diverted the melting snow in the spring away from the sloughs and filled the sloughs with soil from higher ground. Instead he piled rocks in the slough which made future farming very difficult. Something in Neilson's makeup made it hard for him to succeed. To begin with, he had only two years of college education and he wasn't particularly keen about farming. Neilson thought that knowing more about religion might give him a better chance for the afterlife than living the life of a farmer under toil, grasshoppers, and the hot sun – circumstances that diverted his attention from more significant things. He found a Model T Ford and converted it into a makeshift tractor. But it always broke down or got stuck in the mud. Spending so much time on his invention, Neilson had never improved or enlarged his dilapidated two-roomed shack or built a barn.

Marriage wasn't his forte. If you asked his mother, who was smitten with the science of phrenology, she'd tell you that her son could never "read the bumps on the head" of the women he courted before marriage.[5] "Lars hadn't applied himself into comprehending or predicting how to locate suitable moral and domestic propensities on the heads of his potential mates—and especially the organ of amativeness which would benefit the

---

[5] A nineteenth century hypothesis that the "propensity" of human behavior could be determined by "reading" the external bumps on the head.

raising of grandchildren." For this or other reasons, Neilson got off to a bad start in the marriage department.

His first wife slipped away when he went to town one morning to pick up some used furniture that had arrived by rail. He talked her into returning home, but three weeks later she crept out the door late at night and this time never came back. Soon he married again but only for a short time. The new Mrs. Nielson and a secret lover disappeared beyond the Canadian Rockies and left Lars "holding the bag without a lover, cook or clothes wrangler." As he liked to say, "Common sense could prevent a great many divorces. On the other hand, it could also prevent a great many marriages!"

Lars and John shared the practice of worshipping on Saturday. Recently, this preoccupied John because of something he'd read in the newspaper.

It seems a local farmer had planted a wheat field and worked his farm on Sunday, something that was contrary to his Presbyterian faith. When summer arrived and he found a resplendent crop growing there, he put up a sign on the edge of the field that said in large letters "This field planted on the Sabbath." But according to the newspaper, just when the wheat was ready for harvest, lightning struck and completely destroyed it. The only thing left was the sign and it was so scorched by the fire that you couldn't read it. But John had to wonder why God would destroy crops of farmers observing the wrong day for the Sabbath.

John and Lars fell into conversation about the newspaper article and Sabbath observance. "Lars, does it make any sense," John asked, "that an ill omen follows improper Sabbath observance? Why would God spectacularly reinforce a pagan day of worship carrying out the preacher's warnings by burning up a man's field and highlight Sunday observance while at the same time reinforcing the wrong day? Doesn't this leave the wrong impression about the Sabbath?"

Lars was deliberate in his answer. Perhaps he considered the lightning just happenstance or thought that John was trying to ambush him. John liked to humor Lars by portraying him as a praiseworthy Gentile.

While at Battle Creek College in Michigan, Lars had taken a course on how to witness about Sabbath keeping to your neighbors. "The argument goes something like this John," Lars said. "Sabbath rest was for the Jews; the Sabbath wasn't Sunday in the Old Testament; it was the Seventh-day for them. The New Testament abrogated the Jewish Sabbath requirement. Jesus died on a Friday and was laid in the tomb over the Jewish Sabbath. To distinguish their day of worship from the Jews after Christ was resurrected on Sunday, the early Christians adopted the resurrection day or Sunday to celebrate the new covenant following the resurrection."

"There are some today who believe that the shift from Saturday to Sunday was made by Christ and his apostles, not by some arbitrary decision of the Catholic church. The seventh day commemorated Creation, and Sunday, or the first day of the week, marked the beginning of God's new creation, the resurrection. Early Christians also did not like the strict legalism and excessive gravity of the Jewish Sabbath."

Apparently, Martin Luther and John Calvin didn't care which day Christians honored. Sunday was as good as any other day. Puritans eventually brought Sunday worship to this country and very strictly observed it.

Lars certainly knew his history of the Sabbath and it differed entirely from what John had heard from his mother and her kinfolks. It set him to thinking about a story he had read in the Bible about the sun standing still. "Maybe the Sabbath day fell forward to Sunday when the sun and moon stood still during a battle in the Old Testament around Joshua's time?" John couldn't remember the details, but he brought up the story to Lars. "Could this account for the Sabbath moving to Sunday and discredit the Adventist practice?

Like a robber ready to mock a fool, Lars quickly replied, "No, John, that would put the calendar in the opposite direction. The Sabbath would have landed on Friday thereafter, and even the time-stopping darkness at Jesus' crucifixion would have had the same effect." John could not dispute the calculation, but like a long curving staircase where you can't see both ends from the middle, he still didn't understand how God, the noblest and truest friend to man, would use lightning and fires to punish a wayward person.

Because of his education at Battle Creek College, an Adventist educational institution, Lars believed he could refute Darwinian evolution as an explanation of the origin of life and species variation. At the same time Lars claimed that John's theology seemed to be based on a Book that simply dropped out of the heavens and lacked any appreciation of higher criticism and the treatment of the Gospels as mythologies. Lars obviously had more experience with the Adventist message. He once bragged to John that as a student he had actually heard Ellen White and other Adventist pioneers preach in the Battle Creek Tabernacle on the closing events of world history.

As he recalled, "Sister White said the signs were tokens promised by the Savior of his soon return because man desired a sign from heaven. And during her sermon, Sister White dropped the hint that some people who were alive and saw the meteorite showers in 1833 would be alive to see Jesus return. She kept saying time was short, and the seven last plagues were so soon to fall on the world." [6] The reality of prophecy quickened every time Lars told stories like this to John.

"Now Lars," John asked, "There are many sorts of signs in the heavens that can be used to proclaim the fullness of time. And these are supposed to be a guide to our feet and a light to our understanding. If these signs were mixed up—some provided by God and by the great deceiver—how is an uneducated farmer like me going to know whether we have a real one?"

Lars replied, "look at the use of prophecy this way. If you listen carefully to a good preacher worth his salt, he will always conclude his speech with a call for repentance. The end prophecies are always near the present time, not way into the future or back in history. It doesn't matter if the signs and wonders are confused, the important thing is that the end of the world is near at hand."

Then Lars stepped away from the muddy tractor and spoke as if he were closing a sermon: "John, what does the coming of Jesus mean to you? Where do you propose to spend eternity? Will you be found with the spirit of this world, so dominated by the price of a bushel of wheat or oats, that you will be counted as a lover of this world and not the next? Or will you become so acquainted with Christ as your Savior, so filled with his companionship, that you will meet him with rejoicing when he comes? What will it be brother?"

"Well, Lars, for a minute you had me going. I was just about ready to confess my sins, all thirty-eight. I think you should give up pulling tractors out of the mud take up preaching – even as a twice-divorced

---

[6] Around 1930 Adventists stopped talking about any person being alive during the 1833 display.

person without a clear conscience." With the loss of love in his life, Lars dedicated his life to the gospel ministry and headed back to college. He would devote his energies to healing other men's souls.

John asked Lars whether he would sell or rent his quarter. Eventually they agreed on a typical arrangement whereby the renter gets two-thirds of the crop and the owner receives one-third after deducting the cost of the seed. After they negotiated the deal, Lars sold his car, got on the train in Loraine, and headed straight to Union College in Lincoln, Nebraska. There he finished his college education.

He returned for short visits now and then, but never showed any interest in farming the quarter. After finishing his degree, Lars became president of the Nebraska Sanitarium, an auxiliary of the famous Battle Creek Sanitarium in Michigan,[7] and he served on the Union College board. When he passed away his two sons came to John and offered the Neilson quarter to him for $3,600. That is how John Willey came to own the Nelson quarter. Later he gave it to his son Tom Willey in his estate.

---

[7] *Review and Herald,* June 9, 1921, 22. Lars Neilson remained a member of the Union College Board.

THE UNFORESEEN ACCIDENT
CHAPTER TWELVE

"Angels and ministers of grace defend us." William Shakespeare, *Hamlet*

When Civil War general de Trobriand wrote of his military life in the Dakota territory in the late 1800s he described grasshoppers passing over their camps; "flying low, many of them almost touching the ground…lit on the grass, on the roof, on the boards, the walls, on the posts, and formed in places grey, crawling, moving masses…these cursed insects hit us in the face, caught in our eyes or our beards, got into our clothes, and jumped from the ground in swarms at our every step like big hail stones bounding on the hard ground."

The grasshopper infestation overwhelmed the farmers in 1931. Darkening the sky, they destroyed the crops, ate the binder twine on the sheaves of wheat, gnawed on the wooden handles of the garden tools and fence posts, and destroyed clothing hanging on the clothes lines. And because of the depression there was little money to buy poison. One farmer claimed that for every grasshopper he stepped on a thousand showed up for the funeral!

Grasshoppers and Other Nuisances

A homesteader on the way to Loraine once described how he collected the grasshoppers, roasted them, and ground them into flour for pancakes! He then mixed molasses and eggs into the flour. The Willeys heard this story but couldn't rebrand the bugs as edible food, even though the hoppers ate grasses, were largely made of protein, and abounded.

The Renville County Farmer (local county newspaper) reported on rabbit hunts that were conducted in several townships near the Willey's farm. Fifty men formed a large circle, beat the grasses and bushes, and drove the animals into an ever-tightening circle to be killed. "160 rabbits were shot, and one fox fell prey to the hunters." The fox skin brought eight dollars and fifty cents. The rabbits only brought ten cents. Afterwards, the men enjoyed coffee, embellished hunting yarns, and reminisced about exciting moments during the hunt.

All the animals were trying to do was to make a living like the settlers, but they were at peril. In `31 the county paid three dollars for a coyote was three dollars. Forty-four coyotes were destroyed that year. A bounty of fifteen cents was paid on magpies if you presented a pair of wings to the auditor's office. Sixty-six birds were killed in the county.

Ground Squirrels

Gophers (Richard's Ground Squirrels) constituted a particular nuisance, different from that of magpies, black birds, foxes, or coyotes. The gophers dug burrows in the pastures and in the crop fields, multiplied rapidly, and robbed the grains. The county paid a twenty-six-cent bounty for each gopher tail. Neighbor boys earned ten to fifteen dollars a day in the summer trapping and shooting gophers. This was more than a hired man earned in the field.

George and Tom caught gophers with a lasso and then killed them with a rock and collected the tail. They slowly crawled on their bellies to the edge of the gopher's burrows. There they placed a lasso around the opening of the hole. Quietly they eased back, hugging close to the ground. (Gophers sensed ground vibrations, so the boys had to lie quietly, without talking, and wait. Any nearby movement kept the gophers from coming out.) After a time, the gopher stuck his head out of the burrow and gave an "all-clear" whistle. Once the gopher stuck its striped head and front paws through the lasso the boys jerked the twine. Of course, the gophers sometimes escaped. Even gophers learn what it is to have death come calling. They don't need to hear about it from religious radio stations or at family reunions!

On April 6, 1931 George and Tom (both in their early twenties) tried out a new .22 caliber rifle that had just arrived in the mail from Sears,

Roebuck and Company. They targeted gophers, but saw only a few so they aimed at some cans they'd brought along for target practice.

The week before George had purchased a box of .22's containing fifty cartridges. Around noon, as they started for home, he looked down and saw one .22 shell in the dirt. He picked it up and wiped off the bullet. He put the last shell cartridge in the chamber and clicked the safety.

Farmers owned guns to maintain order and honor and protect against violence. The Willey brothers grew up with guns. They used them to kill skunks, badgers, coyotes and other unwelcome intruders. They harvested game birds for food.

Once the brothers stopped shooting targets and walked towards the farmhouse, a seriously flawed script started to play out. They didn't know that their little brother, Billie, was hiding behind a cottonwood tree and planning to jump out and scare them. Had they known what was about to take place, they would have put the gun by the side of the road and retrieved it later.

Without Divine Intervention

No one in the Willey family wants to talk about what happened next. This tragedy was so horribly tragic, and contrary to their beliefs of divine benevolence, Providential care, and protection by guardian angels that it left them speechless. For one electrifying, terrifying instant, the guardian angels dropped their halos and left their posts of duty.

Some family history sets the stage. George and Tom had finished high school a few years earlier. Tom had done exceptionally well in his studies and left his mark in sports, particularly basketball. The class he took in animal husbandry led to farm animal competitions around the state. During his senior year he placed third on the champion livestock team at the Fargo State Fair.

After graduating from high school in 1928 Tom went to Union College in Lincoln Nebraska, an institution founded by Seventh-day Adventists passionately wanting to protect their offspring from worldly influences. There he enrolled with a major in history and minors in religion and education. The teachers seemed noble and were the most literate people he had ever known. However, after one year, Tom returned home and decided to be a farmer like his father. Many students at Union were employed by the church after graduation as missionaries, preachers, teachers, and sanitarium administrators, but no one went to a religious college to become a farmer.

Before high school his brother George had gone to Hutchinson Seminary in Minnesota, a two-year Adventist school. The principal and president of the school, M.L. Andreasen, was a serious-minded, austere preacher devoted to raising the church's educational standards. [1] Teacher preparation seemed like a good option. But George got caught talking to a girl on the stairs to the girl's dorm, a "no parking zone" for boys. For this infraction he was sent home after only six weeks and this made farming his destiny. Both George and Tom could do the work of grown men. They were strong and had their own team of horses for work around the farm. Besides helping out on their father's half-section they were beginning to farm on their own. They took out a government seed loan and rented a neighbor's quarter.

Guardian Angels Inside Out

The Willey children believed that ever-present guardian angels watched over them and protected them. They pictured these angels as glorious personages, a little taller than humans, who traveled back and forth to earth from the royal courts of heaven. No one knew exactly where these spirits lived or how long it took to fly through the cosmos "to get to work every day" and except under the most urgent circumstances, it would not be necessary to learn this. Eventually, children would be introduced to their guardian angel and later, in heaven, they would get answers to their questions. In the meantime, what Ellen White wrote would have to suffice:

> *We shall never know what dangers, seen and unseen, we have been delivered from through the interposition of the angels until we shall see in the light of eternity the providences of God. Then we shall better understand what God has done for us all the days of our life. We shall know then that the*

---

[1] Virginia Steinweg, *Without Fear or Favor* (Takoma Park, MD: Review & Herald Publ. Assoc., 1979), 79.

whole heavenly family watched to see our course of action
from day to day. [2]

This notion of angels or "watchers" may have reflected the deep need of humans for an intermediary to overcome the remoteness of God. No one has seen God or angels, not even prohibition evangelist Billy Sunday, *"Whom, no man hath seen nor can see."* [3] But the belief seemed plausible when one considered that God had his hands full running the entire universe and needed and needed angels to operate between Him and mankind. (Perhaps for this reason the belief in angels is most prominent in monotheistic traditions.)

There were various types of angels. Some sang in the heavenly choir; some recorded the deeds of mankind and maintained records in the Book of Life; and some worked on the prayers that constantly ascended to heaven. The angel Gabriel stood in a place of honor next to Jesus after taking the place of Lucifer (who, after a rebellion in heaven, went to earth and became Satan). There were haunting stories about times when majestic guardian angels temporarily put on human clothes, engaged in timely interventions, and then disappeared without a trace. A person never really knew who it was they had encountered (as was the case with Jacob who wrestled with a spiritual being at the Ford of Jabbok).

A story was told about a farmer and his wife who were stalled by the side of the road in a blizzard. A traveler pulled up, rolled down his window, and asked if he could help. The pair told the stranger they were lost and afraid to go on. The stranger said, "Follow me; I know my way around these parts." Then he led them a few miles down the road and into a farmyard and safety. When they tried to thank the stranger, he was gone. "We saw his tracks coming into the farmyard but there were no tracks going away."

Although nothing like this had happened to the Willeys, they were open to the possibility that divine strangers could appear on the farm, on the road to town, out in the field, or wherever. Their familiarity with God and his son Jesus Christ was intimate and unifying, not some weak sentiment. They believed that God had made lofty covenants with the

---

[2] Ellen G. White., *In Heavenly Places,* 101.
[3] 1 Timothy 6:16. KJV.

children of Israel and now with all who followed His commandants and placed their trust in the Almighty. Traveling through life was precarious, and they needed all the help they could get. The role of angels might sound far-fetched, but to people who attended church and heard about a loving Father, it was definitely not. Each morning during worship the father always gave thanks for the food on the table and then beseeched the guardian angels to watch over and protect his family.

The Devil and His Angels

Unclean spirits, demons, or evil angels also existed. Unlike guardian angels, these could not travel back and forth to heaven. Some said they were bonded to the earth where they swept in, suggested evil thoughts, and created temptations. According to the Bible, the two types of angels had a common derivation in heaven.

Parents very simply described the balance of power between the guardian angels and evil ones: *"Ask and ye shall receive."* [4] Earnestly seek the good angel if you felt the devil was coming after you. Through prayer, overwhelming power could be had, and this reduced the fear of living.

A religious person normally did not address the evil angels, but if the devil or his dark angels were on the prowl one could command them to go away by invoking God's name or using the name of Jesus Christ. In the worst case, one could lay a Bible across the chest of a possessed person and the devil would flee. A framed color print hung in the front room of

the Willey farmhouse showing what a guardian angel looked like. The picture showed two small bare-footed children crossing a rickety bridge over a deep canyon and below a dangerous frothy stream. The handrail was broken and some of the bridge slats were missing. The picture illustrated a glorious guardian angel with a star above its head gently hovering behind the children. The angel stood erect with outstretched arms and eagle-strength wings at the ready in case the children fell off the bridge. The picture left its mark on anyone who saw it.

---

[4] Matthew 7:2. KJV.

Seven-Year Old William Warren Willey

On this April morning seven-year-old William Warren, or Billy as the family called him, badly needed a guardian angel. He operated on a full tank of energy and was approaching his eighth birthday on the day his brothers were down the road shooting gophers. (His keepsake name came from his grandfather William who had homesteaded the farm across the road.)

Billy, the youngest, was the darling in the family, especially to his father and his oldest sister Genevieve. John doted over Billy more than the other children — he had a happy-go-lucky disposition that could charm a badger out of its den. Because his hair was soft people liked to put their hands on his head and tease him by saying he should have been a girl. This annoyed Billy because he felt that girls were inferior to boys. For one thing, females could not keep up when males pitched hay or threw sacks of grain into the wagon. And they couldn't catch a run-away horse.

An exceptional bond with his father began the day Billy was born. A few minutes after his birth, John proclaimed to the rest of the family: "We've got a fine Norwegian boy here who looks like his mother." As Billy grew older his father took him to the field where he let him hold the horse's reins while driving the hay rack and hold a small pitchfork to pick up hay. It was quite a site to see them working together in the field.

Billy came up with all kinds of comical activities. The previous summer he started collecting walking bugs — the bigger, the better. He would tie a thread around a bug's leg and place the bug on the ground within reach of a chicken. When the chicken stepped up to its meal, closed its eyes, opened its beak, and went for the food, Billy would jerk the bug away. His mother said the bug trick came from his father's side of the family!

Billy liked to be around the draft horses when they came out of their stalls in the barn. They were the center of power on the farm—big and majestic. His father warned him repeatedly about the dangers of getting too close to their rear end. A kick from a horse could send a boy his size into the neighbor's backyard, so he stood to the side watching his father or the older brothers hitching the snorting horses up to the singletree and traces in front of the barn. This ritual took place before they headed out to the field.

Billy already took small chances. After a horse was in the traces he would sweep in close to the horse's flank and quickly snap the sidebackers to brass buckles. Someday he dreamed of having his own team and, like his older brothers, he'd drive horses in the fields all by himself.

The Willey farmhouse was set back from the county road with a large front yard where the family played baseball and grew several rows of corn. A row of cottonwood trees next to the road served as a wind break. From the farmhouse one could see visitors coming up the dusty road. This gave Billy time to run to the chicken coop and fetch his pet rooster named Henry Clay. He liked to stand at the edge of the driveway with Henry Clay on his shoulder and with his hands in his pockets when visitors drove into the farmyard, hoping the callers would notice the chicken and himself. He had been trying to teach Henry Clay some tricks that he could show off – such as coming when he whistled. But chickens were about as intelligent as water striders or frogs.

Billy attended first grade in the Larson School located on the corner of the quarter his father owned. This school offered all eight grades in a single room. Because his father had given an acre for the corner school, he was elected clerk throughout the time the school was active and hence was responsible for recording the student's grades and paying the wages of the teacher (about sixty dollars per month). Usually fifteen to twenty farm kids made up the school's roster.

The joke around the neighborhood was that Billy's father once missed the driveway in front of his own farmhouse, ran over the mailbox, and landed in a ditch. Inez told her friends that her husband had been thinking about the pretty schoolteacher he had seen walking up the road. He couldn't explain why he missed the driveway.

Billy was supposed to be in school on the day a stained-glass window shattered. Instead, he had come late to breakfast in his pajamas bearing a red face and a complaint about having a sore throat. What no one knew was that he had put his head over the furnace register in the front room for several minutes before he entered the kitchen. (His sister Marjorie taught him this trick for feigning illness.) He got his mother to verify that he had a temperature by feeling his forehead.

Hearing that George and Tom were going gopher hunting that morning with the new rifle made him fear he'd carried the red face scheme too far. He wanted to go hunting with them instead of staying in the house.

Billy's mother saw through his now-fading illness and almost put her foot down and sent him off to school despite his claims. For one thing, sick boys didn't eat so fast and so much. It was his father who gave in on that Monday morning and let Billy stay at home and play "hooky" from school. He was not supposed to go outside.

Father's favoritism brought disastrous consequences, but no one knew this beforehand. Everyone scurried around the kitchen, talking and preparing for whatever they were planning to do. After a while, George and Tom picked up the .22 rifle and went out the door and father went to the barn to milk the cows and separate the cream. That left only Billy and John, Jr. with their mother in the house. (Billy's two sisters were in Mohall attending high school.)

As the morning wore on, Billy and John Jr. played inside the house. Before lunch Inez sent Billy upstairs to learn his lines for the upcoming spring play at the school. She continued busying herself about the kitchen, washing dishes, cooking, baking, and setting the table. Her husband was in the barn cleaning up the morning chores and feeding hay to the cows and horses. She heard the separator whining and pails banging on the concrete slab as her husband finished the chores. George and Tom would be returning around noon for lunch.

At noon she heard the crack of a rifle out by the road. She thought the older brothers must be returning to the house and for a fleeting second, she worried that they were shooting the gun too close to the house. (There wasn't a window on the north side of the kitchen where she could look out to the road.)

Years later it would be hard to get Inez to talk about what happened next, although she held the memory as clearly as if it loomed over her the week before. At times she seemed trapped in the memory and reeled from talking about it. But in her defense, it was rare for anyone in the Willey family to say much about the accident.

When Inez did talk about it, her voice quivered, and her sentences became deliberate, slow, and full of anguish. Tears flowed freely. Living as she did on a farm, she was familiar with death. Every spring she saw lambs die, sometimes in her kitchen when she tried to save an orphaned one. In the fall the family butchered a sheep for the winter supply of meat. She bandaged cows that got caught in the barb wire.

As she got further into the story about Billy, the telling took on more sadness and sorrow than she could endure, or the listener wanted to suffer. As you listened to her you felt as though a freezing wind was rushing across your skin and sucking the life out of you. It was the kind of emotion that never goes away—never weakens or softens.

This is how she remembered: "I was cooking in the kitchen and I was expecting the two older boys and dad for dinner without thinking too much about what any of them were doing."

Most of her thoughts that morning were about a quarrel she had with her husband about letting Billy skip school. Later she would deeply regret not putting her foot firmly down. Therein resided most of her guilt and shame for what happened next.

"Dad always gave in too easily to Billy," she recalled. "Billy was both the teacher's pet and his father's favorite. Dad let him get away with things the other children couldn't do. Just that morning when it was time to go to school Billy complained of a cough or something like and he was permitted to stay home."

Her words starting to spill out faster. "All of a sudden I heard pounding footsteps on the porch, and then the kitchen door burst open. George came into the kitchen swaying from side to side almost leaping as he passed through the door. It startled me and the hair on the back of my neck stood up. I turned around and saw that George was carrying Billy whose head was limp over his shoulder. Blood poured down George's back and soaked his shirt. My first thought was that Billy must have been run over by a car. Tom came in right behind George, his face white as a birch tree, and saying in a feeble voice that it was an accident. George bent over and carefully laid Billy on the kitchen linoleum. I ran into the bedroom to fetch a blanket. When I came back, I told Tom to go out to the barn and get his father."

"When dad came into the kitchen, he knelt down on the floor next to Billy's head trying to see where he was bleeding. Already there was a pool of blood on the floor, oozing slowly towards the stove. Billy was not moving. He was breathing very slowly and continuing to bleed. I was afraid he was going to die right there on the kitchen floor. Dad pulled Billy's blond hair over to the side. There was a small round hole about the size of my little finger. Something had entered the right side of his head just above his ear. That was the first time I realized he'd been shot in the head. Kneeling there holding Billy, Dad kept saying over and over 'please God don't take him now.' "

"My stars…It was the worst thing you could ever imagine! Dad was beside himself. I thought he was going to fall apart. He knelt down on the floor and hugged Billy, all the while pleading with God to spare him. Billy was lifeless and still and limp as a sack of flour. I saw Tom go over to the telephone on the wall and ring Dr. Fitzmaurice in Mohall."

She continued, "Tom came over to dad and said that Dr. Fitzmaurice wanted us to bring Billy into his office. Dr. Fitz's car was in the repair shop and he couldn't get out to the farm. Dad wrapped a towel around Billy's head as tight as he could, and George carried him to the car. Dad helped arrange Billy in the back seat as George climbed in under Billy's shoulders and held Billy's head in his lap. George held Billy's head in his hands to keep the towel from unwrapping. Tom didn't go with us. I saw him head to the barn. I wondered why he didn't go with us. The savagery of it all was too much!"

On the way to town it dawned on Inez that Tom had done the shooting. She remembered worrying that out of shame, Tom might harm himself in the barn.

ON THE WAY TO THE HOSPITAL
CHAPTER THIRTEEN

"For he shall give his angels charge over thee, to keep thee in all thy ways. They shall bear thee up in their hands, lest thou dash thy foot against the stone." Psalms. 91:11-12

The car turned hastily from the driveway and onto the dirt road towards Mohall. John drove — avoiding ruts in the road, ducking mud that splattered against the running boards and inside the fenders and evading the ditches along the side of the road that were filled with water and with last year's sword-shaped cattails. Billy was stretched out in the back with his head lying on George's lap—not moving, but still breathing. A cutter rug covered his legs. The car was in flight, trying to outrun the Grim Reaper.

Heading for Mohall and Dr. Fitz

Once on the straight part of the road John turned around and looked at George. In an earnest voice he asked, "George tell me what happened." A bloody stain seeped into the towel on Billy's head.

John's voice conveyed fears, the kind that arises when you hear a team of horses running toward you and panic. He was frightened as never before.

George was still stunned. It had been less than fifteen minutes since the accident. He spoke with great sorrow — as if he already knew that Billy would die. He had seen the bullet hit Billy; had seen his eyes open wide and his mouth fling open as if he was trying to yell; had seen Billy's eyes snap closed just before he slumped and fell forward; had heard a crackling sound as the bullet smashed through Billy's skull, like when you break a tree branch. Pheasant hunting came to mind. As a bird lifts in the air and is hit by pellets from a shotgun it just quits flying and crashes to the ground.

"We were down east of grandpa's barn shooting gophers about a quarter mile away," he said. "We used up a box of .22s. As we were leaving, I saw a shell that had fallen out of the box. I picked it up and put it in the chamber. We walked up the muddy road rather than back through the pasture. I carried the rifle. As we approached the house, Tom said he wanted to plug the bottle on the fence post out front — the one behind the mailbox. I gave him the rifle. Just as Tom pulled the trigger Billy jumped out of the tall grass behind a cottonwood tree. Neither one of us had seen him hiding there. I think he was planning to scare us. He was hit the instant he stood up. Billy fell. I rushed over and picked him up and ran to the house. Tom just stood there stammering Oh no! — Oh no! — Oh No NO!"

"Are you sure the bullet hit him in the head?" his father asked, trying to get George to say something more. The car darted into a rut and back out again. John twisted the wheel to stay on the road.

"I'm pretty sure dad, that Billy is badly hurt," replied George. He looked down at Billy's head and saw only the blood. George never swore around his mother or his father. But with a gap in his mind that could not be filled with other words, he murmured under his breath, "God damn it!" and looked out the window.

"What in the world was he doing out by the road on a day like today? I thought he was supposed to stay in the house," John said.

"No, dad," said Inez. "Don't you remember, Billy was playing hooky from school." There was a sharp edge of regret in her voice. She could let you know what she thought even if she didn't say it.

A gossamer sadness settled in the car for the next few miles. Last years' wheat and barley stubble could be seen, and also a farmhouse now and then. John kept wrestling with the car's steering wheel to avoid the ruts and ditches. No one really knew how much harm a small .22-caliber bullet could do to the brain. After all, when dad and the boys hunted deer down at the Mouse River, they used a Winchester 30-30 high-power rifle. (They wouldn't take a .22 hunting because the bullet wasn't powerful enough to bring down a deer.)

Inez broke the silence, "George, is Billy still breathing?"

George did not answer. He was afraid to look down at Billy because there was too much danger in the question. If Billy stopped breathing George knew it was all over.

As they got closer to Mohall Inez felt like she was watching a flag starting to tatter in a hurricane wind. Her life was flying off in shreds. Her fears had grown until they nearly overwhelmed her. Was her little blond-headed boy going to die? Could Doc Fitz save him? Meanwhile, John sat wishing he could barter his own life with God so that Billy could live.

"Hurry dad, Billy might stop breathing," Inez said. All hope rested on getting Billy to the doctor as quickly as possible.

John turned to George and tried another question. "George did the bullet enter his head or just graze his scalp?" John knew the answer to his own question. He had seen the hole in the side of Billy's head where the blood was oozing out. Was he trying to push the bullet in a direction it hadn't taken?

Inez held her hands so tightly that her knuckles turned white. Tears ran down her cheeks and blinded her. She no longer saw the road or the passing fields, nor did she care. She knew that hope for a lesser injury would not change what had happened; Billy had been struck by a bullet in the head and his brains were smashed. John took her hand and in a self-possessed voice quietly said, "Ma, we're going to be all right. Billy will pull through this."

Few things could make George cry. But his eyes now swelled with tears. He worried that he was holding his brother for the last time, and he quickly pushed the thought away. Maybe he'll live. If they could just get Billy to Mohall before he stopped breathing the doctor might save him.

Then George said in a broken voice; "You're scared, aren't you Ma?"

His mother replied, "I guess so, I wish Jesus would come before Billy dies. What will we do if he dies? Why would God take him before he grows up? Why has this happened? How do we claim `God is our helper?' Is there such a thing as divine reason and protection?"

Instead of getting closer to town it seemed they were being pushed away as they moved down the road. Every second was like an hour. Finally, in the distance Mohall grain elevators came into view. George said later that there was something terribly dark and solitary about the trip into town. Yet, the trip took only ten minutes and Billy was still breathing.

The car stopped in front of Dr. Fitzmaurice's pharmacy. Dr. Fitz rushed out and told John, "Drive around back to my office and bring him inside."

Arriving at Dr. Fitzmaurice's Office

George carried Billy into the office and laid him on the examining table. Dr. Fitz took a stethoscope and listened to Billy's heart, then bent over and listened to his breathing. He measured his pulse rate and blood pressure; the rate was rapid and the pressure was low. With a magnifying lens, he looked into Billy's eyes. Inez stood next to Billy holding his hand, feeling calmer now that something was being done to save Billy. But she blamed her misjudgment in the morning and felt guilty of something sinister.

She glanced up and saw a picture on the wall of a country doctor sitting at the bedside of a young boy with bluish-pale skin, evidence of dying. Behind the doctor stood a mother in an apron and a father in overalls. The parents appeared paralyzed in helplessness. The doctor in the picture was calm and contemplative. Inez looked down and saw that she too was wearing her apron. Then she saw John still wore his rubber boots for morning chores. Suddenly, they were seeing themselves in the picture.

She returned to Billy. He was wearing the jeans he wore to school. The shirt Genevieve had made out of a flour sack had dainty green and yellow flowers. Staring at Billy, she "saw" a beautiful child with perfect features. Wouldn't it be wonderful if all she had to do was wash his head and comb his hair? Through her mind flowed a powerful desire for her son to come back the way he was just a few minutes earlier. She was willing to give anything to make this happen. It was the strongest desire she had ever experienced, stronger even than what she felt when she gave birth to him. But now everything was spinning away–savagely. Life was mocking her. She kept trying to harness her faith in God without deploring what had happened.

Inez leaned over and whispered in Billy's ear, "Billy, listen to me. You're going to make it. Dr. Fitz will fix you. We love you son. You've got to pull through. We're praying to Jesus. Hang on until Dr. Fitz can get the bullet out. Be strong! You can make it through this." There was no movement, no intervening miracle, no response of any kind. "Oh, no! Good gracious, isn't anybody listening;" she whispered.

John tried talking too, but he struggled for words. What could he say? He had always felt that Billy was going to die before his time, and now he was watching it happen right before his eyes. (That was one reason why he treated Billy differently.) Can a person trust these kinds of premonitions?

Word about a gun accident began to spread through Mohall. Rumors were that the Willey family was facing the death of their next-to-youngest child.

When John saw that Dr. Fitz was preparing to cut Billy's hair to take a better look at the wound, he said to Inez, "Ma, let's go find the girls and bring them here." He didn't want Inez to see Billy's head. The wound was beginning to swell and once the hair was shaved off it would be easy to see what he had already seen when he pulled back Billy's hair on the kitchen floor.

Before Inez left she turned to Dr. Fitz and in a pleading voice asked; "Is my Billy going to make it?" Dr. Fitz looked at Inez, she said later, "With unoccupied eyes, partly opened mouth and a pail full of words stuck in his throat. He tried to close his mouth but couldn't. His chin was trembling. Doc Fitz knew what we were facing, and he tried to make us feel that Billy had a chance to pull through." Somehow you know it is hopeless even before you learn the truth. You could feel a strength and warmth and integrity in the doctor. But in his mind all hope for Billy was diminishing.

As usual, Dr. Fitz knew more than he was saying. The words were stuck in his mouth. It wasn't easy being a physician when parents are staring death in the face. For the moment he kept his thoughts to himself, waiting for his own melancholy to subside.

The only time Dr. Fitz had ever seen a patient survive a shot to the head was when Peter Nelson, who lived on the edge of town, tried to commit suicide. The bullet grazed the top of Peter's forehead and came out the back of his neck. It traveled all the way under the skin of his skull, a freakish thing indeed. After that Peter changed his mind about suicide and began attending church and Wednesday night prayer meetings. But this story wasn't something for Inez to hear.

When Inez leaned over and kissed Billy on the forehead, it was the last time she saw him alive. Afterwards, she always believed that Billy had felt her kiss. "He sighed and took a deeper breath, though he didn't open his eyes or move."

John and Inez left Billy and walked to the high school a few blocks away to tell Billy's sisters about their brother's peril. Maybe they should come over and see him just in case this would be their last chance.

After the parents left Dr. Fitz asked George to describe what had happened. While George was talking, Dr. Fitz began looking for the bullet's exit spot on the other side of Billy's head. He trimmed the hair around the entrance. While a .22-calibre bullet is small at the entry point, it can do a lot of damage while passing through the brain.

Dr. Fitzmaurice graduated from the Rush Medical College in Chicago. As a medical student he had seen many gunshot head injuries and he knew that recovery was rare. Never did he feel more helpless than when he faced such an injury. Medical procedures for treating such injuries were few. He could diagnose the measles by smell. He could set a broken leg or arm quickly. But there wasn't much he could do for brain injuries. He didn't even have an x-ray machine to see how far the bullet was lodged in Billy's head.

Dr. Fitz had been the Willey's family doctor for more than two decades. When he first came to Mohall he had met John on the baseball field. About the same age with many of the same interests, they had spent happier times together.

He especially enjoyed John's friendship when he showed up in Mohall on Saturday nights to joust and talk farming business with the men on the street corner. Everyone liked to catch up on the news with each other over popcorn and ice cream.

Dr. Fitz knew that family piety ran deep in the Willey family, although he wasn't aware of their peculiar Sabbath keeping. He saw John as a gregarious and popular fellow who told stories embellished with distortions and even outright lies to get a laugh. He imagined Inez as the more serious of the pair: intensely idealistic, a bit old fashioned, and quite European. From what he knew they believed in the prophecies of the Bible, foresaw the Second Coming of a Messiah, and claimed to explain everything in relationship to signs of the times, like economic downturns and earthquakes.

On a personal level Dr. Fitz knew Inez as a dependable pioneer woman who could do just about anything around the farm and cook well besides. When he was farm visiting patients near the Willey farm, he liked to stop in for a conversation and Inez's Norwegian pudding (to which he always added some butter cream). If there was Lefse in the kitchen he ate that too.

When John returned to the office from the high school, Dr. Fitz took him by the arm and said, "John, let's go outside and talk."

Inez could not bear to go back to the office. She sat in the car with her hands over her face and with all of her fear and misery wrapped around her. The cutter rug laid heaped in the back seat where Billy had been. As a child she learned about a Norwegian nökk that all kids were warned to fear. This supernatural evil demon resembled a tangle of half-submerged tree roots that lived around the edges of lakes and rivers and tried to lure children into drowning. Right now she felt she was drowning. In less than an hour her life had taken a gigantic turn into the unknown. How could it have happened so fast? One moment she was cooking in the kitchen listening to a bird singing praises to the morning; the next her life was flipped upside down.

The two Willey girls went into the office to see Billy, who lay stretched out on the table with George watching over him. His breathing remained shallow. Genevieve began to cry, "Oh, Billy, what's happened to you?" It was too shocking to see him like this! George had nothing to say. He covered Billy's head. They gradually withdrew from the horror, saying much later that it was the saddest moment of their lives.

Outside Dr. Fitz spoke to John alone. That was the customary thing— to talk to the man of the house when facing a disaster. As he began speaking, he used as strong a voice as he could muster: "John, this is a bad head injury that may result in Billy's death."

John interrupted him before he went any further. He was trying for a diversion from what he thought Dr. Fitz was about to say. Some people are this way. When they think they are about to receive some appalling news, they jump onto secure ground and try to take hold.

"Aw," John said, "Fitz, don't be afraid to talk to me straight about Billy. Do you remember when dad was dying of cancer? You came out from Mohall and walked into the kitchen, picked up two loaves of Inez's freshly baked bread just out of the oven and put them under your arms. Then you walked into the parlor where my dad was lying in bed dying of cancer. And I heard you tell my dad that he never looked better. After talking to him for a couple of minutes you came back to the kitchen and took me outside on the porch. Then you proceeded to tell me that my dad never looked worse — death warmed over was the expression you used. And that he probably didn't have more than a month to live. I had just heard you tell him how good he looked! Now there we were outside where dad couldn't hear what you were saying, and you were telling me that we should get things in order as he was going to die soon."

It was the darkest moment of his life, and he knew it. This light-hearted story about his father's dying went nowhere. Humor was useless. Except for the leaves rustling in the wind and a car driving by on the main road, silence prevailed. Dr. Fitz didn't have to say anything about his treatment of John's father. He knew it and so did John. False assurances were the medication you dispensed in those days when you had little else to give.

"John," Dr. Fitz began again, "This time I am talking to you straight. Your wonderful boy Billy is going to die here soon in my office if we don't do something…and I mean real soon. I can't tell you with any more force than that."

On the Way to Trinity Hospital in Minot

Dr. Fitz's voice cracked. He had inherited his mother's soft nature and became emotional at times like this. And he almost started crying himself when he heard his own voice. Then he stopped, took hold of his emotions, and looked down at the ground. He could hardly bear to think what John must be going though right then! It probably was like the queer sensation you get in your legs when someone tells you about running pell-mell down a gravel road, tripping and falling down, and sliding across the raw ground on bare hands and knees.

Dr. Fitz went on to explain why he felt this way. "Billy's eyes have started to dilate. He does not respond with a light reflex nor does he withdraw when pinched. His heart rate and breathing are already irregular and impaired. His life is burning itself out. Typically, patients in this state don't live more than a few hours. The brain swells and pushes the vital centers controlling heart and respiration into the base of the skull. The patient stops breathing. And, John, there is not a thing I can do here.

"So, this is what I recommend. You should take him to Trinity Hospital in Minot as quickly as possible. I've already called Trinity and talked to a neurologist there. He doesn't hold out much hope either. But he said he would see Billy as soon as you arrive. He can x-ray Billy's head and try to locate the bullet. Maybe they can do something, but I don't want to get your hopes up. I'm telling you straight because that is what you expect of me. The only chance now is to get Billy as quickly as possible to Minot. You should find the fastest car in Mohall, and you and George make a run for it — cutting off twenty minutes could make all the difference." Dr. Fritz had nothing more to say.

Minot was over an hour away under normal driving conditions. John walked around the corner from Fitz's office to the Oldsmobile dealer on Main Street. The owner was his friend Maurice. (Many years ago, they had owned the Allen car dealership together in Loraine.) John told Maurice what his problem was and asked him if he could borrow a new Oldsmobile for the trip to Minot. He returned to Dr. Fitz's office with the car and found a clean sheet to protect the back seat. They carefully placed Billy in the back, securing him with pillows and the cutter blanket. Then he and George rushed to Minot.

During the trip George truly hoped they were going from a place of misery to a place of magic—only he wasn't sure. The entire trip took fifty-five minutes, good timing for a gravel road in those days. Billy was still breathing when they arrived. The first response of the neurologist wasn't promising, but he did take an x-ray of Billy's skull.

Inez and her two daughters headed back to the farm. When they got there the two girls went to the barn and found their older brother Tom in the haymow. (During summers he and George sometimes slept in the fresh hay brought in from the field. The bedrooms in the house were crowded when all six children plus Inez's mother slept upstairs.

"Tom, you can't stay here," one of his sisters' said.

But Tom refused to come down. Inez walked out to the barn and climbed the stairs to the haymow to talk to him.

"Tom…where are you?" she called out from below after she entered the barn.

"I'm up in the hay, Ma." He called out.

When Inez got to the top of the stairs, she made Tom pledge that he wouldn't do anything to add to the suffering of the family. Then she sat down and told him about the trip to Mohall and Dr. Fitz. "Billy was still alive when they got to town. Dr. Fitz examined Billy and made arrangements to have Billy transferred to Minot to see a neurologist. Dad and George are making a dash to Trinity right now." Knowing her son was prone to worry, she offered more hope than was realistic. (Later she wondered why she'd been untruthful at the time.) Then Inez listened to Tom's side of the accident. He filled in details that George had left out. Then Inez said: "Now Tom, when Billy comes home, we will all have to pitch in and help him. I suppose he may need to be carried around for a time. Dr. Fitz doesn't know how much brain function he may lose."

Inez would have sat with Tom the rest of the afternoon and talked things through some more. But he didn't need that, and probably didn't want it. Besides, how could she endure talking about what might happen to Billy or how Tom would handle his guilt if death were to occur. (Inez knew Tom was capable of beating down defeat and even anger. She'd seen it before on the baseball diamond.)

Before she returned to the farmhouse, she did what most mothers would do: she put her arms around Tom and hugged him. Pent-up anguish made Tom sob in gasps like she had never seen in him before. As for his promise not to do something stupid, she didn't worry that Tom would actually take his own life. Tom would find his way through all the dragons described in the Hebrew Scriptures and other oppressive powers that he'd have to face. Just the same, Tom stayed in the haymow for the next two weeks. Each day the family brought him food and water and pled with him to come down.

Natural Expectation for Blame

After leaving the haymow, Inez worried how the sickening event would play out in her children. How would John come to terms with the accident? From her point of view, if guilt was the issue, the fault of the shooting should be spread around, and not just on Tom or Billy. Then a strange thing began to happen. Everyone seemed to be speculating.

The accident seemed to have God's hand in the timing. Was there a divine purpose given so much precision? At least one could say God had made some kind of tacit agreement, or else how could one explain the removal of protection? The circle of blame began to circle around in her mind.

Inez believed that God could set limits on Satan's power to do harm and conduct his evil affairs. As she thought about the tragic events she puzzled over their orderliness. Because they came together with such unique timing, it must be that they happened in some kind of supernatural way that wasn't being revealed.

At twenty-one years of age Tom was not a praying person. He'd passed through that stage before he entered high school and saw no further need to communicate with someone you couldn't see and who didn't talk back. If he got lonely working in the field riding behind a plow or stacking hay, he'd talk to himself without referring to any other being. His older brother, even more of a pragmatist, didn't let the ambiguous ideas of God agitate his grey cells and keep him awake at night. He thought a God probably did exist, but a God whom people believed in merely to give them peace of mind.

Tom had seen the bullet hole in his brother's head. Actually, he saw more than that, so he wasn't fooled by his mother's optimism. In the accident he had been the one looking down the barrel of the gun and pulling the trigger. That is how he would always remember the shooting — always looking down the barrel. It became his worst nightmare.

When his mother told him about transferring Billy to Minot, he said later, "A deeper kind of anguish began closing in." Minot was an escalation—it was a desperate move. Trinity Hospital was a place of last resort. There was no other place to go. And for Tom, questions loomed. Would he get all of the blame? Could he live on the farm afterwards? Should he go back to college and abandon his plans to become a farmer? Like the biblical characters Job, Jeremiah and Elijah, he was beginning to wish he had died at birth or not been conceived at all.

After talking with her daughters, Inez stayed the night in her own bedroom. Menacing replays of the accident caused her to worry most of the night, as did her fears that Tom might stop going to church.

That same night, under a full moon, Tom sat for hours—he didn't know how long, with his legs stretched across the edge of a door sill in the middle of the hay loft looking out over the farmland. This door was where they threw hay down to the cattle in the corral below. To keep warm, he wrapped himself in a blanket. He looked over the land, the shelter trees, and the fences. He'd walked furrows in these fields many times and he knew the rock piles, the wet places, the sloughs, and the large erratic boulders. He was acquainted with the neighbors' farms and knew a few things about their family troubles. Yes, he knew this place, and yet it all seemed so strange to him now. Was he drifting away to another planet?

Later, he did not recall spending any time in prayer. It was more philosophical; a dreadful time and he was beside himself with thoughts of the accident. And he lost any notion he might have had about angels watching over him and protecting him and his little brother from danger.

The guardian angel thing had been a grand idea when he was a child. Was this actually true or some kind of fairy tale? Where was Billy's guardian angel or what was the angel doing when Billy left the house and came out to the road? Exactly why would the angel turn away at the exact moment when Billy needed protection—the instant he pulled the trigger? Why hadn't Billy's angel held him down against the tree or made it difficult for him to stand? Had Billy done something wrong (like not obeying his mother), to warrant the momentary withdrawal of his angel's protection?

Then, turning things around, Tom wondered why his own angel hadn't protected him from pulling the trigger at the instant just before the bullet struck Billy. Why didn't his guardian angel knock him to the ground, or freeze his finger before he pulled the trigger? Was there something about Tom's own life that caused his angel to forego protection and thus to protect Billy from harm? Supposedly, there were two brothers with guardian angels, and in both instances the angels had turned their backs at exactly the same moment. One of his father's favorite texts from the Bible kept crossing his mind, *"For he shall give his angels charge over thee, to keep thee in all they ways. They shall bear thee up in their hands, lest thou dash they foot against a stone."* [1] Had the angels been released from their duties and responsibilities to obey this covenant?

One time when he was younger Tom saw a picture in a magazine of a man holding an umbrella as he jumped off a bridge. This picture gave him an idea. He took his brother's fancy umbrella and climbed up the barn as far as he could get. Standing on the ledge he held the umbrella tightly over his head and leaped into a straw pile below. Unfortunately, his brother's ninety-eight cent umbrella failed him, and he landed in a heap on the ground. He wasn't badly hurt, just a sprained ankle. Tom joked about his parachuting adventure at dinner that evening, and his father told him how lucky he had been. "If it hadn't been for his guardian angel, he might have broken both legs or killed himself." Could a person get partial protection if

---

[1] Psalm 91:11-12.

they innocently did something stupid or dangerous? Was that what father meant—and how did he know all these things?

Tom could no longer rationalize guardian angels. He felt he was at liberty to follow his own disposition about the matter and accept contradictory statements about angels. His parents had taught him truths as a boy that he couldn't abide now.

Something else worried Tom. How much had his brother suffered? Did the bullet leave a durable pain? Had he gone into surgery to remove the bullet? Would Billy live through the night? If he got through the night what were his chances to improve in the days ahead?

Long past midnight Tom brooded, but finally fell asleep, resigned to the fact that he could not do anything about Billy's death, should it occur, and the fact that the bullet could not be brought back. If only some kind of miracle like you read about in the Bible would come bounding over the horizon. That was all he had to go on.

> *"Thy words have upholden him that was falling, and thou hast strengthened the feeble knees. But now it is come upon thee, and thou faintest: it toucheth thee, and thou are troubled. Is not this thy fear, thy confidence, thy hope, and the uprightness of thy way? Remember, I pray thee, whoever perished, being innocent? Or where were the righteous cut off? Even as I have seen, they that plow iniquity, and sow wickedness, reap the same."* [2]

---

[2] Job 4:4-8.

BILLY'S FUNERAL
CHAPTER FOURTEEN

"A man with a conviction is a hard man to change. Tell him you disagree, and he turns away. Show him facts or figures and he questions your sources. Appeal to logic and he fails to see your point." Leon Festinger, Henry W. Riecken, and Stanley Schachter, "Unfulfilled Prophecies and Disappointed Messiahs," in Jon R. Stone, *Expecting Armageddon* (New York: Routledge, 2000).

When Clara, Tom's high school girl friend, heard about the shooting accident, she drove over to the Willey farm. It was Tuesday morning and she didn't know that Billy had already passed away. As she drove into the driveway Genevieve and Marjorie came out to greet her.

Both liked Clara, but with a touch of jealousy over her beauty and curly hair. Her one sin was that she played basketball as well as the boys. When they saw her drive into the yard they assumed that Clara had already heard about the accident. As soon as Clara opened the car door and put one foot on the ground, they blurted out that Billy had passed away a few hours ago.

Stunned by what she heard, Clara dropped back into the car with horror on her face. There was a long pause while she sat there, bent over, with both hands on the steering wheel. Tom's sisters, realizing they had thrown Clara into a state of desperate travail, did not know what to do next.

Looking for deliverance, Clara asked, "Can I talk to Tommy?"

"He's up in the haymow," said Marjorie, "he went there yesterday and hasn't come down all night. He told Ma he wants to be left alone."

"Why is he alone in the loft? Did Tom have something to do with the accident?" Clara asked, sounding as if she wanted to push away the sickening dread that was creeping over her. "Do you want to go and tell him I'm here?" There was silence.

"Clara, Tom needs you," said Marjorie in a slow, deliberate manner, measuring each word like she was counting eggs in a basket.

No more was said. Clara got out of the car and headed briskly toward the barn. She entered through the side door into the separator room. The passage going upstairs into the haymow was steep, narrow, and foreboding. When she reached the top Tom was just beginning to stand up to brush off his clothes. He'd been lying on a horse blanket in the hay. He looked like he had been assaulted and mauled by the Devil himself. Tom was astonished to see her.

Clara fell on the blanket next to Tom and flung her arms around him. She hugged him while he sobbed and leaned against her. Now their tears flowed freely like large rain drops on a dusty road. It was not Tom's nature to cry, especially in a woman's presence, but just then he couldn't stop it any more than he could stop the flow of an ocean current. Finally, Tom said, "Clara, I accidentally shot my brother yesterday and he died this morning."

In that solemn hour, Tom and Clara desperately struggled with a most wretched and unfamiliar grief. Placing no blame on Tom, Clara took on the heart of his same grief.

The day wore on. It was springtime, a time of renewal, a time of beginning again. Off in the distance a neighbor hammered the bolts on a plow shear, preparing to plow. If only Tom could know, at this darkest hour, that all sins are forgiven in springtime, for springtime brings renewal with mercy, not judgement.

Clara left Tom with a promise to return and wondering what, if anything, she could do to mitigate the sorrow of Tom and his family. She felt Billy's death in herself. It was worse than when a coyote killed and ate her cat.

After Clara left, Tom tried to shoulder all the blame on himself. He felt disgraced as if in the presence of demons. He began to think himself unworthy of Clara, his parents, brothers and sisters, and certainly unworthy of heaven and eternal life. With enough fortitude, he would have gone downstairs, saddled his favorite horse, and ridden off without saying goodbye, perhaps to become a traveling salesman for the North Dakota Farm Implement Company. And yet an inner strength rose to the surface – the event, he reasoned. was an accident, pure and simple, and he would find a way to go on, following truth wherever it led.

In the afternoon father, John, and George drove up, returning from Minot. Tom heard the crunch of car tires on gravel as they came into the yard. When the car stopped, it seemed to Tom as if the whole world had stopped; and when he heard the car doors open and close, it was as if large iron gates had opened and closed.

Then Tom heard the kitchen door open and people walking to the road. He heard his mother sobbing and imagined his father trying to console her. Then he heard his father speak: "Now, Ma go back into the house and wait for me." (John always took some of the fear out of living on the farm—and now he had to wrestle with Inez' grief as well as his own.) Tom surmised that his father and George must have brought Billy's remains back with them.

Then he heard his father ask; "Where's Tom?"

"He's in the haymow," Genevieve said.

"What's he doing there?" John asked. "Bad luck is nobody's fault."

"He's not hiding out, he is grieving," said Genevieve. "We've tried to console him and get him to come back to the house, but he's been there since yesterday. He hasn't eaten a thing,"

"Well, I'll go out to the barn and talk to Tom later, but first we need to carry Billy inside and prepare him for burial. Kinfolk and neighbors will be coming to pay their respects," John said briskly.

George carried Billy's limp body into the house and laid him on a cot in the front room. John took Billy's clothes off and washed his body with formaldehyde, the same formaldehyde he kept in the granary to prepare seed for spring planting. Inez and the girls then dressed Billy and wrapped a clean white cloth around his head. Billy's face appeared smooth and porcelain in the flickering light, looking almost like a department-store doll. As was the custom, the two sisters agreed to sit with Billy's remains during the night.

Marjorie wondered about the differences between life and death as she sat quietly with Billy.[1] Choked and imprisoned with sorrow, she dared to silently whisper, "Oh God, where were the guardian angels you promised?". Although she did not doubt that Billy was dead, strange thoughts tormented her. What if Billy was to suddenly sit up? Would she run out of the room? (She'd heard stories about death counterfeits and people awakening out of brain injury many hours or even days later.

---

[1] Marjorie became a nurse and married a physician who went to war in the South Pacific. She died at an early age of a brain tumor leaving two children to grow up without a mother.

She didn't know if the stories were true or not.) In the old days, doctors thrust long needles under the fingers and toenails of the dead to be certain they were dead. But Marjorie's deepest question involved the separation between the living and the dead—the mystical departure between the two. What was the difference anyway?

How could Billy metamorphose into death, leaving a body with all the parts, but missing the fixings of life? He looked like he'd fallen asleep. The dithering wonderment of life and death kept circling in Marjorie's mind. A person might wish for questions like these to go away, but there is nothing strange about them bothering her tranquility. Under similar circumstance such sensations would rattle anyone. Eventually Marjorie and Genevieve fell asleep. The profound inquiries disappeared into the quiet, mysterious, splendor of sleep. But just before falling asleep Marjorie recited a poem to Genevieve she'd memorized in high school:

> *Because, I could not stop for Death,*
> *He kindly stopped for me;*
> *The carriage held but just ourselves*
> *And Immortality.* [2]

The next morning George went to the barn to care for the livestock. As he passed the hayloft, he saw Tom sitting on the ledge above. After milking the cows, George climbed into the loft. Seeing saw the confusion and helplessness on his brother's face, he felt a deep love for him. "Tom, you frighten me. You know there was nothing we could have done to prevent this accident. The shooting was not your fault. Dad doesn't blame you and neither do I, and neither does God with his compassion, whoever he is or wherever he lives. Dad says we have to go on. You've got to see yourself as part of the family. We've got to come together. You can't live up here the rest of your life waiting for death yourself."

Tom always thought he could "out-think" his older brother, but he wasn't sure now. Whereas sorrow ran off George's back like water on a duck's back, Tom felt the raw distraction of his shame. He said, "George, I'm afraid I will always have Billy's death on my conscience because I was

---

[2] Emily Dickinson, *The Chariot*.

the one who pulled the trigger. It was not you, or dad, or God, or anyone else, it was me. This is going to be my cross."

George left briefly to put the milk container in the cold-water trough by the side of the barn, and then returned to the hayloft to spend the rest of the day with his brother.

Billy's funeral was scheduled for Thursday and the various plans were set. Neighbors came to the Willey farmhouse, offering to milk the cows, feed the chickens, or do other necessary chores. The women brought dishes of food. The whole neighborhood grieved as if Billy was one of their own. Such was the charm of small farming communities.

Charley Tuor, a Swiss homesteader and carpenter who lived just west of the Willey's, offered to make a box for Billy's burial. When he finished building the coffin, he carved an image of a boy and his dog on the cover and painted the coffin the same colors as his barn—ivory white with bright green trim. (He said if he had more time he would have carved more on the lid and added some posies.) Charley's affection surprised Tom; he had always seemed aloof and devoted only to his horses. Exactly why Charley appeared to help during his neighbor's crisis wasn't clear.

Clara, Tom's girlfriend, and her family drove over to the Willey farm to pay their respects. Tom was still in the haymow dreading the next day's funeral. Clara went to the haymow while her folks talked with Billy's parents in the kitchen. When she saw Tom, she tried to coax him into coming down from the haymow and making his peace with Billy. (John would soon be nailing the coffin lid shut.) Reluctantly Tom agreed. As he entered the kitchen, everyone stared at him. He felt like he was walking outside of himself into another world. Tom and Clara stood together, looking down at Billy.

"Oh, Billy, I'm so sorry," Tom said in a trembling voice, taking hold of Billy's hand. "Who could suppose that something like this would ever happen? Forgive me, Billy, please forgive me." At this point Tom covered his quivering mouth with his hand. Then he reached into the coffin and took off Billy's leather belt and put it in his pocket. Clara heard John Jr. come skipping downstairs into the kitchen and asking his mother why Billy didn't talk to him anymore. With all her heart she hoped that Tom hadn't heard what John Jr. had just said.

Then Tom returned to the haymow with Clara, and she told him that he had to stop pitying and blaming himself for the accident. But Tom resisted: accident or not, he felt damned. Killing another human being, he said, put him so deep in mortal sin that God's grace could not reach him. How could he persuade God to forgive him when Billy himself couldn't do so? That said, Tom decided he would not go to the funeral the next day.

That next day dawned. Around noon the family and a few visitors gathered in the farmyard, preparing to go to the community hall in Loraine where the funeral service would be held.

John's sister Jonetta and her husband Terry carried the Tuor coffin out of the house and placed it in the back of a platform buggy drawn by a team of light-draft horses, this being the same arrangement used a decade earlier to take Wm Willey, Sr. to his final resting place in Loraine. Inez noticed that John seemed so busy with the funeral affairs that he failed to grieve. In the midst of a crisis, he always seemed confident and composed. Just that morning during family worship he had read from his Bible; *"We will trust the Lord God of Hosts."* Then he found one of his favorite texts; *"And hope maketh not ashamed because the love of God is shed in our hearts by the Holy Ghost which is given unto us."* [3]

Upstairs in the barn Tom stood in the open bay where the hay entered the barn for storage and slipped across the railings before dumping. From there he saw the cars and buggies coming from every direction on all the roads leading to Loraine. He watched them until the agony of it drove him back into the dark shadows of the barn. There, for some strange reason, he knelt down and asked God to forgive him of his carelessness. He didn't know what else to do. As noted earlier, He was not a praying man.

The Loraine community hall could not accommodate all the mourners. Some stood outside the entrance; others found places close to the open windows. Relatives came from all over Renville County and other parts of North Dakota. Helmer and Grace Twito, John's sister and brother-in-law and their two children drove over from Jamestown. Sid Elder and his family came from Canada. The congregation contained mostly farmers, renters, and hired help – common folk just like John and Inez: neighbors who joined in barn raisings, haying and harvesting; women who sewed and quilted together; men who worked together on road crews, played baseball in the summer, played poker, or boxed each other in the winter.

---

[3] Romans 5:3-4.

They came in overalls, homemade dresses, and heavy shoes. They were gentle, sturdy people with warm, sympathetic hearts. A few were crying even before they entered the hall. The smaller children, not allowed to come into the hall, sat quietly outside in the cars and buggies, safe from the adult's grieving. Loraine and Mohall schools and businesses closed for the rest of the afternoon. Billy's classmates from the Larson School sat quietly near the front of the hall with their teacher, all washed and dressed in their Sunday best.

The home-made coffin, draped with a black cloth, lay on a table up front. (In later years, John could not remember what color the coffin was painted, only that it was covered in black cloth.)

Elder E. A. Piper, the ordained Adventist preacher from Minot, officiated at the funeral. Mrs. Griffith from Mohall played the piano, fearing all along that she would break down and cry during the service. A quartet of singers composed of Billy's teacher, Miss Carlson, and three friends of the family, provided the special music.

As the service began, the congregation sang

In the sweet by and by...
We shall meet on the beautiful shore.

Women sat quietly, some softly weeping; a few strong-looking farmers bowed their heads trying to avoid looking at Billy's coffin or at their mournful women.

The preacher began: "William Warren Willey, a beautiful seven-year-old boy, named after his grandfather, is to be buried only a few rods up the road from here. He would be eight-years old tomorrow. As an energetic and curious child, he turned over rocks and walked into sloughs, looking for tadpoles or frogs or small animals. He was just starting life's journey. His favorite book was a dictionary. He greeted the mailman with a chuckle and a loud deliberate pronunciation of 'Good Morning Reverend Fred!'"

"Billy's life was cut short by a freakish accident. An older brother Tom, who is not with us today, will need abundant strength and encouragement in the months ahead. No family, not one of us, is secure from bad luck or accidents on this earth. We never know when the grim reaper will come calling for each one of us."

"A few days ago, his father held his son and pled with God not to take him yet, even offering to swap his own life in exchange. His mother hoped for a miracle. I'd asked for the same. But it was not to be." The preacher's voice in the telling. Then he went on. "We don't know the reason why things like this happen, but we have the assurance that God's plan is being played out in our lives each day. Billy now waits with his sleeping soul waiting for the day when his heavenly Father will call him home. He will join the Willey family and the rest of us in heaven. There will be no more sorrow or suffering or death; all sadness will vanish. That's the promise of God."

Then Elder Piper opened his Bible and read from the Scriptures, *"I am the resurrection, and the life; he that believeth in Me, though he were dead, yet shall he live."*[4] After that he gave a short prayer and the quartet sang again.

> *Blessed assurance Jesus is Mine.*
> *O what a foretaste of glory divine.*
> *Heir of salvation, purchase of God.*
> *Born of his spirit, washed in his blood.*

Then the pastor announced that interment would follow immediately at the family plot in the Loraine cemetery, a block to the east. Then the boys from the Larson School picked up the coffin, put it on their shoulders, and headed for the cemetery.

At the gravesite, Piper spoke a few more words of comfort. When the general resurrection takes place at Christ's Second Coming, he said, the dead will rise first from the grave and then the family that is alive will be caught up together into the clouds to meet the Lord in the air. He took most of his words from the Bible, including what Job said about the place of the dead until the resurrection morning; *"If I wait, the grave is mine house; I have made my bed in the darkness."*[5]

After that he chose a text for the perplexed mourners: *"Do not be amazed at this, for a time is coming when all who are in their graves will hear*

---

[4] John 11:25.

[5] Job 17:13.

his voice and come out — those who have done good will rise to live, and those who have done evil will rise to be condemned." [6]

Thinking he might have said something objectionable to the family or the visitors, Piper went on to explain that in his understanding of Scripture, young children were not accountable for anything they might have done to keep them out of the Kingdom of Heaven.

It was time to close. Everyone stood around the grave to come closer and hold hands for the prayer. Inez and the two sisters were quietly sobbing.

"Dear Father in heaven, as we stand beside this open grave, in this place where no plow has turned the prairie, we commit Billy to the ground, and we commit his spirit into your keeping, praying that you will deal graciously and mercifully with him and each of us until we meet on the sea of glass in the New Jerusalem through the grace of our Lord, Jesus Christ. Amen."

John stood on the edge of Billy's grave with his arms around Inez, who was crying as she looked into the lonely grave. George and the two girls lingered while the sting of death enveloped them like a low mist, acutely of how easily and unexpectedly the end can come for anyone. Without words, the families turned away and headed back toward their farms. Buggies with silent, sorrowful passengers rumbled over the gravel roads, each family carrying their understandings about what happens after burial.

Harry Gates and his two sons stood with shovels behind a tree on the corner of the family plot, waiting for the mourners to leave so they could cover Billy's coffin. A meadow lark on a fence post across the road signaled it was time to do so.

Other denominations were represented at Billy's funeral. Church affiliation seemed high around the farms. Most church goers, of course, believe in a "soul" that immediately after death returns to heaven and rejoins its Creator. The neighbors knew that the Willey family attended church on Saturday, but this was the first time anyone could remember hearing what Adventist's believed about the soul after death: it sleeps in the grave with the body. At the funeral the people heard it straight from Elder Piper. He cited as one of the pillars of the Adventist faith that "The body and the soul form an indivisible union."

Most religious people around the farms found their solace by believing

---

[6] John 5:28-29.

that the soul immediately returned to God. This state-of-the-dead doctrine along with observance of the Jewish Sabbath and avoidance of meat and coffee kept the neighbors from conversing with John and Inez about the Adventist faith.

Before Elder Piper left the cemetery, one of the Willey's neighbors confronted him — an exile from the Baptist church who perpetually deduced new reforms from the Scriptures. People said he knew too much about the Bible and not enough about farming or raising livestock. What Piper had said about the immortality of the soul during Billy's funeral visibly disturbed him. He told Piper that the Bible says the body made of dust returns to the ground, but the spirit returns to God who created it and challenged the reverend to read Ecclesiastes 12 "where he'd find the truth of the matter!"

People standing around saw Piper casting about for an escape for it would consume a lot of time to discuss the background of his Adventists teachings. Piper waited too long to respond. As evidence that the spirit returns to God, the neighbor proceeded to remind the preacher that just before Saul's death, the deceased Samuel appeared and delivered a prophetic oracle of doom to Saul. Piper could say something about Samuel's after death reappearance had this man been an Adventist — Ellen White the prophetess had an answer (the apparition was an evil spirit). the man's objection, but instead he replied, "The Hebrew from which the Old Testament text was taken reflects a traditional view of human existence reflected in Mesopotamian and Canaanite literature." [7]

Now out of time, Piper said to the man, "I'd like to discuss this topic with you, but I have to get back to Minot before dark. I can tell that you seek biblical knowledge. So, if you don't mind, I'd like to send you a book from my library called *The Great Controversy*. [8] It discusses my church's views on the immortality of the soul, the resurrection, and the final fate of the wicked. It deals with the questions you raised about the resurrection of the soul."

After he obtained the man's mailing address, Piper executed a clean exit! As he headed for Minot, he thought about the heavy reaction he had caused.

Back at the farm John didn't try to order his son to leave the haymow.

---

[7] Ellen G. White, *Patriarchs and Prophets*, 667.
[8] Ellen G. White, *The Great Controversy*.

He waited for Tom's suffering to subside to where he thought he could rationally approach him.

Both night and day, Tom could not dispel the image of a spinning bullet heading for Billy's head. It always started in slow motion with him looking down the barrel of a gun and then watching it crash into his little brother's head. Always in his dream, nothing could be done to stop the bullet's trajectory. He'd try to yell for Billy to get out of the way, but his vocal cords froze. Most terrifying of all was the sound when the bullet struck Billy, a thud like a large rock dropped into the river from a bridge. This nightmare persisted for many years, then gradually disappeared.

One evening John went to the barn with a hot bowl of soup and climbed into the loft. The two sat together on the windowsill, looking out over the homestead, the same place Tom had been drawn to on the first night after the accident. There was no wind, but in the distance a thunderstorm approached with large bellowing clouds. Mice were rustling in the straw and the horses were stomping in their stalls. A coyote fled in the distance.

In due time, Tom asked his father why he believed in God. His father answered quickly, "I believe in God because He can save me from everlasting death and enable me to see Billy again."

Some of his dad's reasoning seemed tortured to Tom, but later he understood why his father had drawn such a simple test for a skeptical world inside his religion. His dad was at peace with his viewpoints.

They moved on to discuss the accident. His father emphatically told Tom that the accident happened by the merest chance without any design or purpose. He didn't try to blame the devil or evil angels or anyone else. Just chance. Perhaps if all of the forces were rightly understood they could account for what had happened, but for now, the family had no first-hand knowledge about God or the devil. For the first time Tom realized that his father had a gentle irreverence and doubt about how the heavenly council operated.

"Accidents like this are simply part of the human condition," his father said. "It does no good to shake your fists at God or the devil or try to make any sense of what had happened. It was an accident pure and simple." Finally, to cap his discussion, he said, "The sheriff dropped by today and said there will not be an inquest and your son Tom is not a murder suspect!"

The conversation forged a bond between Tom and his father that would never be broken. John proved himself a worthy father. He could not have done better than to sit there with his son and discuss how they would deal with the tragedy. Tom imagined the Bible story of Father Abraham and son Isaac. Their fellowship in suffering was now so precious that Tom didn't want to let his father go. Soon he climbed down from the haymow and took his place with the family, replacing his mental duress with matters he could better control.

He kept Billy's belt upstairs under the mattress and stayed away from the cemetery. Never would he feel certainty about grace. His father had helped raise the doubts that would develop later.

THE HOMESTEADER'S
CONCEPTS OF GOOD AND EVIL
CHAPTER FIFTEEN

> "Of course, Martin Luther thought he had seen the Devil and threw an inkwell at his head, but that wasn't possession—it was more like a hallucination. Without in the least disparaging either his intelligence or his huge corpus of theological and philosophical work, it is well known that Luther was an exalted and visionary character, and that he was very high-strung." Gerald Messadié, *A History of the Devil* (New York: Kodansha International, 1993), 326.

From the beginning, Adventists acquired a distinct sectarian identity concerning the investigative judgement in a heavenly sanctuary. Nonetheless the church shared much forensic theology with the evangelical culture that gave birth to the movement in 1844. To set the stage, consider a poignant assertion by Aleksandr Solzhenitsyn: "If only it were all so simple! If only there were Evil people somewhere insidiously committing Evil deeds, and it were necessary only to separate them from the rest of us and destroy them. But the line dividing Good and Evil cuts through the heart of every human being. And who is willing to destroy a piece of his own heart?" [1]

Waiting for the Train in Omaha

In March 1888, [2] Mrs. Eliza Robbins sat in the ladies' waiting room of the Union Pacific depot in Omaha. She was making connections to Neligh, Nebraska, where her mother lived. Her thin garments indicated only part of her struggle with poverty and sorrow, as did the paltry eight dollars in her purse. By her side sat two poorly clad children looking anxiously at their sobbing mother. In her lap, she held the dead body of a

---

[1] Aleksandr Solzhenitsyn, *The Gulag Archipelago 1918-1956* (New York: Harper and Row, 1974).

[2] "Dead in His Mother's Arms," *The Oakdale Sentinel,* March 10, 1888.

third child whose blond hair she gently stroked. (Sammy had taken sick with typhoid fever, gotten worse, and died right there in the train station.) Sammy had not been baptized. Could anyone say he'd been disobedient to God? Would Sammy be heaven? And then the larger question: How did evil in the world originate? Tertullian, the Christian writer, said the origin of evil was "The question that makes people heretics." [3]

Eliza's abusive and neglectful husband lived in Kansas City. After years of mistreatment, she asked her mother in Nebraska for refuge in the home of her childhood. Fellow travelers noted her predicament and collected fifteen dollars — enough for the local undertaker to prepare Sammy's body for burial.

Good and Evil Agents Locked in Mortal Combat

Spiritual warfare between good and evil, along with pervasive tragedies and disasters, plagued all homesteading families. They fantasized invisible good and evil agents locked in mortal combat for the control of human minds. Adventists knew how such combat would finally end and in fact this was one of the benefits of being an Adventist. "The Mighty Conqueror, King of Kings" would appear in the east through the open space in Orion and descend upon a cloud wrapped in flaming fire. (A detailed description of the fearsome closing events was described in detail by Ellen White.) There was no mystery: [4]

> But the day of the Lord shall come as a thief in the night: in which the heavens shall pass away with a great noise, and the elements shall melt with fervent heat, the earth also and the works that are therein shall be burned up. [5]

Homesteaders saw themselves living at a time when the heavenly judgment could abruptly end. Probation would then close, and *"a time*

---

[3] Elaine Pagels, *Adam, Eve, and the Serpent* (New York: Vintage Books, 1989), xxiv.
[4] Wars and rumors of war, knowledge shall be increased, men running to and fro. Found in the book of Matthew.
[5] 2 Peter 3:10. KJV.

of trouble such as the world has never known" would ensue. [6] A decree would go forth to slay God's remnant saints for their bold embrace of the Saturday Sabbath.

At that moment, the saints would flee to the mountains, hide out in bushes, under the rocks, or in caves. The Four Horsemen of the Apocalypse (famine, pestilence, war, and death) would gallop across the sky. The light of the sun would darken, and the moon would turn red. Then, as the King of Kings came blazing across the sky, the righteous would be lifted into the air to begin their journey to heaven. Corpses of the unrighteous would be strewn over the earth and fire would destroy every feature of the earth. After spending a thousand years in heaven, the saints would return to a purified earth, a New Jerusalem where evil could not arise again.

The salient point was that "those who kept the commandments of God and the faith of Jesus" would go to heaven and experience everlasting life. Such ideas permeated Adventist preaching and publications and became the blueprint for life on earth, the end-time events, and the everlasting future in heaven. One pole on the compass pointed to an afterlife attainable only by the blood of Christ; the opposite pole pointed to the finality of death. John and Inez, for whom the devil was as real as the hot summer sun, determined to hold up "God's down-trodden and despised truth."

Daily Living

But large theological issues consumed only a portion of their life. After all, they were an earthly farm family and other things required great care and exertions. There was snow to shovel, a roof to maintain, and cows to milk. Crops needed seeding, cultivation, and harvesting. There were chickens and horses to feed and sheep and children to watch over. Their heavenly vision did not fill the stomach! Realistically they had to "occupy until (He) comes." [7]

The Willey's believed that God's covenant with the Israelites had been extended to modern mankind. When the Israelites obeyed the laws of God as revealed to Moses on Sinai, God blessed them. If they disobeyed God, then curses and calamities resulted.

---

[6] Daniel 12:1. KJV
[7] Luke 19:12 KJV.

This concept of God came from the Bible and the Spirit of Prophecy which meant it came from those who wrote the Bible and a prophetess instructed by God. The question of who actually wrote these truths did not concern the Willey family; holy men of God under the Holy Spirit's influence had done it. The belief system of Adventism, however, could not explain why bad things happen to good people, the daunting problem of evil.

By this time liberal Protestants had discarded many of the miraculous stories of the Bible and much of the fundamentalist eschatology. Still, to the Adventists, no argument against the biblical accounts, and especially the deception of the devil, could be sustained.

During this time, Adventists believed that the original scriptural documents had been inerrantly dictated (inspired) by God, and that Jesus Christ came into the world by a special biological miracle – hard to explain, but He was born without a father. (Some may have speculated that the Holy Spirit was the father of Jesus.) As a grown man, He walked on water, turned water into wine, and fed five thousand people from a loaf of bread and a few fishes.

Explaining the Role of Christ in Heaven

After Jesus' death on the cross, two angels asked Mary Magdalene why she was crying. She said, *"They have taken away the Lord out of the sepulcher, and we know not where they have laid him."* [8] For Adventists, Jesus' birth, resurrection, and ascension were supernatural miracles. After arriving back in heaven, Christ entered the Most Holy Place in the heavenly sanctuary and commenced a mysterious sanctuary judgement. This sanctuary doctrine unlocked the mystery of the disappointment of 1844: that year denoted not a physical event (the Second Coming) but rather a spiritual event. The "safety" of this idea was that it couldn't be verified.

Along with many Christians, Adventists believed that humans were created in God's image and originally placed in the Garden of Eden. After Adam and Eve sinned, fallen humanity got a second chance: under the influence of the

---

[8] John 20:2.

Holy Spirit, they could repent of their sins and bring themselves back towards perfection. *"Without holiness no man shall see the Lord."*[9]

To the traditional Adventist, perfection of character meant putting away detestable traits such as untruthfulness, greed, violence, prejudice, and sexual passion. Man must measure up to God's standards through sheer persistence and must also prepare the heathen and infidels of the world (unbelievers in general) for the return of Christ by preaching the Three Angels' Message.[10] This assumed that most people, although headed to perdition since birth, still longed for God's grace, but needed prompting as to how salvation was achieved.

Camp meetings, revivals, sermons, colporteurs, missionaries and relentless publications all drilled into Adventists that they lived in the most solemn period of the earth's history, and that they were divinely and uniquely chosen to "let their light shine all over the world."

An all-out war with temptation and sin was worth the exertion: *"He who heareth my word, and believeth on him that sent me, hath everlasting life, and shall not come into condemnation; but is passed from death into life."*[11]

Where Did the Idea of Satan Come From?

Although there are several suggestions of demonic forces in the Old Testament, Satan himself did not figure prominently — he was given minor recognition and only brief mention in only three places, [12] and even these have been variously interpreted. Philosophers such as Daniel Dennett account for the variations on the devil in religious concepts between Judaism (Old Testament) and Christianity (New Testament) as coming out of "the psychological and cultural soil in which different nuances first

---

[9] Hebrews 12:14. KJV.

[10] "Fear none of those things which thou shall suffer. Behold, the Devil shall cast some of you into prison, that ye may be tried: be thou faithful unto death, and I will give thee a crown of life." Revelation 2:10.

[11] John 5:24.

[12] Sydney H. T. Page, *Powers of Evil: A Biblical Study of Satan and Demons* (Grand Rapids, MI: Baker Books. 1995), 11.

took root." [13] But it is quite likely that the abstract notion of evil and devils has always existed.

A profound story took care of the origin problem. A serpent in the Garden of Eden, although created by God, appeared as an enemy of God and spoke to Eve as "Lucifer" or "Satan" around the Tree of Knowledge of Good and Evil. Eve fell under the talking serpent's spell and plucked the divinely forbidden fruit. This simple act, Adventists believed, imparted death and suffering to every human. It ruined the Garden of Eden and a flaming sword at the entrance frightened people away.

This description of the entrance of sin in the Garden almost certainly derived from the pre-Christian apocryphal book, the Wisdom of Solomon. *"God created man for incorruption and made him in the image of his own eternity, but through the Devil's envy death entered the world, and those who belong to his party experience it."* [14] Although not considered part of the standard Protestant canon, it supplied some of Ellen White's vision material.

The Origin of the Great Controversy

The Adventist theme of a Great Controversy between Christ and Satan, or between good and evil, did not originate with Ellen White and the early Adventist church. It was in common use by other authors before her time. The earliest sources were probably the books of Daniel and Revelation.

> *And there was war in heaven: Michael and his angels fought against the dragon: and the dragon fought and his angels…*
> *And the great dragon was cast out that old serpent, called the Devil, and Satan, which deceiveth the whole world: he was cast out into the earth and his angels were cast out with him.* [15]

It is difficult to square the monism in the Scriptures — God representing both good and evil in the Old Testament—and the dualism or spiritual warfare between God and Satan in the New Testament. In

---

[13] Daniel C. Dennett, *Breaking the Spell* (New York: Viking, 2006), 102.
[14] Wisdom of Solomon 2:23-24 (RSV). Writings may have appeared as early as the last half of the first century B.C.
[15] Revelation 12:7-9.

Isaiah the God Yahweh boasts *"I form the light, and create darkness: I make peace, and create Evil: I the Lord do all these things."* [16] As one scholar put it, "the best historical explanation of the concept of Satan — in the Old Testament — is the personification of the dark side of God, that element within Yahweh which obstructs the good…Yahweh was the one God, he had to be, like the God of monism, an antinomy of inner opposites." [17]

Unsophisticated farm families like the Willeys who studied their Bibles and spiritual literature on their own puzzled over contradictory texts. They worried whether or not the devil's powers of deception could lure them from God, from truth, from eternal life. To get around this problem, they relied on Adventist publications, such as the *Review,* and on what they heard from preachers during Sabbath worship, and on religious colporteurs who stayed overnight and offered truth-filled literature. But for some answers, they just waited for heaven and the opportunity to ask God or Jesus directly,

The Book of Job was particularly confusing to John and Inez. Because Job described how Satan had no power to do anything independent of God's will, it appeared that God limited Satan's authority to cause evil on the earth. The loss of Job's possessions, his painful sores, and the murder of his wife and children, were all done by "Satan acting as a servant (agent) of God." This "being," was pictured in the book as a loyal servant (a celestial being subservient to God) attending a heavenly council or divine assembly in heaven. Hardly was he inherently evil. Could this be true? It was God who singled out Job as a man of outstanding integrity and piety and laid down the rules on how far Lucifer could go to test his faithful servant: he to stop his torment just short of killing Job. [18] Could those same things be happening to modern day homesteading humans trying to make a living by farming and facing one calamity after another?

Whereas Inez found it difficult to read the Old Testament, John rose to the challenge of problematic texts and pondered whether evil was provoked by Lucifer on his own or while acting as an agent of God.

---

[16] Isaiah 45:7.

[17] Jeffrey Burton Russell, *The Devil: Perceptions of Evil from Antiquity to Primitive Christianity* (Ithaca, NY: Cornell University Press, 1977), 176.

[18] Sydney H. T. Page, *Powers of Evil: A Biblical Study of Satan and Demons* (Grand Rapids, MI: Baker Books, 1995), 23.

Then there was the Old Testament story about Jonah and the whale. "If you want to read a strange story in the Bible," John said, "this one takes the cake!" But it gave John something to think about as he worked in the field. Only briefly did he attribute Bible stories to folkways and legends. In his own life John had not experienced an indisputably supernatural miracle. His ax head did not float on water. Nor did his precious Billy rise from the dead, even as the family entreated God for a miracle.

The Concepts of Guardian Angels

One Biblical expression of God's goodness and justice was the provision of guardian angels, a matter discussed earlier in this book. The Bible said that mankind was not left alone to the wiles of the Devil. Though angels were invisible and weightless, they were thought to have personalities like man. Isaiah said they had wings, faces, feet and the ability to speak. Abraham, "the friend of God," entertained three heavenly visitors and gave them a bountiful meal of butter, milk and a calf, [19] implying that angels were not vegetarians!

Daniel, whom God called "greatly beloved," was thrown into a lion's den, intended as the lion's evening meal. The next morning King Darius returned to hear Daniel proclaim, *"My God hath sent his angels, and they hath shut the lions' mouth."* [20] Then, of course, there were the three Jewish princes, Shadrach, Meshach, and Abednego, who King Nebuchadnezzar threw into a fiery furnace. Afterward: *"the King's counselors, being gathered together, saw these men, upon whose bodies the fire had no power, nor was a hair of their head singed, neither were their coats changed, nor the smell of fire passed on them."* [21] Bible stories like these reinforced the power of protective angels and showed exactly how God entered the lives of his people. John Willey quietly wondered why these conditions had changed since Old Testament times. Such stories didn't comport with his own experience.

As we will soon see, it might have been better had angels not been described as real persons. They "existed" beyond the familiar physical world and trying to reduce them to human risked heretical drift. Angels

---

[19] Genesis 18:1-15.

[20] Daniel 6:22.

[21] Daniel 3:27. KJV.

were not creatures of this world, not even Satan and his band of evil ones. All could be traced back to their creation in heaven. But when guardian angels did not perform as expected, despair resulted.

At an early age the children in this story learned about guardian angels. When the Syrians surrounded the prophet Elisha, he asked God to open his eyes so he could see what forces God planned to use to protect the Israelites from the enemy: *"and, behold, the mountain was full of horses and chariots of fire round about Elisha."* [22] The prophet Daniel said he saw one hundred million (ten thousand times ten thousand, and thousands and thousands) ministering angels standing before God. [23] How hard would it be to create more angels if you needed them? It appears to the average reader that angels, as portrayed in the Bible, could disrupt the laws of nature. As it turns out, however, cosmic warfare happened on a tilted playing field: the contest favored the devil.

Mankind Was Born with a Proclivity to Do Evil

Because of sin, man was born with an innate proclivity to do evil. Thus, if a person made no decision one way or the other he or she ended up by default in Satan's camp. A person must actively choose Christ to overcome man's original sin. The stewards of the religious faith assume that most people understand this cosmic battle and Satan's unfair advantage. Like a cuckoo bird, he could push the rival eggs out of the nest to make sure its offspring got fed by the foster parents, and in the end the hatchling remained a cuckoo no matter what food it was fed, or what care it received from its foster parents.

The Willey children were told that in heaven they would be "introduced to their guardian angels and learn more particulars." [24] The shelter of guardian angels extended to good behaviors; it was doubtful whether mendacious

---

[22] 2 Kings 6:16.

[23] "A fiery stream issued and came forth from before him: thousands upon thousands ministered unto him, and ten thousand times ten thousand stood before him: the judgment was set, and the books were opened. Daniel 7:10.

[24] Ellen G. White, *In Heavenly Places,* 101. "We shall never know what dangers, seen and unseen, we have been delivered from through the interposition of the angels until we shall see in the light of eternity the providences of God. Then we shall better understand what God has done for us all the days of our life. We shall know then that the whole heavenly family watched to see our course of action from day to day."

activities fell within the angelic coverage — perhaps guardian angels turned their backs if the children played cards or checkers; swore, drank, necked, danced; or did anything else that pleased Satan. When the Willey's offspring became teenagers, parents advised them that saloons, circuses, movie houses, bowling alleys, and billiard tables fell outside the safety zone of their guardian angels. If one went to a movie, the angel waited outside. If the roof caved in or a fire broke out, no protection would be available.

Parents often noticed that when children began to understand angels, they speculated about the secret world of such beings. When told angels that could move around silently and go unseen to wherever they wished, children imagined what a thrill it would be to sneak angel-like into private parlors and see what was going on, or maybe take the whole village under surveillance by flying over at low attitude!

The Willey children took care not to "borrow" other people's things or commit actions that an observant angel might record as violations of the "Laws of God." Sexually they were more modest than other farm kids, or so they claimed. But herein is a curiosity: children who won't self-abuse in front of their mothers would quite readily do so in the "presence" of a putative guardian angel who packed supernatural powers and held a celestial record of evil deeds!

Sometimes guardian angels put on "human clothes" and offered timely supernatural interventions. Most people didn't know they are dealing with these heavenly visitors. The Apostle Paul admonished Christ's followers, *"Be not forgetful to entertain strangers: for thereby some have entertained angels unawares."* [25] After such a visit, the angel slips behind a vale and disappears without a trace. They might show up unannounced to rescue people in distress, reform people's habits, or appear in other inexplicable roles. However, a guardian angel has never been known to ring a bell if someone starts an adulterous affair!

No literal angels visited the Willey homestead, but the family remained open to the possibility that divine strangers might show up on the road into town, in the fields, at the lake, threshing, over on the Neilson quarter. A stranger's appearance might be an opportunity to treat an angel with respect, and in the process encounter a heavenly being.

On the farm in North Dakota and elsewhere, evil included natural

---

[25] Hebrews 13:2.

events such as thunderstorms, prairie fires, swarms of mosquitoes, grasshopper plagues, tornadoes, hail and freezing rains, severe winds, blizzards, and run-away horses. It was not clear who was responsible for such natural evils. Insurance companies called then "acts of God." Then there was the evil in the heart of man that pollutes streams, destroys the environment, corrupts politics, abuses children and spouses, bullies people, and steals from the poor.

The Devil Bound to Earth

They would be more interested in the uneasy space where there were hosts of unclean spirits, demons, bad, fallen or evil angels looming around the environment and roaming throughout the earth. These demons had belief systems too. *"Thou believest that there is one God: thou doest well: the Devils also believe, and tremble."* [26] John used to wonder how it was that devils would tremble in the sight of God and still get away with murder.

It was said that the evil angels, belonging to the tribe of Satan, lived on the earth and could disguise themselves as good angels. The possibility of treacherous combinations of good and evil in a single agent unnerved people. A devil acting thusly made evil and suffering incoherent, chaotic, and confusing.[27] Satan and the evil angels intended to deceive the human family. A pathetic species of angels, they never learned to keep to themselves and stop harming people. No one discovered a way to bridle them or soften their ways.

Indefatigable evil angels sweep in and inject bad thoughts, thereby producing temptations, weakening moral structures, removing barriers for protection, and entangling people with earthly treasures. Adventists warned that Satan leads many to think that God overlooks a person's sins, particularly small or minor ones. [28] The very elect could be deceived by this and miss out on eternal life.

But, allegedly, evil angels possessed weaker powers than guardian

---

[26] James 2:19.
[27] "Satan employs every possible device to prevent men from obtaining a knowledge of the Bible; for its plain utterances reveal his deceptions…So closely will the counterfeit resemble the true that it will be impossible to distinguish between them except by the Holy Scriptures." Ellen G. White, *The Great Controversy*, 593.
[28] Ibid. 620.

angels, although often an artist's rendering of the two makes Satan's angels seem stronger and more menacing. In the Adventist view, evil angels possessed powers almost equal to the good angels from the heavenly court. Satan could heal people, work miracles, impersonate the Apostles, or Christ himself. As the end-time approaches, Adventists believe, the work of Satan will greatly intensify. The boundaries and vitality of his activities will expand. He becomes like a frantic wayfarer traveler trying to gather up his luggage as the train comes into the station.

John and Inez knew about these supposed satanic influences in the life of the church. Ellen White once described how she herself had been deceived by Satan. During her first vision when she was taken to the heavenly New Jerusalem, she allegedly met and spoke with two Millerite preachers, Charles Fitch and Levi Stockman. Later she saw her and stopped talking about meeting these two Millerite preachers. It did not fit with Adventist theology on the immortality of the soul. [29]

So, if evil angels could sully the Spirit of Prophecy, they could certainly fool the pew-dwelling saints. Apparently, Satan knew all the tricks in the book. Some Christians thought he could "step out of the shadows" and harm or even destroy a person. The Bible told how Satan had threatened to kill the incarnate Jesus during His forty days in the wilderness. To raise the specter of this possibility Ellen White described a vision in which she was shown how *"God had spared the life of her husband James, although Satan has pressed him sore to take away his life. God has wrenched him from the enemy's power and raised him up to still act for Him."* [30]

---

[29] Ellen G. White, *Early Writings* (Washington DC: Review and Herald Publ. Assoc.), 10. "We all went under the tree and sat down to look at the glory of the place, when Brethren Fitch and Stockman, who had preached the gospel of the kingdom, and whom God had laid in the grave to save them, came up to us and asked us what we had passed through while they were sleeping. We tried to call up our greatest trials, but they looked so small compared with the far more exceeding and eternal weight of glory that surrounded us that we could not speak them out, and we all cried out, 'Alleluia, heaven is cheap enough!' and we touched our glorious harps and made heaven's arches ring." See Malcolm Bull and Keith Lockhart, *Seeking a Sanctuary* (San Francisco, CA: Harper & Row, Publ., 1989), 59.

[30] Arthur White, 1986. *Ellen G. White. The Progressive Years* (Hagerstown, MD: Review & Herald Publ., 1986), II, 98. (See also p. 127 for another example of direct evil spirits in the life of the Whites.)

Grandma Laura was a Strong Believer in the Devil

Tom's grandmother Laura Willey believed in the literal presence of Satan and evil angels. She imagined them hiding or lurking around her as she worked in the kitchen. Often, she'd stop what she had been doing and call out in a loud voice "Satan, get thee behind me." This outburst occurred for no apparent reason other than that things were not going well, or something was preventing the completion of her work.

George and Tom thought such beliefs had warped their grandmother's mind. Why would she keep on ordering invisible spirits to leave since they seemed to return so quickly! "Maybe," George told Tom; "Grandma did this just for entertainment." They avoided going across the road to see their grandma because it frightened them to think that Satan might be near even if no one actually saw him. As Tom got older, he worried less and he'd say, "Granny, you can't see the devil today cause he's gone fishing down on the Missouri River." What he really thought was that individuals use Satan as an escape mechanism: unable to confront the hard facts of the human experience, they invoke a cosmic force.

One evening when Tom was ten years old his grandmother came for a visit and called him to the kitchen table. She said; "Suffer me to read you something Tommy. Sit down. I want to show you a passage inspired by someone who actually saw Satan in a vision, so you don't think I am so strange." She held what looked like an ancient book with the words *"Spiritual Gifts"* embossed on the spine. (The book was one of Ellen White's earlier *Testimonies.)*

Looking at Tom she said; "You don't seem to tremble and take heed as much as you should about Satan and evil angels. So, let me read you something. You need to fill your hayloft with an awareness of the trickeries and wiles of the devil." She began reading:

> *I was then shown Satan as he was, a happy, exalted angel...*
> *He still bears a kingly form. His features are still noble, for*
> *he is an angel fallen. But the expression on his countenance*
> *is full of anxiety, care, unhappiness, malice, hate, mischief,*
> *deceit, and every Evil. That brow which was once so noble, I*
> *particularly noticed. His forehead commenced from his eyes*

to recede backward. I saw that he had demeaned himself so long, that every good quality was debased, and every Evil trait was developed. His eyes were cunning, sly, and showed great penetration. His frame was large, but the flesh hung loosely about his hands and face…He appeared to be in deep thought. A smile was upon his countenance, which made me tremble, it was full of Evil, and Satanic slyness. This smile is the one he wears just before he makes sure of his victim, and as he fastens the victim in his snare, this smile grows horrible. [31]

Tom had no reason to doubt this physical description of Satan. He told his grandmother he had never heard such things before. Not finding anything else to say, he told her about a calf he'd seen one time over in the neighbor's yard: "It was born with a skull that took off just above the eyes and everyone around said it didn't have much smarts because there wasn't enough room for an entire brain. They referred to the calf as microcephalic so if Satan has a low forehead, he must not be very smart."

Other Planets with Sin-free Unfallen inhabitants

In the Adventist worldview the earth constitutes The Theater of the Universe. But there are other planets where unfallen people watch Planet Earth to see how sin would finally play out, to see whether the devil or God would win. No one knows the names of these planets, or their location, or how one might get in contact with them. But according to Ellen White, the personages themselves appear like Jesus and have experienced deliverance from Satan's temptations. [32]

God's judgment in the sanctuary decides on a person's acceptance into heaven. When Christ returns, those who rejected Christ will hide out with the devil until consumed in a lake of fire they cannot change their minds and seek a second chance. Probation will have closed.

---

[31] Ellen G. White, *Spiritual Gifts*, 27.

[32] "The inhabitants of the place were of all sizes; they were noble, majestic, and lovely. They bore the express image of Jesus, and their countenances beamed with holy joy, expressive of the freedom and happiness of the place." Ellen G. White, *Maranatha* (No publication details), 368.

THE INFINITE POWER OF THE
JUDGMENT IN HEAVEN
CHAPTER SIXTEEN

> "Your shadow at morning striding behind you. Or your shadow at evening rising to meet you; I will show you fear in a handful of dust." T. S. Eliot. The Waste Land. 1922.

After morning chores, Inez asked John to drive her to Billy's grave in Loraine. Before leaving she took off the apron with the playful puppies — the one she was wearing the morning Billy was fatally shot, still showing remnants of Billy's blood — and put on a darker, somber one. At the cemetery she fell to the ground weeping and murmuring. She imagined God and the angels peering over the walls of heaven and seeing the unfortunate pair on the lonely Dakota prairie. "The Lord looketh from heaven; he beholdeth all the sons of men. From the place of his habitation he looketh upon all the inhabitants of the earth." [1]

The small cemetery conjured up miserable memories and forsaken relatives but would have to do until Jesus came. Visits by John and Inez continued for about a month after the funeral. But one day John announced that it was time to get back to regular living, so the visits stopped. Hopeful feelings that humankind is not alone, but watched over by a Presence lingered, of course.

A similar wistful ritual took place at the church potluck after Sabbath worship. [2] Inez pulled her friend Sarah Engvorson aside and chatted in Norwegian. John didn't know what they talked about, but he figured they were discussing how the family could have prevented the accident, or why he personally had been spoiling the boy. He still harbored his own raw guilt, the sort that doesn't vanish when you take a bath or rollick in the snow. Inez observed a year of mourning by dressing in black for

---

[1] Psalms 33:13-14. KJV.

[2] There were so few Adventists where the Willey's lived that they met for Sabbath worship in private homes.

public appearances, churning the accident over in her mind with bitterness and grief. Eventually she suffered what John called "half-of-a nervous breakdown." Billy's death was too much to bear.

Tom later recalled a tender image of his father and mother: standing dejected around the pump organ in Sam's Griese's front parlor while singing Adventist hymns, including this poignant one:

> There's a land that is fairer than day.
> And by faith we can see it afar.
> For the Father waits over the way,
> To prepare us a dwelling place there.
> In the sweet by and by,
> We shall meet on that beautiful shore.

Little Rain in the Summer of 1931

Summer brought little or no rain for weeks. The farm was devoid of joy. Even the sun seemed to come up later and set earlier. Mornings began without much food; the roosters quit crowing; life ground on. There were cows to milk, eggs to gather, and manure to shovel.

The wind blew and rattled the windows and thunder shook the neighborhood, but, as noted above, it rained little. The *Renville County Farmer* reported that Bob a blacksmith was found dead in his bed. He went to "sleep and never woke up," which is exactly what Inez longed for.

Because the death rate among farm children from diphtheria and pneumonia still ran high (until the invention of antibiotics), one might presume Billy's fatality would be taken in stride. This was definitely not the case. A child's death can be so emotionally vivid that it defies description. Who knows how to describe a grieving parent's feelings unless you resort to talking about tight spirals or torments formed on top of each other to disfigure the mind and send it into deep structural suffering? This was certainly how Billy's parents felt for several months after the shooting accident.

They needed to recover a semblance of normal life. Noticing that John and Inez had quit coming to town on Saturday nights, Charley Tuor, a neighbor, came to the farm to talk to John and cheer him up. He found him in the shed straightening out a spring blade on a cultivator. "Charley,

I'm glad you came," John said. "I think the oomph has gone out of me. I feel myself losing ground and not caring about milking cows or bringing in the hay. What's the point of living? Why do we keep going?" And he told Charley, "Inez is disturbed in the most serious way. She has decided her sad state of mind will go on forever until she dies."

Car Accident Nearly Took the Life of John

Four months after the death of Billy, the *Renville County Newspaper* carried the headlines; "Nobody Killed in Three Local Car Accidents. Blow-out Causes Elmer Twito Car to Turn Around and Over Wrecking it Badly. John Willey and Sister Get Cut Up, but Not Seriously."

The paper reported that "The Elmer Twito family of Cogswell, and John Willey, Mohall, have been congratulating themselves that they are alive since an automobile accident 2 1/2 mile west of Mohall Tuesday evening at 8:30 O'clock. John Willey has a bad scalp wound and bruise; Mrs. Twito has several quite deep leg cuts from glass. They are brother and sister. Both of them are very sore from bruises and cuts. They were all brought into Mohall and were attended by both the Mohall physicians."

"The Twito family of Cogsell, this state, had been on an automobile trip thru Iowa and South Dakota, and they had taken with them John Willey of Mohall, a brother of Mrs. Twito. They were just a few miles from the Willey home, when a tire blew out while they traveled quite fast. Mr. Twito lost control of the car and it turned over in the middle of the road and on the second turn went into the ditch. The Plymouth car which they were driving is just about a complete wreck. The top is all gone, and the insides of the body seem to be bent beyond repair. All of the glass was broken, and three wheels are broken."

Maybe there were protective angels after all. This auto accident was a very close call.

The Fear of Dying

John and Inez found it impossible to imagine a world without Billy. and how to firmly fetter their anguish now rapid events that took Billy's life. Dread began to envelope Inez. "Human life doesn't mean a thing," she sighed to John. "We're born; we sleep, eat, work and suffer. We live for such a short time and then we're…" Her moist lips froze, her words stuck deep in her throat, her eyes teared up, her voice slowly petrified—she couldn't finish the sentence. She claimed that not even a powerful prayer, or a half a dozen in rapid sequence, could lift her spirits. Hadn't the word of God said it would be like this when the Antichrist arrived and civilization collapsed? Inez remembered a text in the Bible about Hezekiah nearing death and being advised "to set his house in order, for thou shalt die and not live," whereupon Hezekiah beseeched the Lord for more time and received it. Maybe more time was what she needed?

> *I have walked before thee in truth and with a perfect heart and*
> *have done that which is good in thy sight, then he wept sore.*
> *Afterwards, came the word of the Lord to Isaiah saying … Go*
> *and say to Hezekiah … I have heard thy prayer. I have seen*
> *thy tears: behold, I will add unto thy days fifteen years.* [3]

After the serious accident, John's sister Grace and her husband Helmer Twito came from Jamestown to offer solace to John and Inez. "May heaven bless you, Grace," Inez said, "I've been thinking a lot about life and death lately. Here's what is happening, though I don't like to talk about it in the open." Just because someone was listening, she began to feel better. She started to shake off the sticky melancholy that had gripped her for so long.

Inez told Grace, "As we get older there is rising anxiety about dying, and after reading Isaiah about Hezekiah in the Old Testament I want to live and begin living well. I've noticed we're not as agile as we used to be, or as quick to rise or maintain balance. We notice a mounting familiarity over the wear and tear of our bodies. We may acquire a terminal illness or disability, maybe even liver cancer like my mother. We lose a child or a spouse and dying seems to speed up. That certainly happened to John's father and now to mine. Maybe this is what happens. Then one day we just fall off the perch. Eventually what was once a warm and vital person suddenly turns into a cold and lifeless thing that must be buried in the ground. What an awful, painful thought. Under such circumstances, the quicker the better, if you know what I mean. We all share in this quiet

---

[3] Isaiah 38:1-5.

sadness and sink deeper into dread as the time approaches. Billy helped me see the cycle of life. You wanted to know; well, that is what I've been thinking about lately." Inez sounded confused.

As Inez watched the moon rise and observed its pot marks, she thought it must surely have taken a heavy pounding from flying debris, but never had to worry whether the asteroids came from God or the Devil. Religious scholars contend that mankind invented an imaginative concept about God to light the darkness, a powerful notion of a person like themselves and a heavenly abode that helps to placate the human conditions.

Having the Possibility of Everlasting Life

After Christians face life's perplexities and construct a heaven, they create a plan that will work for them and a blueprint that unintentionally limits or restricts membership into everlasting life for others. Every sect or denomination carries some variation on this qualification theme. Humans build churches, inspire religious sentiments through interior illumination, create songs, and write and paint powerful imagery to buttress these ideas. Only humans compose songs of hope and create beautiful works of sacred art. Scholars explain such behavior by the desire to obtain a divine election in some other place with more pleasant surrounds.

Humans have crafted a Supreme Being who in turn created the infinite heavens, the firmament, earth, vegetation, animals and mankind. (Maybe even the dinosaurs.) This happened in six days about six thousand years ago. The same being promulgated the moral standards for living a godly life. These standards, supposedly found in the Scriptures, set the pace for worship of this God and respect for His will. [4]

A pew-sitting Christian cannot debate all the theological issues on which their faith is founded. They take what is given to them, distilled down to them by parents, Sabbath School leaders, ministers of the gospel, or teachers if they attend a Christian school.

Generally speaking, Christians take their traditional view of God from the rather harsh and authoritarian Hebrew canon and then soften their view with the gentle, compassionate, New Testament Jesus. God and Jesus

---

[4] Karen Armstrong, *A History of God* (New York: Gramercy, 1991), and Jack Miles, *Christ. A Crisis in the Life of God* (London: William Heinemann, 2001).

are part of the Godhead along with the Holy Ghost — three persons in one. If you want to start a good debate, find someone who is convicted that there is only one God and put him or her up against a person who believes in the trinity.

By coming to earth Jesus established that another God existed, one not found in the Jewish Scriptures. Thus, devotees must find a way to accommodate a belief that Jesus is divine with an equally strong conviction that there is only one. [5] There is a difference between the two, or so it is said: One is capable of great wrath, the Other is sweet and gentle. As for the personality of the Holy Spirit, little can be known.

So it goes. One person of the godhead, Jesus, became a sacrifice to God for Adam's original sin and the sins of all mankind.

Do We Know What God Looks Like?

Preachers sometimes talk about God as a loving father and sometimes as a destroyer and creator. The Old Testament God describes him thusly:

That they may know from the rising of the sun, and from the west, that there is none beside me. I am the Lord and there is none else. I form the light, and create darkness; I make peace, and create evil: I the Lord do all these things. [6]

God, Jesus and the Holy Ghost, were not shadowy figures in the "hearts and minds" of Billy's parents. If one sat down with them and asked what God looked like, they would offer an elaborate and fairly lucid description. God's likeness contained the human features seen in the fresco Michelangelo painted in the Sistine Chapel at the

---

[5] The first Christian to produce a collection of books that became the foundation for sacred text believed that the God of the Old Testament could not have possibly been the God of Jesus. There were two different Gods, the Jewish God who created the world and the God of Jesus who sent Jesus to save the world. See Bart D. Ehrman, *Misquoting Jesus. The Story Behind Who Changed the Bible and Why* (New York: Harper Collins Publ., 2005), 33-34.

[6] Isaiah 45:6-7. KJV.

Vatican:[7] He lies on his side in a loose clinging tunic, surrounded by angels. His face bristles with energy as He reaches out and nearly touches Adam's finger. He is a tall man with silver hair, a handsome face, penetrating eyes, large nostrils, and a white flowing beard. [8]

John and Inez, faithful students of the Bible and the Spirit of Prophecy, gathered with others on the Sabbath to worship God. (Of course, they had work to do around the farm, even on the Sabbath, and so they didn't worship all the time.) They viewed themselves as part of God's kinfolk. Rather than searching the Bible for loopholes or asking heretical questions, they looked for ways to be born of the Spirit: "That whosoever believeth in him should not perish but have everlasting life." [9] They believed the promise; "Thy kingdom come. Thy will be done in earth, as it is in heaven." [10] They felt as certain about arriving in heaven through the perfection of man's character as knowing that people get wet when they fall from a boat into the lake.

Salvation (the doctrine called soteriology) lay at the core of Adventist's doctrines, but judgement was always the preamble and a single neglect or heedless act could have dreadful effects:

The Judgment is passing. Today someone stands before God in their advocate; in another half hour their destiny is sealed. Yours may come next, and in a few moments your life, your fate, may hang suspended upon the brittle thread of a single decision, – the decision of the Universal Judge. [11]

Where did this pervasive idea of an investigative judgement before salvation come from? On what authority does it rest? Non-Adventist scholars can't find it in the Bible.

---

[7] Adam's Creation on the Sistene Chapel Ceiling by Michelangelo, https://en.wikipedia.org/wiki/File:'Adam's_Creation_Sistine_Chapel_ceiling'_by_Michelangelo_JBU33cut.jpg ; used by Creative Commons CC BY license: https://creativecommons.org/licenses/by/4.0/.

[8] Frank Meshberger, a medical student at Indianapolis School of Medicine, recognized an unmistakable mid-sagittal cross section of the human brain around the artistic elements of Michelangelo's God. See BBC home page for the website describing "the outline of the human brain in the *Creation of Adam.*" It was interpreted as the artist's pictorial declaration of his belief equating the divine gift of intellect with that of the soul.

[9] John 3:16. KJV.

[10] Matthew 6:10. KJV.

[11] *Review and Herald,* October 7, 1884, 640.

The Origin of the Investigative Judgment

It all began when Elon Everts, an acquaintance of James and Ellen White, wrote an unusual letter to the *Review and Herald*. His letter. Published on Jan. 1, 1857, this letter outlined some impressions of the Investigative Judgment in heaven: [12]

> *Dear Brethren: I am passing through a solemn train of thought. The question with me is: Where are we? I answer: More than twelve years past the proclamation "The hour of his Judgment is come." Rev. xiv, 6,7. ... My dear Brethren, from the scripture referred to I solemnly believe that the judgment has been going on in the Heavenly Sanctuary since 1844, and that upon the righteous dead, from "righteous Abel" down through patriarchs, prophets, martyrs, and all the saints who have fallen asleep in Jesus, judgment has been passing. How solemn the thought, that perhaps, our companions, our children, brother or sister, has been passing the great momentous review that will entitle them to a glorious immortal body at the coming of Christ.[13]*

James White took up the subject and enlarged the concept of "the Judgment."[14] By 1884, when Ellen White weighed in with the widely read *The Great Controversy*, the cleansing of the sanctuary through an investigative judgement had become a verity in the church teachings. This concept caused, and still causes, dread and consternation. Influential church leaders, scholars, and teachers hotly debated it because of the

---

[12] While living in Vermont, Ellen White visited Elon Everts and found him to be in the "age to come" movement, which he said he would not give up. Everts later confessed after a vision about the "age to come" showed that he was wrong. See Arthur L. White, *Ellen G. White: The Early Years* (Hagerstown, MD: Review & Herald, 1985), I, 223.

[13] Elon Everts, *Review and Herald*, Vol. 9, No. 9, Jan. 1, 1857.

[14] Arthur L. White, *Ellen G. White: The Early Years, 1827-1862* (Hagerstown, MD: Review & Herald, 1985), I, 354.

insecurity and uncertainty that it fosters.[15] Is it through sanctification, justification, or both that one gets to heaven? [16]

Around the time of Billy's death, many believers stressed obedience (legalism) in preparation for the judgment. Here is how it worked: An Adventist seeking salvation must acquire a "good record" through careful Sabbath keeping, avoidance of certain pleasures, a restricted diet, and total obedience to God's law. Respecting the do's and don'ts produced moral purification and a pass to heaven. Being kind to others might help also!

Fear and Dread of the Investigative Judgment

The whole strategy lacks a clear biblical basis and it places Christians under surveillance. It fosters fear, dread, and insecurity. Not taught in the New Testament, it found its way into Adventism through the writings of Ellen White and her husband. Assurance of salvation correlates with character perfection. But even then, people cannot be certain that their case will pass muster through the scrutiny of God's judgment. It was hard to know when complete perfection had developed. Achieving it was like observing a rainbow: As you walk toward the end of it, it moves further away and stays out of reach. The perfectionist pot of gold keeps moving away, always elusive. Ellen White added this further wrinkle: not one in twenty (five percent) on the church books would be saved. [17]

---

[15] Malcolm Bull and Keith Lockhart, *Seeking a Sanctuary* (San Francisco, CA: Harper & Row, Publishers, 1989), 82.

[16] Goeffrey J. Paxton, *The Shaking of Adventism* (Grand Rapids, MI: Baker Book House, 1977). See also Calvin W. Edwards and Gary Land, *Seeker After Light: A.F. Ballenger, Adventism, and American Christianity* (Berrien Springs, MI: Andrews Univ. Press., 2000).

[17] "It is a solemn statement that I make to the church, **that not one in twenty** whose names are registered upon the church books are prepared to close their earthly history and would be as verily without God and without hope in the world as the common sinner. They are professedly serving God, but they are more earnestly serving mammon. This half-and-half work is a constant denying of Christ, rather than a confessing of Christ. So many have brought into the church their own unsubdued (sic) spirit, unrefined; their spiritual taste is perverted by their own immoral, debasing corruptions, symbolizing the world in spirit, in heart, in purpose, confirming themselves in lustful practices, and are full of deception through and through in their professed Christian life. Living as sinners, claiming to be Christians!"

Young people who hold this view of perfection fear that their chance to be saved could be missed by a single clumsy lie or a secret sinful thought. Here is how it all sounded to an Adventist:

> *The judgment is now passing in the sanctuary above. For many years this work has been in progress. Soon—it will pass to the cases of the living. In the awful presence of God our lives are to come up in review.* [18]

Angels in the divine realm identify sins and record them in a "Book of Life." It conflicted children to think that their guardian angels not only protected them, but also monitored them. Requiring obedience to the Ten Commandments was one thing, but what about strictures not clearly included in the Decalog!

When Inez had seen Billy's casket, she knew that he didn't belong there. She wished for another way to think about the investigative judgment, a notion that turned over in her mind like a roast of lamb before the fire. Until the accident, the family had hoped to follow a clearly marked pathway, unbroken by death, that led from earth to heaven. They had every expectation of being "called up" (translated) at the Advent of Jesus.

Now they stood at the brink of the end with their certainty and security, as to their standing before God, deeply eroded. Was it possible that God had already processed and branded them? Was Billy sealed before he died? Had anyone in the family passed through probation? [19]

Anxious to make it into heaven, John and Inez devoted more time than ever to praying that they would be bound together in sympathy with God and his son Jesus, whom they hoped to know "as one might know a close and dear friend." They feared terrible delusions by Satan that brought "temptation to the very elect." They sought spiritual wisdom in the church's weekly paper, the *Review and Herald*; they purchased Ellen

---

Ellen G. White, *Christian Service,* 41. Sin acquires a new and real terror when this statement is taken at face value by an Adventist.

[18] Ellen G. White, *The Great Controversy,* 490.

[19] "We are now upon the very borders of the eternal world and stand in a more solemn relation to time and to eternity than ever before." Ellen G. White, *Adventist Home,* 549.

White's "Conflict of the Ages" series of books; and they studied *"Bible Readings for the Home"* and other Adventist publications. For one week each summer they attended the Adventist campmeeting in Jamestown where daily sermons addressed the Three Angel's message, health reform, end-time events, and other core teachings.

Ellen White Came Close to Seeing God

The shortfall on God's pedigree was something God didn't want mankind to feel. Hence Ellen White provided some details about heavenly rivers, trees, grasses, homes, streets, and other matters derived from visions. She claimed to have seen the Ten Commandments in the Ark taken from earth to heaven and now residing in the sanctuary. Compared with other Christian faiths, the close-knit Adventists seemed to have a great number of little details.

In visions Ellen White had been to heaven and talked to Jesus. On the way, she visited other planets occupied by sinless inhabitants. Such contentions ensured that lively heavenly images would embed themselves in the minds of believers. On a hundred or so different occasions Ellen White encountered and talked directly with Christ both here and in heaven. On one such occasion she nearly saw God. [20] But Jesus warned her not to look lest she die.

Heaven was not so far away. Sister White could go for a short visit and report back to the believers what they would see for themselves if they were faithful. The knowable attributes of God and his holy residence acquired living color.[21]

---

[20] "I saw a throne, and on it sat the Father and the Son. I gazed on Jesus' countenance and admired His lovely person. The Father's person I could not behold, for a cloud of glorious light covered Him. I asked Jesus if His Father had a form like Himself. He said He had, but I could not behold it, for said He, 'If you should once behold the glory of His person, you would cease to exist.'" Ellen G. White, *Early Writings*, 36.

[21] "Wings were given me, and an angel attended me from the city (New Jerusalem in heaven) to a place that was bright and glorious. The grass of the place was living green, and the birds there warbled a sweet song. The inhabitants of the place were of all sizes; they were noble, majestic, and lovely. They bore the express image of Jesus, and their countenances beamed with holy joy, expressive of the freedom and happiness of the place. I asked one of them why they were so much more lovely

One thing came out of the first experience of death in the closely-knit Willey family. It suggested that maybe God did not exist in the simplistic sense they held before, but rather amid the activities of the sanctuary. Jesus was the pathway to heaven city, and His death on the cross fulfilled an ancient promise to the Jews and now to them as Christians. Why it was necessary for Jesus to die for man's sins was not so clear. [22]

For weeks after the tragedy John held Inez while she cried herself to sleep at night. Then he'd get up and ponder what to do about the tragedy. Eventually the two crept back to regular living. John accepted the powerful reality that he would never again drive his hayrack by the house and whistle for Billy to come with him to get the cows in the pasture or pick up a load of hay. That joy was gone, gone forever.

John tried to be courageous. He didn't talk much about the tragedy, but let it quietly cast about in his thoughts as he worked on the farm. One Sabbath he decided to share some concerns with the preacher. He drew the minister aside and told him that maybe Billy had been the lucky one: "He certainly never lengthened his time on the earth before he drew out his ultimate destiny." Then he quoted Shakespeare: "He that cuts off twenty years of life cuts off so many years of fearing death." He waited for the preacher to react.

---

than those on the earth. The reply was, 'We have lived in strict obedience to the commandments of God, and have not fallen by disobedience, like those on the earth'...Then I was taken to a world which had seven moons. There I saw good old Enoch, who had been translated...I asked him if this was the place he was taken to from the earth. He said, 'It is not; the city is my home, and I have come to visit this place.' He moved about the place as if perfectly at home. I begged of my attending angel to let me remain in that place. I could not bear the thought of coming back to this dark world again. Then the angel said, 'You must go back, and if you are faithful, you, with the 144,000, shall have the privilege of visiting all the worlds and viewing the handiwork of God.'" Ellen G. White, *Early Writings*, 26.

[22] "If there truly is only one god and if that one god is the God of Israel, then everybody has Israel's God whether Israel likes it or not, and Israel as a result has to deal somehow with everybody." Jack Miles, *Christ. A Crisis in the Life of God* (London: William Heinemann, 2001), 219.

Is the Second Coming Existential or Historical?

When there was no response, he asked the preacher whether the Adventist phrase "the Advent is soon" was existential or historical. But when John moved to this deeper level of questioning, he could see his spiritual guide was not prepared to comment.

The preacher really knew little about the abrupt ending of a person and the soul's journey, if any, afterwards. This surprised John. He thought ministers knew how to explain the human soul and how the body and soul unite at the Second Coming.

John believed that the righteous dead would rise from the ground and become glorified at the Lord's return. But it was hard for John to believe that Billy "totally" ceased to exist and that his restless spirit returned to decomposed dust along with the body. Did Billy's spirit fly away as the spark of life went out, or did his spirit quietly flicker out like a wick in an empty lamp? It was precisely this idea about the human soul that perplexed him. Was the soul aloof or plugged into the body's economy? Did it sit in the brain like a king on a throne? Did the bullet destroy or damage Billy's soul? Was all this fevered imagination about the human soul due to a fear that the doctrine of immortality might not be true? The Bible itself seemed to be unclear or even confusing on this point, and John could never quite accept that the words of Ellen White were equal in importance to the Bible.

So next John tried quoting a passage in Jude where Michael, the archangel, disputed with the devil over the body of Moses. The pastor was impressed that John was reading his Bible. From the Bible, it seemed clear to John that man was not immortal by his nature, but that death might be conquered, nonetheless. What was Jude talking about in these Scriptures? Did the soul depart from the body so that Michael and Satan could continue a property dispute over Moses' body? Was the soul part or separate from the body as this text implied? Which did the devil contend with; the soul or the body? John's skepticism that Sabbath with the Minot minister didn't produce any satisfying result.

FARMLAND BASEBALL
CHAPTER SEVENTEEN

"They were the `world' and we were the `remnant.' They smoked, drank, and played cards. We were vegetarian, observed Sabbath on Saturday, and played Five in a Row. Our worlds did not intersect except where necessary. We had to shop with them, wait in the dentist's office with them, and jostle with them at the Field Museum. Otherwise we spent our time with other members of our little group." Gary Land, editor, *Growing Up with Baseball* (Lincoln, NE: University of Nebraska Press, 2004), 44.

According to the 1928 Yearbook of Agriculture published by the United States Department of Agriculture, wheat exports declined by six percent compared to the previous year. Related problems for wheat growers were many. The price of wheat declined by 23 per cent compared to the previous year. From the postwar boom in 1919-20 forward, prosperity on the farm declined steadily. Unfortunately, land values also declined — land being the ultimate source of a farmer's wealth. Meanwhile, young people left the farms and migrated to urban areas, partly because tractors reduced the need for workers. Other forces also contributed to the changes on the farm, including cheaper cars and trucks, better roads, cooperative organizations handling surpluses, and local banking difficulties.

The distribution of men, women, and children on the farm was often thought of as predictable and certain, but this was not the case. Changing human numbers were less known than land values, field crops, commodity prices, and the price of livestock, but by 1928 the public noticed the rapidly decreasing farm population. The net loss across the country from 1925 to 1928 was estimated at 400,000 persons per year.

America had just laughed its way through the "monkey trial" in Dayton, Ohio, where thirty years before in the same judge's chambers, Adventists had been tried and imprisoned for Sunday labor. [1] In the

---

[1] *Review and Herald*, August 13, 1925, 2.

"monkey trial" John Scopes was charged with denying Biblical creation and thereby breaking Tennessee law. Some thought that the fundamentalists had abandoned the teaching of virtue and instead were hunting "scientific witches" teaching evolution. The religious press asserted that evolutionists were destroying the orthodox faith of the youth.

Following the account in the newspapers, Tom learned about modern evolutionary biology, but he didn't become a crusader for Darwin or long-term geology. According to the *Review* the truth of the last days was revealed during the trial when Scopes' defense lawyers tried to harmonize the Bible and "this theory of evolution." Clarence Darrow, the noted agnostic lawyer from Chicago and the main defense for Scopes, wanted the judge to order that signs in Dayton saying "Read Your Bible" should be taken down. The public felt the newspapers seemed to be propagandists for the theory of evolution. In the end, the defense for Scopes lost the case, but this was no time for creationists to rejoice about deliverance from evolution.

Tom graduated from Mohall High School in 1928 with marks of 90 or above in three subjects and a place on the honor roll.[2] He devoted his senior year to learning more about agriculture and accounting practices in farming. In 1929 left the farm for Union College in Lincoln, Nebraska.

After his graduation, Inez gave him an expensive Elgin Watch. To pledge his affection to his high school girlfriend, Clare, and affirm that they were "going steady," Tom gave her the watch. When Inez discovered this, she went to Clare's home and insisted that she return the watch!

When Tom was ten years old, his grandfather Wm had given him the book *"Pitching in a Pinch"* by Christy Mathewson, the famous baseball pitcher.[3] Tom prized the book and read it several times. He fantasized about being a baseball player someday and catching for a pitcher like "Matty."

"Matty" played for the New York Giants and by 1911 had become the greatest right-handed pitcher of the day. He carried his parents' values to the ball field, refusing to gamble, booze, womanize, or pitch on Sundays. He maintained high ideals throughout his life.

---

[2] Renville Country Newspaper, February 2, 1928.
[3] Christy Mathewson, *Catcher Craig* (New York: Grosset & Dunlap, 1915).

While Tom still cherished "Matty's" book, his mother encouraged him to become a minister. Conditions for farming did not look positive. So Tom went off to college in 1929, but returned after his first year and settled into farming. He'd been an average student except for a "D" in Rhetoric both semesters. Working his way through college by milking cows affected his grades.

Upon returning to the farm in 1930, Tom picked up a catcher's glove and began catching for the local Mohall Athletics baseball team. He entered a playing field of baseball bats, masks, protectors, and hospitable players, umpires, and local fans. The team disbanded at the end of the summer and resumed after planting the crops.

By the 1931 baseball season, Tom had come to terms with Billy's death. The terms were more practical than religious. He stopped dwelling on God's judgment or thoughts about Billy rising from the dead at the Second Coming (though, of course, it did matter whether he'd see his brother again in the New Jerusalem). Trying to get over the accident, he didn't want to think or talk about it anymore. He put the whole affair behind him in the same way a person does who was just about to go over Niagara Falls in a barrel and found no benefit from looking up the river behind him. Besides he didn't want to please the devil by constantly tormenting himself. Feeling sorry about something he couldn't change was madness; if not properly tucked away, it could turn into lunacy. It didn't help to cradle the guilt in his brain and turn it over and over like a roast pig over the fire.

When people whispered or stopped talking in his presence, it seemed they were talking about him and the accident, but perhaps not. He found himself trying to mask his suspicions with belligerent posturing. His girlfriend Clara helped him get past this phase. She told him he'd have to learn to strap his suspicions to his back, go on, and stop worrying about what other people thought. "Get on with your life. You have so much promise." That was pretty much what sister Marjorie said also.

During the first few months of that summer, John spent more time with him, and they shared their grief in unspoken ways. Tom surmised that some remnants of guilt must have landed on his father. His dad said as much, when they were talking in the haymow just after the accident.

Together they repaired the barbwire fences on the east side of the pasture, and then they built a new sheep shed near the barn to protect the animals from the winter snow. John showed him how to set up a shotgun trap for the coyotes that crawled under the fences and killed the lambs.

While talking one day, Tom became apprehensive when his father suggested that he return to college and resume his education. He never said anything like that to George. At this point, Tom owned a quarter section of land and was just beginning to farm on his own. His brother also owned a quarter section. The two helped each other and more-or-less treated the half section of land between them in joint ownership. Knowing that it pleased his dad that his two older boys were starting to farm together, Tom assumed that the college ideas must be coming from his mother, perhaps because she sought atonement for Billy's death.

Tom felt that if his mother had something to say about the topic, she'd probably bring it up to his father and that he'd hear about it from him in a subtle and tactful way. He'd known other times when his mother spoke through his father. He and George had taken a government loan for seed and he did not intend to douse his hopes to become a farmer by going off to college. By now he was working with his own team, Jim and Tipsy. But little did he know that powerful forces of nature would soon make him return to college: farming was in distress because of the failure of adequate moisture,

Tom always imagined himself living on a farm near the place of his birth. Tom found security from such a place. For him "civilization" was only as big as the county where he lived, maybe as far as the county line and village, and it spread out over the land where each homesteader had taken out a claim, and across the small rural towns where the necessities could be purchased. No one ever found diamonds or gold where they lived, but he knew how to drive a straight plow line, milk a cow, pitch hay in the summer, tend the livestock, hunt ducks in the fall, clean the barn of manure, thresh grain, and hitch the horses! A farmer didn't need rhetoric or mathematics beyond high school geometry. Doing heavy work and getting dusty from the field were honorable pursuits. He wasn't a poet or a musician, nor had he any other way of making a living like being a schoolteacher or lawyer. For the time being he would put aside his father's query about the future and go back to planting and haying and all of the things a farmer does to make a living.

At breakfast one morning John announced that henceforth there would be no farm work on Sundays except for morning and evening chores and the harvest. It sounded like tolerance for another day of worship, and a pagan day at that!

Tom laughed about this with George. It was as if his father had created another religious holiday without any priestly authority. This puzzled Tom and George because they knew how their father esteemed the Saturday Sabbath and how opposed worship on the Pope's day. But his father explained himself: "Sundays would be elevated to baseball or other leisure's such as fishing, pheasant hunting, or just visiting friends and neighbors." And taking Sundays off would reduce the neighbor's complaint, stimulated by working in the field on Sunday, that the Willey's weren't religious. Moreover, John liked the magical grip that baseball had on both Tom and George. Sports was in their blood, although Tom was the more athletic of the two.

When the Harlem Globetrotters came to town, owner Abe Saperstein met Tom in the hallway of the high school and tossed him a basketball. Then Saperstein went down the hall and told Tom he could play on the all-star team against the Globetrotters if he could dribble past him. Tom began dribbling the ball back and forth and moving closer to Saperstein who kept backing up. Then he suddenly sprang past Saperstein, looping the ball behind his back and over Saperstein's head.

Long after the game that ensued, the town people told how Bernie Price, a black Globetrotter, had lured Tom into a corner of the court and spun him around like a top, while Tom belligerently tried to take the ball away. Price didn't mean any harm; he just saw an opportunity to take a young gung-ho basketball player and show him a thing or two about dribbling the basketball.

When it came to baseball, Johnny Mach, the high school coach, thought Tom had the makings of a professional player. But an Adventist couldn't play ball on Saturdays. Besides, Adventists didn't countenance about competitive sports: amusements like baseball, basketball and cricket were the devil's domain. [4] Other religious groups also felt that baseball clubs that played on Sunday were "organized bands of criminals stalking over the country, breaking the laws of the land." [5] It wasn't just Adventists: many churches that Satan used these diversions to lead men away from God.

Small-town baseball played a big role in society. Nearly every town had a team and people took pride in their teams, whether deserved or not. The fans needed the diversion of intense rivalry. The sport was conducted in a "semiprofessional manner" in larger towns such as Fargo, Minot, Bismarck, Grand Forks, York, and Jamestown.

Unlike the major leagues, blacks played in these Midwest baseball teams. One of the most talked about baseball teams came from Bismarck. In the summer of 1935, the city of Bismarck entered the National Semiprofessional Baseball Tournament at Wichita, Kansas. Among the "baseball blacks" on the Bismarck team were Satchel Paige, Hilton Smith, Chet Brewer, and Quincy Trouppe. Bismarck took first place and the team brought back ten thousand dollars in prize money, plus a bumper crop of joy and pride that spread through the whole town. [6]

Further north in Mohall there were no "baseball blacks," but the players knew about Satchel Paige, referring to him as "Fire Ball Ace." Paige delighted fans because of his entertainment behind the mound. He would field the ball, bend over, dry his hands on a rosin bag, and then fire a bullet to first base to catch a runner by an eyelash. Paige had a "hesitation pitch," a pitch where he would stop mid-delivery for a split second, then finish his windup and throw the batter off balance. Paige might even tell the fans,

---

[4] "Satan is delighted when he sees human beings using their physical and mental powers in that which does not educate, which is not useful, which does not help them to be a blessing to those who need their help. While the youth are becoming expert in games that are of no real value to themselves or to others, Satan is playing the game of life for their souls. taking from them the talents that God has given them and placing in their stead his own evil attributes. It is his effort to lead men to ignore God. He seeks to engross and absorb the mind so completely that God will find no place in the thoughts." Ellen G. White, *Messages to Young People* (Southern Press), 213. "Examples to the Church," *Review and Herald,* January 2, 1936.

[5] *Advent Review and Sabbath Herald,* December 17, 1889.

[6] William C. Sherman ed., *Plains Folk. North Dakota's Ethnic History* (Fargo, ND: North Dakota Institute for Regional Studies, North Dakota State Univ., 1988), 387.

"they will get no mo' runs" and then he would settle down and use every trick in the book. When he visited North Dakota, he was advertised as the "fastest pitcher ever seen." The crowd went wild when he appeared.

During the week, "Sunday athletic" farmers stacked hay and developed muscles as hard as fence posts. Then, with the arrival of the baseball season, players demonstrated their prowess, showing how far they could hit the baseball or how fast they could run the bases. If you could hit and field the ball well, nationality, social class, and intelligence did not matter.

Small towns in North Dakota romanticized baseball as something that improved a person's character and united the community. There was some truth to this: the games fostered justice, courage, strength, fair play, equality, and friendship. They were played like spiritual warfare with the forces of evil. Teams didn't put on the armor of God or possess sacred relics, but "Holy zeal" was definitely their forte.

Unlike the rules in religion, baseball was simple to play. It only took was a diamond-shaped field in a small pasture, a fence backstop, a couple of bats, gloves, and nine players to a team. One team battled the other with each player hoping to bring glory to the team or to their own name with a home run or an outstanding catch or a sweeping pitch to strike out the batter. Baseball spawned short-term heroes and a few outstanding players.

Sunday Blue Laws still existed in many states, including North Dakota. Some towns strictly enforced them. When a "law and order league" in Nebraska City, Nebraska, swore a warrant for the arrest of the two teams breaking the Sunday laws, an angry crowd followed the players taken by the sheriff to the justice's office. A riot followed. (The day before, the citizens had by "practically a unanimous vote" declared in favor of Sunday ball.) Thereafter enforcement became irregular and Sunday baseball was accommodated with the proviso that games be played between two and six in the afternoon.[7] Precisely at six, games would end and the score would revert to the last full inning. No one cared if players were Catholic, Methodist, Baptist, or agnostic; or whether they farmed, worked at the blacksmith shop, or drove a truck hauling freight. One preacher exclaimed over the lack of prejudice between the players and teams and saw the baseball diamond as a "church" for spiritual growth. Baseball fostered small town core values and community spirit. During the depression,

---

[7] *Advent Review and Sabbath Herald,* July 29, 1902.

baseball helped turn people's thoughts away from drought, insect plagues, falling farm prices, dust storms, and foreclosures.

The 1931 baseball season lifted Tom's spirits from the misery of farming. The heat lasted so long that the world seemed on fire. Wind and dust compounded the hardships. People yearned for better times; they wanted relief from sheriffs and deputies trying to collect on loan payments and mortgages. Baseball was the antidote.

Tom admitted that playing baseball that summer helped him "get over" Billy's death. One might even say that baseball was his weekly redemption. He played with the immodest ambition of walking down Main Street in Mohall and hearing people say, "There goes the greatest ball player who ever played for Mohall." Tom could rise up from behind home plate and throw out a runner trying to steal second base before the runner began his slide. That brought pure thrill to him. Fearing Tom's arm, opposing first base coaches warned their runners not to lead off too far.

In the first game of the 1931 season, Tom hit a home run with the bases loaded to help Mohall win the game 17 to 8. By the end of that summer Tom batted just over .350 to lead the team in hitting. He batted eighty times with twenty-eight hits and five homers.

There had been very little grain for the past two years. In 1932 the *Renville County Farmer* reported, "It's the wind that has caused most of the damage and the same movement disclosed the new 'crop' namely arrowheads, relics of the Indian man. The wind has torn at the topsoil with such enthusiasm (sic) that, in spots it is down to 'hard pan,' bedrock or something equally as hard and cheerless." [8]

The Catholic priest, Father J. Heinz of Mohall, umpired behind home plate for the Mohall games. The players liked Father Heinz — he was a genial and fair person, with a wonderful sense of humor. With a "Holy Father" making the calls there were fewer arguments and much less yelling from the fans to "kill the umpire!" Father Heinz was clearly in charge. It was futile to challenge his decisions.

During these hard times the Catholics couldn't contribute much to their church. Father Heinz suggested raising pigs and selling them for gain. By the first of May, Father Heinz had one hundred and fourteen pigs under

---

[8] *Renville County Farmer*, August 18, 1932.

the Lord's "manufacture" and over one hundred acres of flax for the fall harvest. This harvest was a considerable contribution to his church

A special, unspoken bond developed between Tom and the priest. Father Heinz knew about Billy's accident but never uttered a word of criticism or advice to Tom. He was equally kind to the other players and continually talked up the "spirit" of the team. Although very conscientious about umpiring, the priest made no mention about the swearing and drinking at the edge of the field, apparently believing in some kind of separation of church and baseball. Before a game Father Heinz would grab a glove and ask Tom to catch for him at the plate. He began throwing the ball from the pitcher's mound. Then he'd walk down off the mound a few feet closer to home plate and throw more pitches. Soon he'd be about thirty feet away throwing as hard as he could. By this technique he improved Tom's reflexes and taught him to sharpen his movements and stand without fear behind the plate.

Father Heinz' lessons went beyond the game of baseball. He gave Tom psychological sustenance too. One Sunday he said there were just as many seams on a baseball as beads on a rosary which, he added, should "give you strength to play as hard as if you were praying for grace and salvation." These brief conversations didn't last long, and Heinz never urged Tom to join one of the larger denominations such Baptists, Methodists or Catholics. He knew little about Adventism, just the rumors that it was a cult. And frankly Tom did not let his light shine, something Adventists were admonished to do. The high point in Tom's relationship with the priest occurred when he asked Father Heinz near the end of the summer if he could visit him in his church and afterward go down to the basement with him. "What for, Tom?" asked the priest. Tom was too reluctant to say.

Here was Tom Willey, the Seventh-day Adventist, admiring a Catholic priest and putting aside his presuppositions about Catholics as the "antichrist," apostate Christians lead the persecution of the Sabbath-keeping Adventists at the time of the end. And the Adventist and the Catholic got along as righteous people were supposed to. One day Tom mentioned the Protestant belief about torture chambers in the basement of Catholic churches. Father Heinz told Tom to come and see for himself. In the church basement they found a furnace that hadn't worked for several years, some abandoned coal, and a few old chairs!

Despite being illegal, moonshine liquor showed up behind the backstop at these games. Called "mood softener," it was brought across the border from Canada or provided by a brave farmer who made liquor in his barn or under his house. If the sheriff lurked, it had to be hidden from view or made to look like lemonade. Tom and George, who never drank, knew that Prohibition was in full swing in North Dakota and that possessing beer or liquor could land a person in jail.

This is what happened to Miles See, who lived south of Mohall on the Stevens farm. Snagged as a "liquor manufacturer" by the Federal Prohibition officer, he was sentenced to six months in jail, plus fines. His bondsmen got cold feet and he stayed in "jail longer than necessary." Leona See, Miles wife, once held the sheriff at gun point in the farmyard giving Miles time to destroy the majority of his liquor in the basement. The trouble was that the liquor only slowly evaporated and sank into the ground. [9]

Tom remembered something about humanity that had to do with skin color. Iver Johnson, a local Mohall fan, scheduled a leading Negro team called the "Ghosts" to play an all-star team comprised of Sherwood and Mohall players. The newspaper advertised the event as "the best game of the season." But the "Ghosts" arrived so late in the afternoon that the six o'clock rule precluded much of a game — to the great disappointment of the crowd.

By the end of the summer of '30 other things were driving away the thoughts of Billy's death. Old timers still talk about the Great Depression when times were unbearable for people everywhere. Farming changed fundamentally, particularly in the manner of controlling soil erosion.

Reverend Gene Aal from the Zion Lutheran Church in Mohall admonished his congregation to boycott Sunday baseball games: "Afternoon Sunday baseball interfered with the observance of the Sabbath." Devotion to the game indeed took on the form of a religious practice.

Lutherans and other denominations believed that God wanted everyone to honor a day called the Sabbath. This was all that the pastor was trying to tell his people. What complicated matters was the liberal Protestant redefinition of "Sabbath worship" to include baseball as "divine living."

---

[9] Ibid. February 23, 1933.

THE DEPRESSION & END OF TIME
CHAPTER EIGHTEEN

> "In 1932, the United States, with its diversity of needs, according to its own locality and hazards, had reached its darkest hour where this representative government had come to a standstill cannot be viewed and appraised in forty years of hindsight, and we can see with some clarity that the machinery needed change for the necessity of its growth and expansion, rather than failure of man. However, the people never noted for kindness to our public servants were in an angry and bewildered mood." Blanche Hembree, *Fate, Destiny, Necessity on Renville's Prairies* (Self-published, 1977), 248.

During the summer of 1931, the crops in Renville County completely failed for lack of rain. By the middle of June, the local newspaper, *The Renville County Farmer Press,* was ready to throw in the towel;

For weeks we tried to say as little about the weather as possible, believing that the less said about it the better for all concerned. But at last the point has been reached when we may as well admit that after three days of the hottest dust storm possible, the damage to the crop is irreparable.

There has been no rain in this territory this spring and so little snow last winter that the grain could not make a fair start. Every week it has been 'If it will only rain this week, we might get a little from our seed.' But still it did not rain and now the common opinion is that only by an act of God could any crop return be made, or the livestock saved from death by hunger and thirst...It is truly enough to bring everyone in this section of the state to their knees imploring an answer as to what to do next.

That was exactly what the farmers did. The Catholic, Methodist, Lutheran and Nazarene congregations in Mohall met in their respective churches on June 17, 1931, to pray for rain. Special prayers entreated the Lord, "to turn the minds of the people to God in their extreme need of rain for both crops and livestock." Father Heinz said later, "There was better attendance than usual tho (sic) people are always regular in attendance." The congregation at the Methodist Church almost tripled in size when it met to invoke the power of prayer. Every business in Mohall closed during the services.[1] People manifested an instinctive, superstitious attitude about nature. When the water table in Mohall kept falling, some began to think about the end of time.

Then, low and behold, it rained! Maybe God was paying attention to the needs of these hapless, crop-less farmers after all! But winds came up and sucked the precious, God-given moisture back into the clouds. Did some rejoice too loudly? Did some not give God His due? The winds blew so hard that fishermen on Lake Metigoshe gave up and went home. Dust descended like an Egyptian plague.

The Farmer's Press stated that "the little moisture probably has helped some, but it has not been of sufficient quantity to warrant putting in any feeds of any kind which the people desire to do." The Mohall High School football squad of thirty-six boys took their sponge bath in one tub of water.

The county commissioners gathered to consider what, if anything, they could do about the drought, but they quickly adjourned, admitting they were at a "loss as to how to solve the questions." An old timer told of worse conditions in the past, but this brought no solace. And, as expected, the City of Mohall called off the Fourth of July celebration.

Tom's brother, George, and the next-door neighbor, Bruce Carlson, became "hobos" and took to the railroads in their search for work. Maybe there were threshing "rings" elsewhere in the state or in South Dakota.

Riding the railroads could be dangerous. In the summer of '31 a posse removed nine African-American boys from the railroad on trumped up charges of assaulting two white female transients. The boys were tied together with a plow rope and taken to jail in the county seat of Scottsboro, Alabama. The court handed down death sentences to all but one. One of the defendants described the courtroom as "one big smiling white face."

That same summer, Mohall experienced an interracial confrontation. "Sheriff H. R. Gieselman was asked by the Ward County sheriff in Minot to arrest Wm. Bryans, a Negro, should he make appearance in Renville County. Bryans was found, arrested, and held in Mohall for a few hours until the Ward county sheriff came and took him back to Minot. The white woman he was traveling with was allowed to go. The newspaper said the "charge will be either the White Mann Act or the adultery charge." The Mann Act (a federal law) outlawed interracial marriages in America.

---

[1] *Renville County Farmers Press,* June 18, 1931.

When arrested, Bryans was only twenty miles from freedom and sanctuary in Canada.

George and the neighbor boy Bruce, the two "hobos", found work at seventy-five cents per day during haying and as much as a dollar a day during harvest in the southeastern part of the state. On one farm, they went to work for a German immigrate farmer, but found him too demanding. Life wasn't what they had expected, and so they returned home.

The hot sun, wind and dust lasted the entire summer of '31. On some days, the thermometer rose to a sizzling 115 to 120 degrees. The land was barren and parched, denuded and thick with dust. The only standing grass was on the margins of the sloughs. Some farmers said "Migratory birds flying south better bring their own provisions with them as there is nothing to eat on the ground here in North Dakota."

One of John's neighbors owned a herd of sixty Holstein cows, his "pride and joy." One day he and his wife picked out the best ones and herded the rest to the corner of the pasture. The cows stared at him, not supposing what he was about to do. Then the neighbor laid his rifle across the side of the wagon and began shooting —with tears running down his face. The sickly cows dropped like a rock when shot. His eight-year old son called this "the first time he'd ever seen his father cry."

Day after day John looked to the sky for clouds and rain; mornings and evenings he pled with God to consider his family's needs. Instead of a garden next to the house, they planted potatoes and other vegetables on the edge of the slough near the barn. Then came the grasshoppers to voraciously devour the remaining vegetation. They darkened the sun, swirling to earth in a surging, pelting, devastating storm, and disgustingly spitting out their "tobacco juice." After feasting, and in anticipation of another dry year, they laid mounds of eggs. Then, they flew off, looking for more vegetation to conquer.

The next year, the earth became a moving carpet. Across the dry and seared ground came the army worms, marching from south to north. They gave no warning of their coming, unlike the jaunty grasshoppers. Noiselessly, they occupied the housetops, trees, fence posts, fields, and highways. Cars and horses ground many into a slimy mass, but their numbers were such that the loss of a few million gave them no reason to pause.

To meet these insect challenges, Tom and his father constructed a two-foot fence of chicken wire around the garden and staked the chickens on the inside perimeter to eat the oncoming grasshoppers and worms. Fortunately, the hens, nourished by the grasshoppers and army worms, continued to lay eggs. Tom told his father he was amazed that chickens could eat nothing but inserts and still lay decent eating eggs! The family sold some of these eggs at the grocery store in Lorraine.

A church pastor with strong fundamentalist leanings suggesting ringing the church bell every day at noon to awaken God. But church members feared that this would let the Devil himself know how bad things really were; he'd bring in his collaborators and make things worse. Just the same, it seemed reasonable to ask whether this was the time spoken of in the Bible when men's hearts would "fail them for fear and for looking after those things which are coming on the earth?" The US Secretary of Agriculture Henry A. Wallace came close to saying as much: "The millennium is not yet here although the makings of it are clearly in our hands." [2] People attending church no longer prayed for the cure of an alcoholic spouse, or for firewood, or even a job; they prayed for food, clean water, and life itself.

When the county property taxes came due in October, John owed $45.17 for his half section of land and couldn't come up with the money to make the payment. The newspaper listed nearly every farmer in the county in the same straits. The common problem was the lack of rain and the dry winds, conditions over which no one had control. Few people east of the Mississippi River understood or even cared about what was happening out on the Plains. Without wheat and other crops, the whole nation was in jeopardy.

The Better Farming Association hired graduates of agriculture schools to visit farmers throughout the state and urge them to diversify their crops. But farmers didn't take kindly to well-dressed kids financed by

---

[2] John C. Culver and John Hyde, *American Dreamer: The Life and Times of Henry A. Wallace* (New York: W.W. Norton & Co., 2001), 129.

businesses, banks, and railroads trying to show them how to farm without first walking the dry furrows with them.

Unrest spread and deepened. Farmers faced shrewd operators and business people who understood markets better than they did. A study of the Minnesota Grain Exchange where farmers sold their grain revealed that farmers were being cheated in a number of ways along the shadowy causeway of economic transactions. It was not only the state Banker's Association that found this; the federal Interstate Commerce Commission concurred.

North Dakota farmers benefited from the high demand for their wheat, mutton and beef during World War I, being the largest producers of hard red wheat and supplying many livestock as well. The price of wheat rose to nearly three dollars a bushel. Farmers used their prosperity to plow marginal land into production, purchase new farm machinery, and buy cars. The end of the war seemed to promise a bright future. New strains of wheat were developed to increase production and the value of land increased. Steam engines and easy credit began arriving on the farms around 1920. But then, the price of wheat and livestock began a downward slide.

Depression set in very soon after the war of 1914-1917. Foreign grain and livestock markets contracted as unity of purpose and hopes for a better world buckled on the world scene. Prosperity for North Dakota farmers declined around 1921 and wheat prices stayed below a dollar per bushel for the next twenty years. Hence when the stock market collapsed in 1929, North Dakota farmers were already suffering mightily. Things only got worse. No other felt the depths of the depression like North Dakota, or for so long.

When deflation and land values, grain production, and commodity prices fell, heavy indebtedness left the banks holding the bag. Bank closures hit North Dakota in the '30s. About 573 of the 898 institutions collapsed. Fifty million dollars of hard-working depositor's money evaporated. Before this, a North Dakota farmer could pay off a $5,000 mortgage with 3,300 bushels of wheat; a decade later, when grain prices were slack, it took 16,600 bushels of wheat to buy down the same debt. But by then, of course, the drought had withered the crops and the little available money went to essentials like food and gasoline. In a word, the "Dirty Thirties" hammered down hard on the North Dakota farmers.

When times were good farmers and bankers had not stopped to think that wealth was based on a single-crop economy and that the boom and bust cycles were influenced by many factors outside the control of the producers of the wealth on a farm.

The Odlands faced a foreclosure from the bank just as the children celebrated their parent's fiftieth wedding anniversary. All nine children, including John and Inez, arrived at the old homestead in Norma, North Dakota, for the occasion. But there must have been too much excitement for Inez's father; Thomas Odland died suddenly at age seventy-two from a heart attack. Instead of eating cake, toasting, and sharing joy, the family solemnly buried Thomas Odland at the Rosehill Cemetery near the family's homestead.

Tom Odland, along with his son Thomas, farmed a half section of land, each quarter of which was under a mortgage held by American Life Insurance and the nearby Norma State Bank. By 1922 Inez's oldest brother Jake had made a name for himself in banking at the Norma State Bank. Fiercely determined to leave his mark, he called in the Odland note held by his bank, and with a sheriff's lien, Jake foreclosed on his own mother, who held the property after her husband died. Next, the American Life Insurance company did the same and called in its note on her son Thomas! The farm and two quarters were sold at auction.

With nowhere else to live, Isabel Odland came to live with her daughter Inez in the Willey farmhouse, where she spent the last fourteen years of her life. She talked to God about her son who had foreclosed on his own mother and brother. How could he do something so atrocious? For comfort, she read the Psalm: *"It is God that girdeth me with strength, and maketh my way perfect."* [3] She implored Jesus to recommend her to the Father so that she could occupy a mansion in heaven. "This Great Hope" was all she had. She died of liver cancer after a long illness. Her last request was to see her sons again, but both lived too far away to reach her in time. Inez resented what her brother Jake did to her mother, and never again spoke to him.

The *Renville County Farmers Press* reported the good news that "A Newark, N. J., insurance company announced the suspension of all foreclosures on owner-occupied farm lands in the United States and Canada. The action was effective immediately and it involved 37,000 farms and an investment of $200,000,000, or one tenth of the resources

---

[3] Psalms 18:32. KJV.

of the company. An association of life insurance presidents, representing more than 91 per cent of the nation's life insurance companies, reported that farm mortgages held by those companies at the end of 1932 was estimated at approximately $1,666,000,000." It had been a policy of some of the insurance companies in this territory during the past two years not to foreclose if the farmer remained on the land and attempted to take care of his land. (One of the real reasons for this policy was that, after foreclosure, insurance companies ended up owning land without operators, which caused the land to depreciate further and become non-productive.)

Life began to ease up on the foreclosure scene when debt holders looked kindlier on foreclosures.

Then later the *Renville County Farmers Press* announced to it readers that, "With an aim of speeding up recovery in the Northwestern drought area, the American Red Cross will furnish individual collections of garden seed to all its beneficiaries in Montana, North Dakota, South Dakota and Nebraska, who are unable to secure seed from any other source." Others from the east were shipping boxcars of clothing, hay, and grains to the people of Northwestern North Dakota. Obviously, things had gotten so bad that help was needed from afar.

Preoccupied with The Three Angels messages, John and Inez decided to sponsor a religious campaign in Mohall. They could point to economic events that ostensibly foretold the end of time and the soon coming. A minister of the Seventh-day Advent church in Jamestown conducted a series of evangelistic meetings in the community church for an entire week. The presentations covered biblical prophecies about the end-time. Tom remembered the kindly priest who umpired the baseball games and asked the evangelist not to say anything negative about Catholics. According to the newspaper, "The services are being well attended," [4] but the minister didn't convert or baptize anyone. Many years later, Inez lamented that after 50 years on the farm she had not "brought one soul to the altar." (In her parochial mind, only Adventist converts, that is, converts to the one true church, counted as "souls brought to the altar." Adventists did not even have a church building of their own.

In March 1933, while thirty people milled around a homestead in Renville County that was to be auctioned off, a farmer came up to State's

---

[4] *Renville County Farmer Press,* November 2, 1932.

Attorney Sorenson and Sheriff Gieselman of Mohall and said: "I am a good Christian and believe in God and the laws of the United States just as far as it is possible to support them, but we believe sincerely that some adjustments must be made to save our farms, homes, and farm equipment." Hearing this sincere speech, but noticing that many farmers were brandishing guns, the sheriff called off the sale to let things cool down.

By 1933 foreclosures were averaging sixty-two per thousand farms in the Great Plains, almost double the national average. Nearly seven thousand Dakota farmers were forced off the land every year during the depression. The drought on the Willey farm extended from 1931 until rains finally came and relieved the parched soils in October 1940. [5] The 1933 state legislative session passed a law that gave farmers two years' grace to redeem their property.

President Roosevelt and the New Deal legislation of the Congress began relief and rehabilitation programs to get farmers back on their feet. Slowly the effects of these programs were felt. A program, that began as The Resettlement Administration later became the Farm Security Administration. Meanwhile, farmers organized themselves into cooperatives, constructed credit systems, established market controls, and diversified income and production. A way out of endless despair seemed at hand.

Officials asked farmers around Mohall to voluntarily cut their wheat acreage to encourage higher prices. The local newspaper reported that Renville county totals for 1933 would be allotted 881,276 bushels. Under this price control, John Willey reported in 1930 that he farmed 220 acres and produced 2,228 bu. In 1931 he seeded 210 acres that produced no bushels, and in 1932 he seeded 210 acres that produced 600 bushels. His allotment by the Wheat Production Control Board for the three-year average would allow 210 acres to be planted and he would be reduced to producing 913 bushels. Unfortunately, the voluntary acreage reduction had little effect on farm income, because Russia flooded world markets with cheap wheat. [6]

The depression finally dashed Tom's farming dreams and he returned to

---

[5] Michael Johnston Grant, *Down and Out on the Family Farm* (Lincoln, NE: Univ. Nebraska Press, 2002), 17-21.

[6] *Renville Country Farmers Press,* November 3, 1933, and Charles and Joyce Conrad, "50 Years North Dakota," *Farmers Union,* 1976, 79.

Union College in Lincoln, Nebraska at the beginning of spring semester in 1935. His sister Marjorie went with him and began her training in nursing. (George stayed behind to farm his parched quarter section.) At Union College Tom met Ruth Cowin, whom he married after graduation. Her homesteading family lived in Nebraska north of Lincoln. Her grandfather, John Cowin, emigrated from the Isle of Man where the distinctive tailless cat had its origin.

JOHN COWIN FROM THE BRITISH ISLE OF MAN

CHAPTER NINETEEN

> "Now therefore amend your ways and your doings, and obey the voice of the Lord your God, and the Lord will change his mind about the disaster that he has pronounced against you." Jeremiah 26:13.

Ruth LaVon Cowin's grandparents homesteaded in Nebraska in 1869 (two years after Nebraska became a state). Ruth grew up on this homestead, but sometimes longed for the city. It is a universal story—people fantasizing about the lives of others and "thinking the grass is greener on the other side."

The Cowin family endured what thousands of Nebraska homesteaders experienced: they arrived with utopian dreams of a stable and productive life, but they had to modify their expectations and adapt to something close to subsistence living. Farming was not a refuge for the righteous. Ever since Adam and Eve left the Garden of Eden, mankind lived by the sweat of the brow.

John Cowin (1847-1895), the original homesteader, came to America at age 18 from the British Isle of Man. He caught an "infection" going around at the time called the "America Fever!" This contagious disease settled in the minds of restless and ambitious individuals like a bite from a malaria mosquito. Hundreds of railroad agents passing through the British Isles spread the "fever" by handing out glowing descriptions of cheap, fertile farmlands in America. They scattered testimonial letters, pictures of bumper crops, and promotional pamphlets.[1] According to these pamphlets, "If you wished to go near a wheat field, you'll have to carry a compass and a hatchet because the crop grew so high, trailblazing was necessary." (The agents hoped to dispose of the free land given to the railroads by the government to finance construction.)

---

[1] William C. Sherman, ed., *Plains Folk* (Fargo, ND: North Dakota State Univ., 1988), 11, 13.

Prosperity being within easy reach, John and his brother Frank headed for "flowery meadows where grew abundant and plentiful crops." Their parents had recently suffered a potato famine like the one in Ireland, and so figured the boys might have better promise in America. In route, the brothers hired out as "cabin boys" on a freighter.[2] Upon arriving in New York they became separated, and John never saw his younger brother again.[3] (It was presumed after a time that Frank had picked up and returned to his homeland.)

For the next three years John Cowin took odd jobs and saved money to fund his homesteading dreams. The agent's pamphlet recommended having at least a thousand dollars as a grub stake before taking out a homestead. This would buy a "pair of horses, a wagon, some tools, a cow and a pig." The railroad offered a one-way ticket westward at half-rate; but the price to return was double.

After reaching Chicago by rail in 1869 John pushed on to Omaha, Nebraska. From Omaha, he walked a hundred miles into the northwest interior of Nebraska, heading for Norfolk where he would file a claim for a homestead. On the way, he saw his first jack rabbit, his first antelope, first buffalo, and his first wolf (coyote). He followed the flood bench west along the Elkhorn River, named by French trappers from the shape of the river's path. The Elkhorn was not large, averaging only seventy-five feet in width, but it was rich with trout. [4] When John arrived at Norfolk, he heard about some bountiful lands thirty miles further to the west in the direction of the Elkhorn Valley. With this exciting information, he took out a claim at the land office and purchased the essentials to settle his homestead. His claim was a mile north of the Elkhorn River in Antelope County — close to where a small town named Oakdale, Nebraska, would be developed later.

---

[2] Margaret Pierson, *The History of Antelope County* (Dallas, TX: Antelope County Historical Society, 1986), 394.

[3] The family believed the younger brother got cold feet and returned to the Isle of Man.

[4] Terry W. Ahlstedt, "You Take the Low Land and I'll Take the High Land. Land Settlement in Antelope County, Nebraska 1868-1891," thesis presented to the University of Nebraska, 2004, 53.

Drawback to Homesteading

According the homestead Act, a claimant could not obtain mortgage funding during the first five-years of residency. Nor could he take temporary employment or market lumber obtained from the claim. Consequently, many claimants were initially short of capital. They often delayed completing the filing of their patent to keep the property off the county tax rolls.

Where John's claim was situated, he could hear the rushing waters of the Elkhorn and, at night, the chirping crickets. He could watch swifts and swallows flit about the edges of the river catching insects. And by necessity, he kept a watchful eye on the Indians – who could inflict grievous pain as they protected their hunting grounds. The county had been home to buffalo before the homesteaders arrived. There were also prairie chickens, quail, grouse, beavers, timber wolves, coyotes, badgers, raccoons, and wildcats. (By 1900 most of these animals would disappear except the coyotes and the game birds.)

The shrub plants that grew along the creeks and rivers were subject to frequent and devastating prairie fires. (The ash residue, of course, helped to enrich the soil and strengthen the prairie grasses.) Winter winds blew snow off the unprotected hills, creating great drifts in the ravines and gullies. When it melted, erosion, deficient ground water and poor grass cover resulted. The summers were hot (as high as 115°), and the winters were cold (as low as -38 degrees). The last frost occurred in May and resumed in late September. Periods of abundant rainfall were followed by heartbreaking drought that could last as long as ten years. Then heavy rains followed, lasting five to ten years, causing flooding and erosion. Powerful, unpredictable thunderstorms with extremely high winds, hail and occasional tornados which resulted in property damage and loss of livestock. [5]

John knew little about farming, but it didn't seem to matter; he was under the spell of owning land and becoming independent. He immediately built a small sod house and a corral for his two horses. He used trees near his homestead to build a log cabin and improved it when the sawmill was established. As he became familiar with his surroundings, it was clear that almost every railroad promotional description about this lonesome prairie had been greatly exaggerated. Only with a lot of energy could he triumph over his immediate disappointments.

---

[5] Ibid. 51.

John Marries Almira

Within a short time, John met Almira (1853-1906) the fifteen-year old stepdaughter of a neighbor.[6] Almira thought John was a gallant gentleman and liked his English accent. He was six years older and appeared to be a man not given to compromise. But some aspects of John's character bothered her: "he was melancholy, worried too much and distressed too easily. Worries tiptoed into his mind like a cat quietly stalking a mouse and left him depressed and with an upset stomach." John possessed an unromantic view of work and a wary uncertainty about pleasure. Having lived through the potato famine on the Isle of Man, he accepted self-denial as a fact of life.

After they were married John carried her trunk to his log cabin, where "they took up together." Almira was short, petite, fine-boned, strong-willed, and spiritual. John could have said like Bunyan, his favorite English author, "This woman and I—we came together as poor as poor might be."

If she married John in 1871[7], an unsettling blemish becomes evident: marriage may have followed the birth of their first child Jenna Anna in July 1871. Then again, there might be another explanation. Of course, on the frontier, people sometimes "married" unofficially, and then months or even years later found a traveling minister to legalize things. Premarital pregnancy was common. It was standard practice to go to a sexual partner and talk him into marriage. [8]

Not surprisingly, unmarried pioneer men were eager to marry. A woman's remarkable work around the farm was never done. Year around she labored in the kitchen, did the washing, raised children, and helped during spring planting and fall harvesting. It was not uncommon for the women to milk the cow, take care of the chickens, and raise and cultivate a garden. They remained loyal and obsequious to their husbands. By giving birth to children the family sank deeper roots into the homestead and made sure that the land would go to their offspring. Homesteads were almost always titled in the man's name. If a husband died, the wife retained

---

[6] *Oakdale Sentinel,* March 16, 1906.

[7] Ibid. March 23, 1906.

[8] Deborah Fink, *Agrarian Women* (Chapel Hill, NC: Univ. North Carolina Press, 1992), 87.

a dower right to one-third of his property. Up to the point of marriage, Almira's life had not been easy, and she probably would tell you it didn't improve much after she married John.

Seven Children Were Born to John and Almira

Seven children were born to the John Cowin family, four boys and three girls. (One of the girls, Stella, died in infancy.) The first was Jenna Anna. Three years later came Harry in 1874, and then Frank in 1877. William or Weaver, as he was called, arrived in 1882. "Mother's sunshine boy," Henry, came in March 1885, and, finally, Julia in 1887. High fertility rates played a critical role in the survival of a farm. Studies of fertility on the farms showed higher birthrates than in cities, a fact associated with the greater economic value of children as workers in rural settings.

Homesteaders Wanted to be Near a Town

Generally, farmers and their families wanted to be near a town to purchase resources such as barbed wire, well equipment, windmills, and finished goods such as food, farm supplies, clothing and luxuries. And towns functioned as local markets for farm produce. Later the railroads provided a vital link to outside markets, and grain elevators began to appear at sidings along the tracks for moving grains to distance markets. The Cowin's homestead stood approximately three miles from Oakdale, adjacent to woods along the river and next to a county road that connected to Nelige and Tilton. A grain mill established along the Elkhorn River in both Oakdale and Neligh allowed farmers to market surplus grain. Wheat and corn could be ground into flour and flour brought a better price than unmilled grains, plus being cheaper to transport to outside markets. Homesteaders did not want to live more than seven miles from the nearest town.[9]

Two significant events hampered further growth in Antelope County. The 1873 financial panic caused economic distress. When Jay Cooke & Company, a heavy investor in railroads, began to fail, other banks

---

[9] Ibid. 111.

experienced a run on deposits and over one hundred banks, from the east coast into the Midwest, suddenly failed.

The second event occurred a year later with the outbreak of the grasshoppers. It was not uncommon for a farmer to lose his entire crop to these insects, and by 1875 many families were so destitute they began asking the state for help.

And yet, homesteading people could be, or appear to be, happy and contented. It is wrong to think otherwise. They were friendly, benevolent, and largely self-sufficient. Their system of borrowing and bartering to secure goods and assistance often came through church fellowship. It was an unspoken sentiment that on Judgment Day the agricultural virtues practiced on earth would be the ones that got souls into the Kingdom.

History of the Commercial Life Near the Cowin Homestead

The county population continued to swell. Whereas there were only a few settlers in 1869, three years later, in 1872, 13 persons submitted to taxation.[10] The largest number of settlers resided near Twin Groves where the Elwood family erected a store and a dwelling house. The first doctor located in Twin Groves. Methodist Episcopal circuit riders performed the first church services there. And the first tragedy unfolded there too – a three-year-old boy was found unconscious, lying face down in a shallow pool of water, and no one could revive him.

At the first Fourth of July celebration in Twin Groves, an assortment of settlers delivered speeches about how they had come to the country. John from the Isle of Man put on his clogs and did a jig for the crowd. The highlight of the day came when Uncle Jessie Bennet walked through the celebration with tears streaming down his face and urged the crowd to "forsake their crooked by-ways, which lead to sin, for that shining path which leads to glory." [11]

---

[10] A. J. Leach, *A History of Antelope County Nebraska* (Henderson, NE: Service Press, 1909), 53.
[11] *Oakdale Sentinel*, September 28, 1928.

Indians Are Stealing and Homesteaders Go After the Thieves

Indians poked around the farms, silently coming through the trees near the river or appearing on the hills as silhouettes. Sometimes they entered farmhouses uninvited. They didn't speak English and always seemed to want something. The women thought they were murderers, which brought out their protective instinct. They kept a vigilant eye on their children and kept a gun behind the door. Mostly the Indians meant no harm, but homesteaders could not understand their customs and tribal etiquette.

One day two Indians appeared near the front door of the Cowin home and wanted to feel the hair of her daughter, which was lighter in color than theirs. Almira called out to John in the barn and he came running. The Indians jumped on their horses and fled!

One Indian entered the yard of John's neighbor and asked to trade three of his wives for the settler's wife, because she made "better biscuits." They begged persistently. [12] Settlers looked down on them as inferior, needful of Christianity. They felt somewhat the same way about white people who couldn't speak English, or practiced strange customs, or wore clothes from other countries. Apparently nearly everyone outside the close-knit community needed Christian refinement.

John's first encounter with Indians happened in November 1870, and only by a slim margin did he escape with his life. The trouble began when Indians broke into Robert Horne's cabin in Cedar Township south of John. Horne found moccasin tracks in the spilled flour outside his cabin, and his clothing and household goods had been carted off. A small group of settlers decided to punish the Indians and rode over to Judge Snider's cabin to recruit additional men to go after the thieves. But Horne had lived all his life in the city prior to coming to the frontier and was dubious about what they were setting out to do. He tried to tell the agitated group that the Indians were human beings, not animals, and that all he wanted was to get his personal things back without killing anyone.

A party of twenty men including John set off in pursuit of the Indians. First, they inventoried their fire power, an assortment of muzzle loaders,

---

[12] Everett Dick, *Sod-House Frontier* (Lincoln, NE: Johnsen Publ. Co., 1954), 166.

carbines, shotguns, squirrel rifles, and pistols. Then they decided to act and stop the larceny. Said one, it "felt like they were riding down into a volcano." (Indians would peel off the top layer of your skull if they caught you and then take your hair as a trophy.)

Smoke was seen rising from a grove of trees in the bend of the river. Examining the area with glasses, they saw Indians lying flat on the ground. When the two Hopkins brothers slowly approached on horseback, a large athletic Indian jumped up and in sign language indicated he was the chief. The Indian also held up three fingers signifying that if it came to a showdown, he would take three of them. The Indians wore Horne's garments and leggings fashioned from Mrs. Horne's black and orange dress.

Suddenly the Indians leaped up and started shooting. The Hopkins brothers galloped off into the nearby trees. The others began firing at the "three-finger" chief who seemed dismayed and bewildered. Then the chief went down.

At the start of the shooting John sat on his horse just behind the Hopkins brothers. As he turned to take cover, he felt a sharp pain in his leg and looked down to see that an arrow had gone through the back of his leg and then lodged in the flank of his horse. Horne, who was nearby, jumped off the wagon, bounded over in full view of the Indians, broke the shaft of the arrow, and pulled John off his horse. Then they both took cover in the grass as John tried to pull the shaft from his leg to stop the bleeding.

Suddenly, the Indians charged down the hill screaming war-whoops and rapidly firing their arrows. Faced with this new threat, John stopped what he was doing and began shooting. One Indian plunged with a heavy thump into the grass near him. John saw the wide-eyed expression on the Indian's face, and smelled his perspiration. "This Indian is going to kill me and is as terrified as I am."

Then as suddenly as the firing had begun, the Indians jumped up and fell back, dragging their wounded a quarter mile away. They sat down and sang a death song—probably supposing their "three-finger" chief had died. [13] Meanwhile, the settlers decided to retreat, thinking they'd made their point.

They reached a settler's cabin and stayed up all night retelling what

---

[13] A. J. Leach, *A History of Antelope County Nebraska* (Henderson, NE: Service Press, 1909), 74.

had happened. John Cowin dressed his wound, took some ardent spirits, and put wagon grease over his horse's injury. The women and children were too frightened to go to bed. Might the Indians return during the night? Guards stood around the cabin.

The next morning a few of the settlers walked up the river. They did not find the "three-fingered" chief nor any Indians fastened in a tree as was the Sioux custom for disposing of the dead.

John limped around the farm for several months afterwards. Almira admonished him to "leave the Indians to the Army." After this close call with the Indians, John realized he was not afraid to die. (The brush with the Indians had taken place about six years before "Custer's Last Stand" on the Little Big Horn River in Montana.)

Twin Groves lost its prominence in favor of the new town of Oakdale in August 1872. [14] The site was about a mile and half south and east of Twin Groves and on the other side of the Elkhorn River. By 1874 Oakdale featured a blacksmith's shop, millinery, land office, hotel, doctor's office, druggist, a saloon, a bank, and flour mill. A baseball league formed that same year. The local newspaper reported; "The sound of the hammer and saw makes pleasant music in our town these days." [15] Oakdale became the Antelope County seat until 1883.

Although never one to shrink from a fight with an enemy, John nearly threw in the towel when the great grasshopper plague arrived on his property in 1874 – the so-called "Grasshopper Year." He had expected a good year following the awful previous one. There had been a severe blizzard for three days in April 1873 [16], during which a gale blew down the telegraph wires along the Union Pacific railroad, destroyed sheds, killed livestock, and even caused a neighbor's death. No blizzard would strike like that again until 1888. [17]

---

[14] Norma Launt Schauer, "A History of Oakdale, Nebraska," thesis presented to the Department of History, University of Omaha, 1962.

[15] *Oakdale Journal,* June 4, 1874.

[16] The blizzard of 1888 was documented in W.H. O'Gara, *In All Its Fury: The Great Blizzard of 1888* (Lincoln, NE: J & L Lee Books, 1988).

[17] Ibid. This blizzard was called the "School Children's Storm." It hit around noon when the children were heading home. Many people lost their lives trying to rescue the children.

PESTIFEROUS LOCUST
CHAPTER TWENTY

"They do not fly high in cloudy weather but will go from one wheat-field to another. Do not fly high in hard winds, and never are seen flying except between 8 a.m. and 7 p.m., generally from 10 a.m. to 4 p.m. If they fly nights no one knows it. If they go to roost in the same spot the next morning, and do not move until they have breakfast and the dew is all off. They only float with the wind when flying high and go just as fast as the wind blows. With a strong glass I can plainly see locusts and cottonwood seeds flying together, and they keep the same rate of progress; but the locusts will leave the cottonwood seeds to the right and left and go before and above them, showing that they make use of their wings to keep up and gyrate in flying; but I think they propel ahead none at all after they get high, but fly forward and upward very fast when rising from the ground to fly away or for short flights." Report by the United States Entomological Commission, 1880, *94*.

The lure of "free lands" offered by the government compelled many to stake their claims in the Midwest, where, by the sweat of their brow and the power of their horses, they could follow their dreams of becoming wealthy landowners.

Each region developed different methods of agriculture. In North Dakota and Nebraska, the farmers grew wheat and other grains that could be turned into flour, marketed locally, and shipped abroad (transported by the railroads to distance millers). Later these same farmers found that livestock could increase their income. Demand for corn grew as corn became "food on the hoof." Over time, technology and mechanization improved production and created less demand for manual and horse labor. Farmers developed hybrid grains that resisted disease and tolerated of climate extremes.

The goal was always to increase profits: farmers had not come to homestead simply to subsist. Horse-drawn machinery fell away when tractors arrived, and horse-drawn wagons gave way to trucks. Inventions like the McCormack Reaper made farming more profitable and less labor intense. But quick profits were rare. As one historian put it,

> *As noble, earnest pioneers conquered a hostile land, and*
> *with that conquest, transformed the plains, achieved with*
> *the help of a benevolent government which bestowed upon*
> *the 'humble dweller of the plains' the rich gift of free*
> *land through land grants like the Homestead and Timber*
> *Culture Acts.* [1]

To succeed in this environment an individual had to be savvy, practical, and perhaps, lucky — not like one farmer's wife who, believing strongly in faith cures, threw away her false teeth, expecting new ones to grow in. Six months later she had a "mouthful of pearly incisors and molars put up by the best dentist in town." [2]

The Summer of 1874 Was One of the Driest on Record

The summer of 1874 was one of the driest on record in Antelope County, Nebraska. That same year title to the Cowin homestead arrived in the mail. As he shocked his wheat, John began to see himself coming out of financial difficulty into economic respectability – this was why he came to America in the first place — to live independently on the land and make a good living. Meanwhile John and Almira were expecting their second child.

One day as John was leaving the field, he decided to stop by and talk to Judge Snider, a man he admired not just because of his ingenuity and insights, but also for his optimism and integrity. As he drove into the judge's farmyard a huge yellow-brown cloud in the northwest sky caught his eye. It looked like a dust storm, but it was higher and reached across the entire horizon. His team suddenly jerked and twisted as if they wanted to return home, but John pulled hard on the reins to keep them from breaking away. Soon the cloud filled the sky, the sun darkened, and he heard a dreadful humming sound. The locusts were back!

---

[1] Terry W. Ahlstedt, *You Take the Low Land and I'll Take the High Land.* (Lincoln, NE: University of Nebraska Press, 2004), 170
[2] *Oakdale Sentinel,* December 20, 1895.

Dropped by to See Judge Snider When the Locust Appeared

Within minutes, insects the size of a man's thumb dropped from the sky, filling the air like driving hail and swirling around like dead leaves in an autumn whirlwind. Fearing the insects would be drawn in with his breath, he shook the bothersome, crawling locusts off his arms and legs. With a quick wave to his father-in-law, he returned to his barn.

There he stood dumbfounded as an awful reality settled in his mind: his dream of prosperity now shattered by a locust holocaust. Everything went from prosperity to hell, and he must now think about famine and starvation (most of the food on his table came from the vegetables grown in the garden).

Vegetation coursed through every part of a farmer's life. Gardens, fruit trees, wind breaks, shrubs around fences, crops, and pastures provided primary sustenance — all of which ultimately came down to energy from the sun and growth and nourishment from the plants.

Some settlers thought God gave man the right to "take dominion" over the creatures of the earth, but if that were true John wondered why God now allowed the locusts to take dominion over man! Did locusts have a special dispensation? Did they have an evil intent, or did someone with an evil intent send the locusts? Were they sent by a benevolent God to teach some kind of lesson?

Almira ran outside screaming and beating the ground with a broom, slipping all the while on squirming locusts. The hoppers crawled up her legs and got in her hair; they shredded the blankets she had spread over the garden. The whole prairie was a writhing mass of them. They now did the threshing and harvesting, and they were making a clean sweep of it. [3]

Within a few hours no vegetation was left standing in the fields – not the corn, or wheat, or onions and turnips, or marijuana, or even the dandelions. John and Almira became refugees in a devastated, war-torn zone.

---

[3] Locust found in glaciers in the Rocky Mountains showed repeated swarms passing over the glaciers preserved in the ice more than a thousand years ago. (See Jeffrey Lockwood, *Locust* (New York: Basic Books, 2004).

After their destructive work, the locusts closed their mandibles, spread their wings, and headed south to another property. What they had done equaled the damage caused by prairie fires and hail storms.

Department of Interior Established Entomology Division

Homesteaders had been in a hurry to put in crops, build houses and barns, bear children, and become debt free. But in their haste had they neglected their duties to God? As the Reverend George Barnes, a Baptist preacher, commented:

> *Everything was made to bend that way. The Sabbath was painfully disregarded. You could hear the whiz of the saw, and the click of the hammers, at all hours of the day and night for the whole week. The Lord's day found only a few who honored its claims.* [4]

The Nebraska frontier may have been churchless, but it was unswervingly Christian. Naturally, therefore, the locust swarms reminded Almira, who was raised a Methodist, of the Egyptian plagues spoken about in Exodus. The Bible said God deliberately hardened Pharaoh's heart, so He could manifest His great power and cause it to be known among the nations. [5]

As noted earlier, God was possibly testing their faith or punishing moral wrongs. Almira thought this might be the case, but John felt it made no sense. "This whole idea of locust punishment is an exaggeration. We haven't staged any extravagant cotillions or house parties to excite the wrath of God. It simply would be presumptive on God's part to send such a devastating swarm to remind us in general to stop storing up worldly goods. By no stretch of the imagination could anyone accuse us of living a self-indulgent life or being too fond of riches. We are living near the brink of extinction." "Besides," he added, "locusts had been coming here for centuries before we showed up."

---

[4] James C. Olson and Ronald Clinton Naugle, *History of Nebraska, 3rd Ed.* (Lincoln, NE: Univ. of Nebraska, 1997), 99.
[5] Exodus 10:1-14. KJV.

John and Almira had no choice, but to stick it out. After the locusts were gone Almira thought John reflected too much on self-doubt, worry and failure. "He complained there was always something thrown up to torment his ambitions." What she didn't know was that John was even wondering what it would be like to drown himself in the Elkhorn River. As his despair deepened, he thought about giving up and returning to the Isle of Man.

The migratory Rocky Mountain locust swarms extended from southern Canada to the Mexican border. At times, they flew in the opposite direction as if circling back to make sure they hadn't missed any vegetation. In a summer outbreak, locusts numbered around 15 trillion insects and spread over 500,000 square miles. Once on the ground they metabolically burned up 4,000 pounds of vegetation per hour. [6] Entomologists in the U. S. Department of Interior estimated that from 1874 to 1877 the Rocky Mountain locusts caused $200 million in crop damages. (The equivalent today would be $116 billion.) Only birds, a few parasite, and mites could tolerate them. [7]

The Northern Pacific Railroad stood in the migratory pathway of the locusts. When settler immigrations slackened because of the plague, commerce dropped away, and railroading collapsed. Indirectly, the locust plagues put financier Jay Cooke's firm in Philadelphia in bankruptcy. [8] During the Panic that followed 1874, which was one of the worst economic depressions in the nation's history, almost a hundred railroads went into receivership and 18,000 businesses, including banks, failed. [9] Banks and savings were also lost. It was a colossal disaster.

Mosquitoes and Sleeping Sickness in Horses

Other insects caused additional hardships. Obnoxious mosquitoes got on your nerves, biting and sucking blood. One day John complained to a

---

[6] Jeffrey Lockwood, *Locust* (New York: Basic Books, 2004).
[7] First Annual Report of the United States Entomological Commission for the year 1877 relating to the Rocky Mountain Locust. Gov. Printing Office. 1878.
[8] Jay Cooke was financing the Northern Pacific Railroad.
[9] Jeffrey Lockwood, *Locust* (New York: Basic Books, 2004), 253.

neighbor that the mosquitoes got so much of his blood he accepted them as relatives!

In August John noticed that his horses were showing signs of "sleeping sickness," a condition (equine encephalomyelitis) that probably resulted from mosquito bites. The sickness would last only three to four days and within that short time the horse would be dead. As a neighbor remarked, "Even if the horse survived the animal might become crazy or show other signs of brain damage." Now John faced the gigantic expense of replacing his horse power.

Dreams turned out to be "such fragile things." Nature could easily and quickly destroy what the settlers intended to preserve and protect. Seemingly, the sun never shone on anything that did not require the exercise of immense toil, great patience, and indomitable courage.

Almira was still optimistic and wrote to her brother in South Dakota describing the "sheer beauty as the sun rose like a gold tide racing across the land left bare by the locusts." But other calamities and ordeals beyond locust plagues continued to occur. The *Oakdale Sentinel* reported that "Mr. Garrison was seriously injured recently by falling from his wagon, the wheels passing over his body. Hopes are entertained for his recovery." [10]

Trying to Make Ends Meet

John tried hard to turn a profit on his homestead, but it troubled him that his efforts were not more successful. The question in Bunyan's *Pilgrim's Progress*, "What dost thou here, Christian," came to mind. Exactly what was he doing here? Rarely did he have enough cash to pay taxes, buy farm implements, replace his stock, and purchase seed. He was living from harvest to harvest, or, as they used to say, "hand-to-mouth, or from the farmer's hand to the grasshopper's mouth."

The monopolistic railroad charged high tariff rates, which made it hard to deliver his crops to market. Almost all economic forces aligned against him. When the price of corn was low, he used corn husks to fuel the cookstove so as to avoid purchasing coal. Encouraged by bankers and agricultural agents to borrow money, John accepted debt and mortgaged his farm three different times over a decade of farming, each time paying

---

[10] *Oakdale Sentinel*, September 22, 1877.

high rates of interest. By the 1880's census John held sixty-five acres under cultivation and ninety-five acres in pasture, but he could only afford two horses. For family use he milked four cows and fed three pigs.

Things were tough indeed. In July 1882 John borrowed $21.20 [11] at ten percent interest from the Antelope Bank in Oakdale to purchase two cows and a John Deere plow. A year later he borrowed $19.75 to purchase two more cows, again at ten percent interest. In 1888 John drilled a well on his property and installed a pump for fifty dollars – on which he made installment payments. A few years later he drilled a new well with two-inch pipe and a ten-foot "back geared windmill put up." [12]

In spite of ups and downs in growing crops, John did not waver in his determination to make his farm a success. In 1895 the *Oakdale Sentinel* predicted a strong future for farmers, as seventeen of the past twenty-five years had produced good crops and only four were major failures. Unlike wage earners, John could set his own pace much of the time, although as one historian of homesteaders commented "it was drudgery from daylight to dark, day after day, month and year after year." [13]

Oakdale Continues to Grow with Transportation Business

Nearby, the town of Oakdale grew rapidly. When gold was discovered in the Black Hills of South Dakota, the town became a natural thoroughfare to the mines. Freighting companies formed to haul supplies. By early 1880 regularly scheduled trains operated through the Oakdale depot and one could travel back and forth between Oakdale and Omaha in a single day by train.

Oakdale was close to the Cowin's homestead. Neligh lay to the northwest, Elgin to the southwest, and Tilton to the east. It was where the children went to high school, participated in community entertainment, and purchased items for the farm. In the small town, wooden frame houses lined square streets amid cottonwood, oak and elm trees; and along Main Street in the center of town stood stores. Oakdale took pride in its baseball

---

[11] $405.21 in today's dollars.

[12] *Oakdale Sentinel,* September 20, 1894.

[13] Michael McGerr, *A Fierce Discontent* (New York: Oxford Univ. Press, 2003), 17.

team and high school. Most Saturday evenings in good weather farmers and their families congregated in the town square to exchange friendship. In a nearby cemetery the dead were buried amongst relatives and friends.

The local newspaper kept its finger on the pulse in the same way that a physician measures the heart rate of his patients. Reporting was direct and to the point. When one man's marriage failed, the *Oakdale Sentinel* told how the husband arrived home late one night and failed to attract a kiss from his wife. "Instead" the paper said, "she kicked him out the window naked and threw his clothes after him, shoving him into a cold and wicked world." The paper went on to report that "He told his friends down at the hotel that he and his wife only had a mutual separation." But the woman maintained an ugly disposition: [14]

> *He thinks it unfashionable to be decent, and good breeding to be impious. I know him to be a stupid sottish fool who cares for nothing on earth but perfuming his own hair and curling his big whiskers and making love to all silly nursery maids he meets. He has but to whistle after any woman and she is his—so he believes, but like many other frail mortals he is deceived by his self-love.*

Secret Service and Thoughtless Women Writing Letters to Men

The paper once described how "a runaway team lead (sic) a merry dance through our streets on Wednesday, leaving pieces of the wagon scattered along at suitable distances apart." [15] As for the younger women in town, the newspaper said they participated in "runaway" sexual misadventures also "scattering debris at suitable distances." Later, the Secret Service came to Oakdale to investigate these young women.

> *A habit very common with a number of our thoughtless young ladies, who do a great many things quietly which they would not like to have known of at home—a habit deserving*

---

[14] *Oakdale Sentinel,* Oct 6, 1877.
[15] Ibid. Feb 8, 1896.

of the strongest condemnation—is that of promiscuous correspondence with gentlemen, whether the gentlemen be married or single...We are not really sure that this does not come less under the heading of an undesirable habit than a sin; for there is an indelicacy about it quite amounting to immodesty, of which no girl who respects herself or who desires the respect of others will be guilty. [16]

Family misfortunes appeared in print, too. "The three-year-old child of Anthony Gerst, living east of Elgin, was burned to a crisp on Tuesday...the fire was started by the children while the parents were at work in the field, and the father arrived too late to save the child, being badly burned in the attempt." [17] "W. O. Jones had a cow killed by lightning on Tuesday morning." [18]

Terrible Violent Way to Treat a Horse

A horrible example of human violence came to Mrs. Newton of Blaine Township. As the newspaper reported, "One night recently some fiend in human form set fire to the barn and burned up three horses, the corn she had herself gathered on shares to feed her stock with, and other property in and around the barn. He also rode another horse some distance away and kerosened (sic) and set fire to him. The poor animal came rushing home at a furious rate. The galloping, equine torch streaked down the road in wild gyrations and leaps, bursting into the farmyard with eyes bulging. After the horse calmed down, and the fire extinguished, it was so badly burned by the primitive and merciless fire the animal had to be shot." [19] It was never determined who did this to Mrs. Newton.

Moral evil beyond comprehension appeared from every direction. "Mr. Dalrymple was standing on a load of hay which he had just loaded by hand to the stack when the team started forward, and he fell backwards, striking on his shoulders and the back of his head. He was taken up stuned (sic) and helpless and remained so until death released him of his sufferings...

---

[16] Ibid. Feb 29, 1896.
[17] Ibid. April 7, 1894.
[18] Ibid. Aug 4, 1894.
[19] Ibid. Nov 9, 1895.

his sudden taking off is greatly regretted." [20] One winter, "Boys were skating...and Raymond, the seventeen-year-old son of the Mr. and Mrs. Frank Bradley, broke through the ice...When the accident happened young Bradley was around the bend in the river about a quarter of a mile from the rest of the party. His cries for help were heard by his playmates and they hastened to his rescue but were too late, as he had become chilled and exhausted and sank under the ice." [21]

Tracing Evil Origin to Garden of Eden

Conservative theologians and practicing preachers trace evil and human suffering to the Garden of Eden and the alluring tree of knowledge of good and evil, but this account completely ignores the fossils that were embedded in the earth's crust millions of years earlier. These show the effects of parasites, predation, harm from natural causes and other evidence of evil. How does this all fit together? Maybe it doesn't.

A fable tells about a scorpion that asked a frog to take him across a river. Before the frog agreed to do this, he made the scorpion agree not to poison him through his sting. After the frog began swimming with the scorpion on his back the scorpion stung him anyway, and as they sank the frog asked the scorpion why he did it. The scorpion replied, "It's in my nature." Maybe that is the simple way to account for evil in humans.

---

[20] Ibid. Sept 15, 1877.
[21] Ibid. Jan 6, 1894.

DEATH OF JOHN COWIN
CHAPTER TWENTY-ONE

"There is only one way to be born and a thousand ways to die." – Serbian Proverb

Almira became a Seventh-day Adventist in 1876 without any promptings from colporteurs, bible workers, firebrand evangelists, or anyone coming to the farm to visit her.[1] Her acceptance sprang from the primordial spirit of Methodism and its apocalyptic vision of the world. The idea of the soon coming of Christ sent chills up her spine, especially the notion of everlasting life. She had grown up with the view of history as a cosmic conflict between God and Satan.

Isolated on the farm she had not known that in August 1870 Dr. Paulson from Battle Creek, Michigan (a colleague of John Harvey Kellogg at the Sanitarium) came to Oakdale, Nebraska, and converted several families to the Seventh-day Adventist faith. They subsequently met in individual homes and remained quiet about their beliefs. In June 1878 an evangelistic tent campaign in Oakdale generated so much interest that the Methodist minister cancelled his Sunday sermon to attend!

Almira learned from her reading that Adventists sought to separate from the rest of society and bind themselves as "God's true church," or, as they were accustomed to saying; "they were the remnant bound for heaven." Believers were told to come out of Babylon and leave worldly temptations behind. Almira liked the Adventist practice of Christian morals and higher values. They held a strong eschatological (end-of-the-world) springing from a belief in a loving heavenly father and an evil Satan who warred against Christ and the faithful. [2]

---

[1] There were 166 Adventist ministers, of whom 96 were ordained in 1876. Malcolm Bull and Keith Lockhart, *Seeking a Sanctuary* (San Francisco, CA: Harper & Row, Publishers, 1989), 208.

[2] The Devil is not fully developed in the Old Testament. "I create the light; I create the darkness," boasts the God Yahweh in Isaiah 45:7. The Hebrews were explicitly monotheistic, unlike the Christian religion that became implicitly dualistic. Jeffrey

They believed that Christ, the incarnate son of God, could destroy Satan, and that Christ would return to earth at any moment and take Sabbath-keeping saints to a home in heaven, leaving the unwashed masses and pleasure-seekers behind in the malicious hands of the devil. At Christ's Second Coming the earth would be destroyed by fire and brimstone. After a thousand years in heaven, the saints would return to the restored Garden of Eden on earth, a New Jerusalem. (While in heaven the righteous would spend the thousand years validating why their friends and relatives were not in heaven, thus assuring that justice had been done.) In the meantime, Satan and his evil angels, sin, and evil would be completely eradicated.

The foregoing details, all worked out by theological experts in the church along with messages from the church's prophetess, made Almira a trusting believer. This whole scheme organized her life and helped mitigate the rage, lust, grief, sorrow, and disappointment that crept into her life at times when her husband became depressed.

Almira Becomes an Adventist by Reading Discarded Review

You might say that Almira entered the faith through the back door for she was converted by "undelivered Adventist literature." Someone had thrown away a discarded stack of Adventist publications at the Oakdale post office [3] and the postman said she could have them. To her they conveyed "truth-filled literature." Not until almost a decade later did she meet another Adventist believer. But she subscribed to the *Advent Review and Sabbath Herald* which she faithfully read every week.

After Almira embraced the Adventist teachings she began to "live up to all the light she had." Her children noticed that her prickly temperament turned milder. The Adventist dietary restrictions and simple dress customs without jewelry and makeup became evident. Dietary laws had been a sign of Israel's special relationship with God in the Old Testament. She accepted the credo of the health message that was attached to Adventism, pointed

---

Burton Russell, *The Devil: Perceptions of Evil from Antiquity to Primitive Christianity* (Ithaca, NY: Cornell University Press, 1977).

[3] The *Advent Review & Sabbath Herald* and *Signs of the Times.*

out in the Review: *"What? Know ye not that your body is the temple of the Holy Ghost, which is in you, which ye have of God, and ye are not your own?"* [4]

Coming from Methodism, Almira already believed that the world was only a few thousand years old, that original sin had entered through Adam and Eve, and that the world would end soon as depicted by the horsemen of the Apocalypse in Revelation. The doctrine of "holiness" or even "perfectionism" did not seem radical to her: freedom from sin was within reach in this earthly life, or so she thought. As in the days of Noah, sinful humans would be destroyed again — only this time by fire and brimstone, not by a flood. After the Noachian flood a rainbow was given as a promise that God would not again cover the earth with water; the final destruction of Satan and his followers would not require assurance that it would not happen again.

From her reading, she conceptualized the judgment in Heaven that was currently underway and would soon be concluded, after which the saints would be sealed on their foreheads. (She thought, however, that the seal on the forehead was only a figure of speech.)

She learned the traditions of the church as yeast cells leaven bread: a small amount swells and brings the loaf to rise. Once the judgement activities in the heavenly sanctuary ceased, probation would close. Then Christ, the son of God, would return to earth, appearing in the sky on a small black cloud and surrounded by angels. Every eye would see Him coming. Then He would raise the righteous dead from their graves and together with the living saints gather them up and take them to the sea of glass in heaven. The journey would take about a week. As they were leaving, flames would rise out of the ground and fall from the sky. Mountains would burn. Creatures would run to and fro and birds would fly with their wings on fire. The wicked would scream and holler for God to help them, but He would not answer; then they would cry for the mountains and rocks to fall on them. All of the above "end-of-time" events could occur soon and quickly. To faithfully abide by God's Ten Commandments and hold fast to the promise of everlasting life – that was the cornerstone of her belief system. To think, or believe, otherwise would be blasphemy for the Almighty through an inerrant Bible revealed

---

[4] 1 Corinthians 6:19.

it. Only the blood of Jesus could atone for sinners in the sanctuary. An angel told Ellen White:

> *I saw that the time for Jesus to be in the most holy place was nearly finished and that time can last but a very little longer.* [5]

The prophetess in the church added more details such as the lamb-like beast, a two-horn dragon of Revelation that represented the United States in prophecy. [6] Divinely appointed as the one true remnant church, the Adventists knew they had received Truth through a modern-day prophetess.

Oakdale Sentinel Defends Religious Liberty

According to the *Oakdale Sentinel* in Antelope County, a Methodist newspaper defended religious liberty to worship on Saturday when Adventists fell victim to Sunday (blue) laws. The *Sentinel* reported that "all these Sunday cranks are either blind bigots, blinded by excessive religious zeal, or they are iniquitous worshipers of the beast of persecution. Sunday laws are wrong. Sunday is a Roman Catholic feast day; the mark of the papal beast, since it was the Catholics that changed the Sabbath from the seventh to the first day of the week; even Cardinal Gibbon claims this to be so. In the light of Bible prophecy, is it any wonder, then, that Sunday laws caused persecution?" [7]

It could not have been better said by an Adventist publication. A few years later the *Sentinel* reported, "Several letters have been received asking for Sunday games with the Oakdale baseball team. It was decided at the beginning of the season that the team would take part in no Sunday games at home or abroad, and this decision will be adhered to strictly." Regarding matters of religion, consistency was apparently something you could not count on.

The Spirit of Prophecy foretold world-wide persecution for the

---

[5] Ellen G. White, *Early Writings*, 58.

[6] For a discussion of the inerrant word of God in the Bible see Bart D. Ehrman, *Misquoting Jesus. The Story Behind Who Changed the Bible and Why* (New York: Harper San Francisco, Division of HarperCollins LLC, 2005).

[7] *The Oakdale Sentinel*, March 24, 1894.

enforcement of Sunday worship, followed by mass conversions to the seventh-day Sabbath. If one did not take this last chance to accept the Adventist message, they would find themselves aligned with apostate protestants, Spiritualists, Catholics, Gentiles, and others, and these would all be lost. Achieving a perfect character by Sabbath-keeping and otherwise did not seem easy, but it was probably within reach: [8]

> *The standard of Christian perfection is a high and holy one. Says Jesus, 'Be ye therefore perfect, even as your Father which is in Heaven is perfect.' Is it possible for mortals to obtain this high state of perfection? Yes, it is possible, or it would not have been required of us. And nothing short of this perfection will entitle us to a place in the heavenly inheritance.* [9]

The Mormons Come to Oakdale

The Latter-Day Saints (Mormons) sponsored the first religious services in the County in the summer of 1871. Before Almira became an Adventist, a small group of Mormons from Missouri proselytized in the vicinity of Oakdale. Residents who heard them charged that the Mormons were "openly blaspheming the Highest God, and casting contempt on His holy religion by supposing revelations from their human prophet Joseph Smith." Almira herself wondered if the same skepticism applied to her own prophet.

Mormons held that the prophet Smith had received direct revelations from God:[10] he went into the woods near his home to pray when two persons dressed in white robes descended from heaven. One spoke to Smith, saying, "This is My Beloved Son. Hear Him!" When Smith recovered, he

---

[8] That was one of the attractions of Adventism. Physical righteousness was an outgrowth of perfect spiritual righteousness. It was even thought at this time that people who kept the commandments of God and practiced faithful health reform would never die but be translated. Meat eaters could not be translated.

[9] *Advent Review and Sabbath Herald*, April 1, 1873.

[10] Smith's prophetic role was similar to Ellen White's. White was seventeen years old when she had her first vision in December 1844. Unlike Joseph Smith Ellen White did not proclaim her revelations immediately but wrote about them later.

inquired, "Which church is the right one?" The Personage replied, "Don't join any of them. They were all an abomination in my sight." "These visions," Mormons said, "began the restoration of the Gospel and the commencement of a new dispensation on earth."

The notion of a modern-day prophet meant that God was not ignoring his people so long as they would listen. After the Mormons left town, with a little prodding from the people jeering them, Almira wondered why Divine providence hadn't stepped in and quieted the hecklers. Since Adventists believed that their own human prophetess had visions from God, such messages were not limited to one denomination.

Husband John's skepticism and irreverence greeted "the Mormon things about golden plates, the Urim and Thummin, the Egyptian translations into the book of the Pearl of Great Price, and that the Native Americans were descendants of the Lamanites." (Back home on the Isle of Man he had heard about disreputable Mormon elders.) Mystical religions that embodied supernatural experiences that others could not validate got no sympathy from him.

Extravagant claims by prophets of whatever variety brought to light the difference in religious temperaments between John and Almira: Presbyterian liberalism attracted John, whereas Almira preferred the simple piety of evangelicals, the power of dreams, experiences that witness to God's spirit and restoration, and the dark symbols of the Apocalypse.

In the meantime, James White, essentially the head of the Adventist church in Battle Creek, suffered his fourth paralytic stroke.

> *"He was anointed with oil and then engaged in pray for his recovery. The Lord came near by His Holy Spirit. My husband was greatly blessed. His arm was strengthened. We felt assured that by the blessing of the Lord he would recover."* [11]

---

[11] Ellen G. White, *Manuscript 6*, 1873. Soon after this stroke, the Whites left for their "hideaway home" in Washington, Iowa. See Arthur L. White, *The Progressive Years 1862-1876* (Hagerstown, MD: Review & Herald Publ. Assoc., 1986), 383.

Encountering the "Supernatural"

Almira had heard about Joseph S. Curry in Georgia, the self-proclaimed "Elijah the Prophet of Jehovah" who was charged with adultery and fornication, found guilty, and banished from his home. because he took to himself too many wives. [12] She also knew about a certain Nicholas Hart who on his birthday each year fell into a deep sleep and upon awakening told of a journey to heaven.

Such stories appealed to Almira's "intricate mystic soul" and continued to speak to her like the stories of the Old and New Testament. She longed for reunion with deceased relatives and friends.

Almira introduced John to Bunyan's *Pilgrim's Progress*, a popular book at the time and one that resonated with him. John admitted to having been in the "dungeons of Doubting Castle" and to being a great sinner who feared the wrath of God.

Almira made John aware of his sins! His "wickedness" card playing, baseball games on Saturday, dancing at community fairs, and hunting for pheasants near the Elkhorn River. Like Bunyan, John accused himself of sins as well. But he didn't squander money on alcohol or gambling. Along with his two oldest sons, Harry and Frank, John signed an "Anti-Whisky Pledge" in 1885 and kept this temperance pledge throughout his life.

John Joins the Presbyterian

Nevertheless, John resisted the intensive, polarizing, religious instructions of his wife. (Regarding spirituality, men in general were thought to lag behind their wives.) Eventually he told Almira that the "strict orthodoxy of the Adventist church did not appeal to him." Further, he said, "I am not persuaded that the Adventists have it right claiming so few will be saved and so many of the unjust will be consumed in the lake of fire. The revelation of God's love through Christ does not measure up to consigning millions of people to eternal torment while saving only the 144,000 mentioned in the Bible. There is something wrong with a religion that wants to see so many damned and burned up while ignoring the good people in other churches."

---

[12] *Advent Review and Sabbath Herald,* April 29, 1873.

When the more fashionable Presbyterians built a church in Oakdale and established a Seminary in 1881, John joined up. Presbyterians looked down on the enthusiastic religion of Methodism and, of course, Adventism. Just the same, Almira and the children settled into a small company of Adventist believers. (They did not build a church in Oakdale until 1905.)[13]

Financial Depression in 1893

A financial panic on Wall Street impacted the Plains, including Nebraska, in 1893. The silver mines in Colorado closed. Reading Railroad went bankrupt. Other railroads failed as did hundreds of banks and businesses. The stock market plunged. European investors pulled their funds out of the United States. Distressed farmers abandoned their farms and migrated east or further west while, at the same time, agitating against the railroads and the monopolistic corporations known as trusts.

During the early 1890s rainfall was lower than usual and temperatures could top 110 to 115 degrees. A drought peaked in July 1894. In one stretch, Kansas and Nebraska had no rain for over thirty days. Not enough wheat was produced, people joked, "to winter a flock of chickens." Forest and prairie fires, often caused by sparks from passing locomotives, added to the drought.

In 1894 farmers for the first time seriously discussed how to bring water to their farmlands when seasonal rainfall did not suffice. Several ideas were bantered about, such as pumping water out of the Elkhorn River, digging a canal, and even detonating explosives (the latter based on the fact that rains had followed the Civil War battles). The people of Grand Island, Nebraska hired an Australian rainmaker who promised to deliver three-quarters of an inch in four days for $2,500. They watched from the sidelines as he brewed pots of chemicals and sent gas into the wind. But after four days only a few sprinkles materialized and the rainmaker hastened to Cheyenne, Wyoming. [14]

Meanwhile, four million people across the nation lost their jobs and thousands of businesses collapsed. President Cleveland showed little

---

[13] Ibid. April 13, 1905.

[14] Catherine Renschler, "The Drought of 1894," www.adamshistory.org/drought1894.html.

interest, believing that the business cycle was a natural occurrence to be left alone — a form of Herbert Spencer's theory of social evolution. Of course, the *Oakdale Sentinel* disagreed. "There may be something in the rumor that President Cleveland is sick. His administration doesn't look like the work of a well man. Perhaps we ought not to expect much of a president who gets his inspiration from Buzzard's Bay, Loon Lake, Hogg Island and Dismal Swamp." [15]

Cornfields were not productive in the summer of 1894 because of drought and an infestation by the European corn borer. Instead of working the fields, John sat in the shade of the barn or under a large cottonwood tree and watched the wind pile up leaves along the fences. Cattle and pigs in the county were shipped to market at a loss because hay and feed corn were in short supply. Farmers were admonished to "trust in Providence and plow deep."

One evening two men on horseback stopped at the Cowin's home and asked to stay the night. They planned to leave the next morning. It was not unusual to put up visitors needing a place to overnight. But during the night they cut short their stay, stole John's team of horses, and fled north to their hiding place. Sensitive about thieves, John became "mad as hell" that such hombres could so blatantly desert the principles of Christian life and common-sense decency. There was no sheriff to help in the recovery.[16]

Among the farmers in the county, John was the first to sink a deeper well on his land and to begin crop irrigation with a windmill to pump out the water. During September of that year he put down a well with a two-inch pipe and installed a ten-foot back-gear windmill. [17] His plan was to pump water at the northern edge of the field and let it trickle down the rows of corn toward the river wash.

John's Stomach Illness

On January 26, 1895, Dr. Minton, a physician from John's church, made a house call at the Cowin farmhouse because John complained about incessant stomach pains. The doctor couldn't determine the cause of the

---

[15] Ibid. March 24, 1894.
[16] W. Clem Cowin, "From Douglas to Oakdale," (Personal Notes).
[17] *The Oakdale Sentinel,* Sept 29, 1894.

ailment, but a few days later the newspaper reported that he was doing better. [18] Worries about rain, debt, and the previous year's crop failure must have been eating away at the lining of John's stomach.

In the meantime, the Reverend Hicks, a weather prophet from St. Louis, tried to dispense some optimism to the farmers in advice columns of the newspaper. "We frankly say to all such that we do not believe the drouth (sic) of '94 will continue through '95 in all its rigor in the same sections, but that a gradual return to fruitful conditions may be expected. We think it unwise to abandon any part of the country simply on the score of drouth." [19] These were uplifting words, especially for John who incessantly fretted over the weather. But it didn't really matter much, for John wasn't planning to abandon his farm. He was bound irrevocably to the land.

John continued to suffer an undiagnosed stomach illness and tried treating himself with Haller's Sarsaparilla, an herb touted "As a renovation of the system to cast out impure and wasted matter." It must have done some good: the *Oakdale Sentinel* soon reported seeing John "occasionally walking into town." In town one day John met an old grizzled Indian wearing worn out moccasins with red paint on both cheeks. With bubbling laughter, the Indian gave John some sacred water to cure "bowel troubles," and this too seemed to help. Afterwards, the newspaper reported John was "looking much better.

The first shipments of clothing and food from charitable people in Iowa reached Oakdale in March. After dispersing the charity to the needy, another meeting was held in which a delegation solicited feed and seed from Iowa.

John Cowin's stomach troubles intensified. On April 20th the *Sentinel* reported that he went to Lincoln, Nebraska where for medical treatment. He stayed for a week and returned home without discussing his illness. Then, unexpectedly, heavy rains flooded Oakdale and washed out the sidewalks and bridges. This should have alleviated John's worries, but he looked up and in a particularly gloomy spirit remarked, "It won't do any good; the spot price for corn is too low."

Town people noticed that John walked around with a dour face and a

---

[18] Ibid. January 26, 1895.
[19] Ibid. Feb 16, 1895.

slow gait. The family feared that stomach cancer might be the problem. He seemed confused and often repeated himself. A murder trial in the State of Tennessee obsessed him.

On May 30 (Memorial Day), Almira convened a family powwow and asked her two oldest sons, Harry (age 21) and Frank (age 18), to "Keep a watch on your father today. Don't let him out of your sight. Of all things he's been talking about ending his life." She went on, "Your father is focused on a new set of worries. He is rambling, not making sense. And I pleaded shamelessly with him not to do anything rash because of his children."

Harry took down the gun from over the kitchen door and hid it, along with the butcher knives from the hallway cabinet. He sat back down at the table with his mother and brother trying to determine what they could do to overcome their father's despondency. Where was this taking them?

Death by Hanging

Around eight o'clock, thirteen-year old Weaver came bursting into the kitchen screaming; "Daddy is hanging in the barn and he is jerking around like he's trying to get down!" (Weaver was on his way to school and had gone to get his bicycle in the barn.) Quickly Harry and Frank jumped up from the table and ran out the door, followed by Almira. Once across the yard Harry slowed, turned, and ordered his mother and Rosa, Frank's wife, back into the house. Their father had hung himself in the ten minutes of being away from the family.

The two older boys entered the barn, stopping just inside the door to adjust to the darkness. Then they saw their father hanging from a rope across a beam. His legs jerked now and then as if he was trying to reach the ground with his toes to save himself. The skin started creeping up Frank's back. He ran over and wrapped his arms around his father's legs, then called out to Harry, "Get the barrel over in the corner and cut him down." Harry rolled the barrel into position, jumped up, and cut the rope. Frank and his father fell to the ground tangled in the rope—mixing with the dust and the straw on the floor. Almira came through the door wringing her hands in her apron. She fell to the ground and pulled John to her bosom. Turning her eyes to her husband's face she burst into a flood of tears and wept. He hadn't even said good-bye, and grief poured out of her. She held him tight until the last beat of his blood had flowed through his body. She knew he was gone. She pleaded with him to start breathing. But it was too late—John's neck was broken. To reach a place where "there would be no more worries, suffering, pain, or fear of the future," he abandoned everything, including his farm, his own family, and his own life. For the rest of the family, the account of how he took his own life by suicide in the face of his symptoms and struggles caused excruciating pain. They carried his hanging in their minds forever.

Almira recognized the importance of prayer and knew that John had stopped praying two months earlier. No preacher, no theologian would ever be able to say whether prayers could lift anybody with the burdens John was experiencing. Was God listening, or what could the angels who answered prayer do about John's situation? Had John been affected by a crisis in his religious faith that prevented the Devine Realm from listening?

The *Sentinel* reported, "Although he had been in ill health and a severe sufferer for some time past, his many acquaintances were hardly prepared for the news that he had hastened his end by hanging himself in his barn. No doubt his acute physical suffering, for which there seemed no relief, unbalanced his mind to such an extent that he finally committed the rash act while temporarily insane...The funeral will be held this Friday afternoon at the Presbyterian church at 8 o'clock." [20]

For a long time, Almira could not bring herself to sing one of her favorite Adventist songs. It didn't help that a lady in town, "I hope your husband had a right relationship with Jesus." Doubts about precisely this could penetrate deeply.

> *Will there be any stars, any stars in my crown?*
> *When at evening the sun goeth down.*
> *when I wake with the blest in those mansions of rest.*
> *Will there be any stars in my crown?*

Almira had hoped to convert her husband to her faith and hoist a bright shining star in her crown representing John's acceptance of the Sabbath. They could then be in heaven together. Now she faced an imponderable: can a suicide be acceptable to God in view of violating the

---

[20] Ibid. June 1, 1895.

Seventh Commandment? Is suicide an unpardonable sin, even if driven by insanity from illness?

Death by suicide lingers in the thoughts of the remaining family. Try as they might, they can never stop wondering why it happened and if there was anything they could have done to prevent it. John's family bore the burden of his suicide for many years.

The editor of the *Review* wrote a troublesome piece that ground sand into their emotional wounds:

> *The papers are full of records of suicide, and those who perish by self-destruction include persons in all stations of life, the high as well as the low, the rich as well as the poor. We read of the rich and the great taking their own lives; but we never read of a Christian committing suicide, that is, one who by faith has laid hold upon 'the hope set before us.' Such a person may have all the hardships and trials in life that the apostle Paul had, but he will think and speak of them just as Paul did. Is not the Christian's hope worth more than anything else in the world?* [21]

A judgment like this ignores the intolerable misery connected with chronic pain, overwhelming depression, incurable mood disorders, or tragic genetic abnormalities. And more significantly, people cling to life with every ounce of energy they have without being a Christian or having any religious inclinations. Was John any more damned than a man who picked up a hitchhiker and was robbed and killed while trying to help a fellow traveler?

John clearly knew what he was doing before hanging himself. He shaved, put on a pair of clean coveralls, and quietly slipped into the barn. Then he threw a rope over the beam he planned to use, tied a knot and put the rope over his neck. He climbed up on a ladder leading to the hayloft, tied the rope over a beam, and jumped off.

Young Julia was eight years old at the time and the family explained to her; "Your daddy just had problems he couldn't resolve, and he got to the point where he couldn't stand to live anymore. He was sweet-natured, a

---

[21] *Advent Review and Sabbath Herald,* July 5, 1906. p. 24.

hard-working man, someone you could look up to, but he wasn't strong the day he walked into the barn, hung himself and didn't come out alive." All his friends knew of the melancholy and depression that one day, through the heartless, mindless threads of genetics would show up in his son Frank.

Recall that John came to Nebraska under the utopian misconception that by sweat and toil he could achieve financial success. Twenty-five years of horse farming amid perilous conditions dashed his ambition. He had been humiliated by his own dream. Every difficulty he conquered gave way to three or four new difficulties.

Was he just homesick? There was no chance he'd get back to the Isle of Man to see his parents, his sister Jane, or his brother Frank. He wanted to go, but the lack of money and sizable debt had shattered any hope of such a trip. As far as we can tell, the Isle of Man ancestors do not know what became of John Cowin.

John Cowin was forty-nine years old when his Nebraska family buried him in an unmarked grave at the Oakdale cemetery behind the town. [22] After the barn was torn down, and the timbers auctioned off, farmers refused to buy the stacked wood calling it "blood lumber." Maybe John Bunyan was right.

> *When days had many of them passed away, Mr. Despondency was sent for; for a post was come, and brought this message to him: 'Trembling man, these are to summon thee to be ready with thy King by the next Lord's day, to shout for joy for thy deliverance from all thy doubtings. And,' said the messenger, 'that my message is true, that this for a proof'.' So he gave him the grasshopper to be a burden unto him.* [23]

The suicide of their father planted a virus in the minds of Frank and Weaver (William). It is said that children never escape the influence of a father's life, good or bad, and mental stain around their father's hanging

---

[22] In 1900 life expectancy for the working class was around 48 years. In the summer of 2005, the author purchased a tombstone for John, Almira, and Henry Cowin. They now have a marked place in the Oakdale Cemetery.

[23] Verse taken from Ecclesiastes 7:5. John Bunyan, "The Final Summons," *The Pilgrim's Progress*, 359.

settled quietly and deceptively in both boys like grain filling a bin or a railroad car. Son Frank was most affected. The memory of his father hanging in the barn came to him at night when he couldn't fall asleep. It struck him during storms, or in the fields, or at church. For the next twenty-one years after his father's hanging, son Frank, the one who held his father's hanging legs, continued farming the homestead. (By then the homestead had been divided into three parts shared by two other family siblings.) Life went on — sort of.

Frank was baptized into Adventism in 1889, and in 1899 married Rosa Neil Hunter, a local girl whose relatives were cattle ranchers in Oakdale. They had four children.[24] By order of birth they were Lloyd, Darrell, Verle and Ruth LaVon. Our story now advances to the life of Ruth LaVon, starting with her high school years at Oakdale.

---

[24] *The Oakdale Sentinel,* "Frank Cowin Found Dead," November 21, 1940. Rosa's mother (W. H. Hunter) was born in Germany in 1846, came to America at nine years of age, and suffered all her life with asthma. She died of dropsy and other complications in November 1896. She gave birth to three children in her first marriage and five children in her second marriage. Rosa was born in the second marriage to George Hunter. *Oakdale Sentinel,* November 28, 1896.

TOM & RUTH MEET AT COLLEGE
CHAPTER TWENTY-TWO

> "Only the human adds to his real enemies the pain of imaginary ones who blast his life with superstitious terrors. Only the human invents guilt, by inventing demons who turn his own pleasures into crimes." Susan Neiman, *Evil in Modern Thought* (Princeton, NJ: Princeton Univ. Press, 2002).

Disaster struck the Cowin family one year after John Cowin died. This time son Henry Cowin, age nine years and nine months, died on Saturday December 19,1896, as a result of a "peculiar accident." He was attempting to perform some athletic feat that badly strained him and caused his bowels to telescope. Today we know this condition as prolapse of the large intestine. It can be surgically repaired, but at the time there was nothing Dr. Minton could do but administer pain killers.[1]

Almost a year later an apparently successful operation was performed on Will Wagner, who suffered from the same telescope bowel prolapse as Henry Cowin. The doctors restored normal conditions in a surgery that was considered remarkable for the time. [2]

Subsequently Nettie Shurts, age eight, was playing around a haystack when the sharp point of a hardwood pole entered her abdomen and caused the internal bleeding that killed her. Accidents of one nature or another occurred often on the farm, affecting both children and adults.[3] The press regularly carried this tragic news to the public.

Occasionally the reports were amusing. Dr. J. R. McHugh, a phrenologist, lectured in Oakdale in 1898 and in one of his presentations he paired up the men and ladies according to the principles of phrenology. Incredibly, instead of Rose Hunter being matched with her husband-to-be, Frank Cowin, Dr. McHugh matched her to her brother George, and Frank ended up with Mable Olson, to whom he hadn't spoken for three years.

---

[1] *The Oakdale Sentinel,* December 19, 1896.
[2] Ibid. October 1, 1898.
[3] Ibid. October 8, 1898.

In 1906 Almira Cowin, wife of John Cowin, passed away at age 53. The newspaper and the *Review* called her a "faithful member of the Adventist church in Oakdale, being the first in the community to accept the present truth." She left behind a family of five children, all of whom accepted "the belief of the third angel's message. They sorrow, but not without hope." [4] She had outlived her husband John by twelve years.

Almira distributed her estate to three of her sons. Frank ended up farming 40 acres. He married Rosa Nell Hunter who bore four children — Lloyd, Darrell, Verle, and Ruth.

Their youngest child, Ruth LaVon, attended Oakdale high school and Shelton Academy. As a senior she performed in competitions involving drama readings, plays and singing. She qualified in the "Elimination Declamatory Contest" at the Oakdale High School and gave a reading called "Mickey's Marker." In the same competition she sang a solo. Later that year, the senior class presented a play in which Ruth had a major role.

At the Junior-Senior banquet in April 1934 Ruth received "a Gregg Certificate of Proficiency for having written for five minutes at one hundred words a minute and having transcribed the shorthand notes neatly and accurately on the typewriter." Ruth graduated a month later from high school. [5] A week later Ruth returned to the farm in Oakdale. By August, she was in Lincoln preparing for college.

After one year at college Ruth returned home and took a job with the law firm of Attorney Butterfield in Neligh. [6] But she returned to Union College in January 1936. (She borrowed $60 from her uncle George and promised to pay it back at $2.50 per month.) Soon she began dating Tom Willey, and they were married on July 31, 1937. Their first born, a son, arrived October 30, 1938 He was sweet natured and active and rarely cried. Ruth and Tom named him Thomas Joseph Willey.

---

[4] *Review & Herald,* May 3, 1906.
[5] *The Oakdale Sentinel,* May 31, 1934.
[6] Ibid. September 12, 1935.

RUTH SUCCUMBS TO HODGKIN'S DISEASE
CHAPTER TWENTY-THREE

"From the admission that God exists and is the author of Nature, it by no means follows that miracles must, or even can, occur. God Himself might be a being of such a kind that it was contrary to His character to work miracles. Or again, He might have made Nature the sort of thing that cannot be added to, subtracted from, or modified. The case against Miracles accordingly relies on two different grounds. You either think that the character of God excludes them or that the character of Nature excludes them." C. S. Lewis, *Miracles,* 71.

In June 1825 Thomas Hodgkin (1798-1866), a physician in Guy's Hospital in London, became "Inspector of the Dead and Curator of the Museum of Morbid Anatomy." There he caught the attention of the great clinician and British surgeon, Sir Astley Cooper, who understood the importance of postmortem examinations and recognized Hodgkin's potential for advancing the emerging field of pathological anatomy.

As a Quaker with a strong social consciousness, Hodgkin set out to promote healthful living in the working classes. He took an active role in the temperance movement during the Victorian period and recommended a vegetarian diet that the Adventist health gospel would later replicate.

Hodgkin's renown in medical history rests on his discovery of what we call Hodgkin's Disease, a rare cancer that starts in the lymph nodes and spreads. It is more common in males than females. The cancer usually presents as enlargements in the nodes around the neck and upper body. Some nodes may swell to the size of an egg. If the cancer is unchecked death results. The swelling gradually stifles a person's breath or progressively closes off the circulatory system. But if diagnosis is made early and treated with x-rays and chemotherapy, many patients survive the disease.

In 1939 Tom became principal of Denver Junior Academy (near Campion Academy), an Adventist school with an enrollment of 120 students.

In September 1939 Ruth told her mother that "it looks as if the end of time is drawing near. We have been listening to the radio all day practically and now Britain and France have gone into it for good and earnest, and Britain has just taken the German liner Bremen. I just wonder now how long it will be before the U. S. goes into it. It may be less than a year, and Tom says he may not be able to finish this school year…" [1]

The Willey's moved into an upstairs apartment three blocks north of the academy. Ruth was pregnant again, hoping for a girl this time, and expecting around December. Tom took his job seriously. Now married over two years, his tie to Ruth was strong and affectionate, and her affection for him was loyal and admiring. Of course they were poor – trying to survive on the sacrificial wages of the church.

There wasn't the slightest doubt that the family of nations was playing out the Biblical prophesies. The Adventist prophetess had explained:

In the warfare to be waged in the last days there will be united, in opposition to God's people, all the corrupt powers that have apostatized from allegiance to the law of Jehovah. In this warfare the Sabbath of the fourth commandment will be the great point at issue, for in the Sabbath commandment the great Lawgiver identifies Himself as the Creator of the heavens and the earth. [2]

But unless God had changed his mind, Hitler was not trying to corral Sabbath keepers in the United States and force a different day for worship. Most Adventists did not see Hitler as the antichrist: the antichrist was the Roman Catholic Church.

In the middle of September Tom and Ruth had thirty cents between them! Because Tom was not paid until the end of the month, they could

---

[1] Ruth's letter to her mother, September 3, 1939.
[2] Ellen G. White, *Selected Messages, III*, 392 (1891).

not handle an outstanding debt and a new baby coming shortly. When talking about money, Tom gazed into space. Most frustrating of all was the church's tendency to delay salaries because of its own lack of resources. Tom asked his father for financial help and generous friends loaned furniture, a washing machine, and other necessary items. They were scratching out a living, trying to establish a home on the heels of the depression.

Ruth told her sister in Lincoln, "Tom has some bad students in school using tough language. But he was on to their case and had warned them to stop talking this way or get out of school." Satan may have been influencing the youth, but Tom preferred to blame the restless hormones he'd learned about in psychology at Union College.

The boys admired his joking nature and baseball skills. The girls liked the new principal because he taught them the planetary system and showed them how to jump-shoot a basketball. One girl told him after gym class, "You're pretty nice, Mr. Tom." Another girl thought she could out-run the principal, but in a race around the block he beat her.

Like many newlyweds Tom and Ruth succumbed to a high-pressure salesperson who talked them into purchasing cookware on time. The product was hard to keep clean and slow to heat, and Ruth admitted they had been duped. So Tom talked to a lawyer about breaking the contract. But the lawyer only warned him of buzzards that circled newlyweds.

As a stay-at-home mother, Ruth cleaned the house, washed the clothes, provided a warm, happy environment, and worried over the moral training of two children in an evil and wicked world. She'd be the first to tell you she was naïve about raising children.

The January 4, 1940 issue of *Review* told its readers,

> *As men scorn the hand of the Prince of Peace, God waits to send forth His Son the second time to redeem those whose hearts are perfect toward Him. Surely that time cannot long be delayed. The hour is late, and the end of all things earthly is near and hasteth (sic) greatly. The long controversy between the forces of good and evil is almost ready for its terrifying and eternal climax.*

Ruth remembered the warning of persecution to come at the end of time in America and the need for commandment keepers then to flee to the hills and hide.

A daughter Marcia Jean was born at the Denver Porter Sanitarium and Hospital in December of 1939. Ruth stayed ten days in the hospital and her mother Rose came by train from Nebraska to help care for Tommy Joe and prepare meals for Tom. When Ruth got home, Rose returned to the homestead. Tom and Ruth now had two adorable children and every intent to raise them to love "the message" in spite of wicked influences.

Ruth awaked Tom one morning and an said that there was something wrong with her. She complained of bumps under her armpits, constant fatigue, sweating at night, itchy skin, and shortness of breath. Warm tears ran down her cheeks as she mentioned symptoms.

On Saturday evening, February 17, 1940, Tom and Ruth attended a social function at the academy gymnasium. She hadn't wanted to go but Tom talked her into showing off the new baby for an hour or so, especially because their college friends, Alma and Charles Teel Sr., would be there. It cheered Ruth to hear the happy responses of everyone to her new child Marcia Jean.

But Charles Teel sat down next to Ruth and said, "You don't look well, sister." (Extending a salutation using "sister" or 'brother' in Adventist circles was an old-fashioned greeting. Church leaders were referred to as the "brethren.") He went on, "You look like you've lost weight. Haven't you been feeling well?" Alma inquired if perhaps Ruth was still recovering from childbirth.

"To tell you the truth I've not felt good for a month," Ruth replied. "I think I have an infection in my neck. My glands are swollen. Tommy thinks I might have the mumps or something like that."

Charles quickly asked, "Well sister, what are you going to do about it? Why don't you go see the doctor and get yourself checked out?"

"We don't have any money for that," Ruth blurted out, dropping back to a whisper. Without hesitation Charles reached into his pocket and took out a twenty-dollar gold piece and gave it to Ruth.

"Promise me tomorrow you will go see Dr. Beebe at the Porter San and get yourself checked out. You and Tom pay me back later when you can." In spite of economic hardships during the depression Charley carried gold in his pockets as an unassailable means to get things done. He had a reputation as a wheeler-dealer!

The next day, Sunday, Tom and Ruth arranged to see Dr. Nathan L. Beebe at the Porter Sanitarium. (Dr. Beebe was a family physician who graduated from the College of Medical Evangelists — now called Loma Linda University Medical School — in 1921 and who delivered the two children of Tom and Ruth.)

After Beebe's initial examination, he expressed concern about Ruth and a need to consult with another physician. Beebe then arranged for Ruth to return shortly. As they were standing in the hallway, Beebe told Tom "It might be tuberculosis, but it definitely is not the mumps. But we will hold off guessing until we get further studies."

They returned to Porter Tuesday afternoon. Neither Tom nor Ruth knew what to expect as they went from one examining room to another. Blood samples were taken and x-rays of Ruth's chest. After this was completed a female specialist entered the examining room with Beebe. She felt Ruth's neck and measured the swelling under her arms, and then explained to Ruth that her lymph nodes were abnormally enlarged without any signs of inflammation.

The specialist and Beebe went into the hall and began an earnest discussion with troubled looks on their faces. After a while they came back and Beebe told Ruth that she had a "blood disorder." He was reassuring and said, "not to worry, we'll find a way to treat this illness." He implied it looked like an early infection of some sort.

Beebe then asked Tom if they could speak privately. Outside the room, Beebe said, "Tom, while Ruth is not in pain, we have a really bad diagnosis from the hematologist for Ruth. We need to begin talking about this possible diagnosis. It is our considered opinion that Ruth should not know, at least for now, what we suspect. Keep this to yourself for the time being. Let it ride for a time. But here is what we know."

Dr. Beebe went on: "Ruth has a disorder like leukemia called Hodgkin's disease, a blockage of the lymphatic system. That is why her neck glands are swollen. If this is the case, we are looking at a serious disease. Now, what can we do about this? We need to begin x-ray treatments right away in the hopes of clearing it up in a few weeks. However, I want to tell you that the treatments with x-rays are considered experimental—and there are no assurances that radiation will work to reduce the swelling or destroy the cancer. We'll probably know this outcome in a few weeks."

Beebe paused, stepped back, and looked as if he was trying to decide what to say next. After taking a deep breath and letting it out slowly, he said, "I believe I should tell you from the beginning that Hodgkin's patients often have only six to twelve months to live after the first signs. That is for the really severe cases. We don't know if we have caught Ruth's early or not." He went on: "Hodgkin's is not contagious, if that is what you are worried about you can put that aside. After we get things started, she can occasionally return home after a treatment. By using radiation, we are trying to arrest the growth of the cancer. But here is what can happen: we might see it go into remission for a while but then it might show up again. Unfortunately, we don't have a foolproof treatment for Hodgkin's."

Beebe's words struck Tom like a violent earthquake. His feelings may be more easily imagined than described. They had the viscosity of the fear he felt in the haymow when Billy was dying. Suddenly his world was changed. Hopes and dreams had yet to be accomplished in their new marriage. With a wonderful wife and two new-born children he had found a vibrant world of happiness, but what did the diagnosis actually mean? Could Ruth die at her young age of 23 years?

After what Beebe just said, Tom could have raged through the hospital hallways in terrible pain, but instead he asked, "Are you sure Ruth has Hodgkin's?" It seemed such a hopeless cancer.

"Yes, Tom, we are sure."

Beebe recommended that Tom check Ruth into the Boulder Sanitarium and start radiation treatments the very next day. (Boulder was about forty miles from Denver.) Beebe then asked about the children. Was there someone in the family who could take care of them for a few weeks? Tom said they would work things out.

Beebe told Tom that radiation often leaves patients sick and unable to keep down their food. They talked a little more about what to expect. Clearly Beebe, with a little stoop to his shoulders, was weary from confronting an untreatable disease that could take the life of a young woman.

The Boulder-Colorado Sanitarium where Ruth was taken for treatment was a branch of the world-renown Kellogg Sanitarium of Battle Creek, Michigan. It was constructed largely from Adventist tithe money, a detail Ellen White later condemned: "The light which the Lord has been pleased to give me is that it was not right to build this sanitarium upon funds supplied by the General Conference." [3] Initially begun as a tubercular sanitarium, the Boulder San soon became popular among people desiring the lifestyle changes promoted by the colorful John Harvey Kellogg.

Ruth began her first radiation treatment immediately. As for the children, Ruth told her mother that "If we had the money, we would pay your way out. So many people came to take the kids when they found out about it. We had more places than we needed to put them. Tom has been out of school the last couple of days. He has been so worried."

But hearing that the children were passed on to others, Ruth's mother Rose came on the train and took the two children back to Lincoln. When she arrived in Lincoln and came down the platform carrying Marcia Jean in her arms, Tommy Joe, a year and a half old clutched her shirt and sucked his thumb. The children would see their mother off and on, but never would return to Colorado and be under Ruth's sole care.

During her treatments at the Boulder Sanitarium Ruth did not ask for the complete truth of her diagnosis. But she likely understood the gravity of her illness by overhearing conversations among the doctors, nurses, and technicians, and by undergoing endless tests and examinations. At one point she came close to guessing her condition from an article she read in a health magazine in one of the waiting rooms. She found the uncertainties hard to live with, but she feared learning the outlook. No disease could destroy her so long as she followed the medical treatments and prayed. In one of her letters to her mother she closed by saying, "I'm so sore and tired. I do so want to get well. I miss my children. Let us live so that God will hear our prayers."

---

[3] Letter 93, 1899. Source: Robert W. Olson, "Ellen G. White Comments on the Use of Tithe Funds."

Ruth endured eighteen separate x-ray treatments over several weeks at the Boulder San. They left her constipated, burned from radiation, and short of breath.

Good things also happened. One day when Tom brought Ruth back from the San, the boy next door offered his pet rabbit. He said, "I was going to give this to my aunt, but I'd like to give it to you to keep you company." (This was the same boy who once said his ears were so good, he could hear the grass scream when he mowed the lawn.)

In May 1940 Tom and Ruth took a public bus from Denver to Bismarck and then on to Minot. Their trip was relaxing and comfortable. In Minot Tom bought Ruth a new hat, and they had an intimate supper together as they relaxed in the best hotel in town, the same hotel where Tom's grandfather stayed when he came to North Dakota to take out a homestead claim. They waited at the hotel for Tom's sister Genevieve and Alan Rasmussen to take them to the farm in Mohall. Ruth wrote to her mother about the trip, "I've been thinking a thousand times about my darling babies and grandma how you withstood the trip back to Lincoln. Were they good?" Fortunately, during their two-week visit to North Dakota there was only a little pain associated with her tumor. Ruth and Tom had a wonderful time visiting with Tom's parents and traveling into Canada.

Back in Lincoln, the children became separated. Tommy Joe went to the Frank Cowin farm in Oakdale. (While there he got the chicken pox.) Marcia Jean went to Ruth's brother Darrell and his wife Willie Dee in Lincoln. Before they parted, someone took pictures of the two children and sent them to Ruth. Her reaction was that, "Everyone is wild about the pictures." Ruth showed them around to her friends and the clinic staff.

In July Tom and his brother-in-law Lloyd Cowin went to the fireworks display in Denver. As Ruth remained at home in bed, she wrote a letter that was to remain sealed until after she passed away. The letter contained her instructions on the future of her children. Obviously, this time Ruth had a premonition that she was going to die. Here is a portion of that letter. [4]

---

[4] "If I can't live, I told Tom your folks (the Willeys) are entitled to them first, to take my place. They will soon make a cute pair." Letter undated.

I am writing this because I do not know just what might happen. The Lord may see fit not to spare my life, but I feel I am ready for whatever is His will. I feel so ill at times I am afraid I will not surely live and I am writing this while alive. I think of my dear sweet babies who may be left without a mother. That is the bitterest thought of all. They are so dear and innocent and ready even for instruction. I want them to be as happy of life as possible, and yet I want them to learn the lessons of life in a way that will benefit them…whoever cares for them, please love them as your very own. It is my desire that they not be separated. I want them to grow up together and love each other… I want them to grow up in a home where the parents are true Christian Seventh-day Adventists. Give them the love like I would like to give them. Love them and teach them the truth. I pray that God will bless all who undertake to carry out these instructions…My tears flow fast, but God will wipe all tears from our eyes. May we all meet in that first resurrection.

On July 16 Ruth and Tom left Denver by train and traveled to her sister's home in Lincoln. There Ruth began treatments that extended to the end of September.

Ruth was evaluated by Dr. Rinehard, who had trained at the Rockefeller Institute in New York, and by Dr. Roeme, an expert on radiation, after they studied her x-ray pictures and blood tests. A ten-day hospitalization seemed likely. When Tom pleaded about the expense, Dr. Rinehard said, "Don't worry, fellow, you play square with us and we will with you." Together the two physicians reached the same conclusion that the Colorado physicians had reached at the Porter San. Rinehard reassured Ruth wth a pinch of hope that she might survive the disease. During her x-ray treatments, Ruth was to remain quiet in her bed and not walk to and from her treatment rooms. After a week of daily treatments, the swelling in the lymph nodes had decreased. Soon she left the hospital and returned to her sister's home.

Ruth's brother-in-law Ted had prepared a room upstairs for her. Ruth had not lost any ground during the summer. "Now if I can just get complete relief won't that be grand! I don't see why God wouldn't see fit at this time to cure me." But her chest area was "terribly sore and swollen."

In her next letter to her mother Ruth lamented that Marcia Jean "doesn't act like she recognizes me. I'm so disappointed, but I suppose it will have to be that way for a while." Nearing the end of her letter she said, "Love my Tommy Joe for me, how I miss the dear little kisses, study your Bibles, and pray without ceasing."

During August she wrote to her mother that she was "feeling pretty good except my left side." The two physicians told Ruth that they should know in a few weeks whether the x-rays had destroyed the tumors. They decided to use a "Fluroscope" to evaluate the changes in her lungs. After this last bout of treatments Ruth took a turn for the worse and could not see visitors. She wrote, "I'm so sick at my stomach I can hardly keep anything down. Even lost my fruit juice and pills this afternoon. I am afraid if I can't eat, they will let up on the treatments and that won't do. I have tried so hard to keep stuff down but I'm getting so I can't look at food."

John and Inez came to Lincoln for a visit near the end of September. Since Ruth's birthday was coming up in October, they bought her a black dress. Later, Ruth wrote to thank them for the gift and update on her progress. "Well, I hardly know what to write. I know you want to know how I am. I wish I could tell you I'm feeling just grand and will be with you soon. But I can't say that, not yet, and it just about breaks my heart. I'm tired and sore, breathless. But there is always something to be thankful for. I'm happy to say there are no new pains and aches, and I'm learning to handle myself better; with more patience I will make it yet. I'm still saying, "by the 24th of Oct at least."

The day before Ruth's 24th birthday she wrote to Tom in Colorado. He was thinking of taking a leave of absence from his new preceptorship at Campion Academy, but Ruth didn't "really want him to do that as her sister and her husband might find the arrangement an added burden if Tom were to come to Lincoln." She valued the love between them: "I have always wanted to make you happy and as I look back our happiest moments were those when we were alone in our own room at home, talking and planning together. Oh, Thomas, I find so much happiness in thinking back over our happy times together. We used to talk and plan for the future, but I find no pleasure in that anymore. So, I sit and dream of the past and smile when I think of some incident you would enjoy recounting with me."

Elder A. L. White, grandson of Ellen White and secretory of the trustees who oversaw the writings of the Spirit of Prophecy, visited Union College October 9 to 14. He spoke to the student body for chapel, Friday evening vesper service, and Sabbath morning church service. Following these meetings, he displayed "some of the White manuscripts, her first writings of the Testimonies to the church, and other books. He showed the "big family Bible which Mrs. White, as a young seventeen-year-old girl, was alleged to have held outstretched on one hand for a half hour while she was in vision and reading separate verses." This Bible was printed by Joseph Teale in Boston in 1822 and weighed eighteen pounds. The story became an Adventist legend used over the years as a supernatural proof of Ellen White's visions. [5]

Somehow around October 12 Arthur White learned of Ruth's steady decline and brought the "big family Bible" to her the bedside at brother-in-law Ted and sister Verle's home. According to her cousin, Shirley Burton, who was present, White placed the eighteen-pound Bible on Ruth's chest and then, with Elder M. L. Howell, anointed her and prayed that God would heal her – this being the first known use of the "Big Bible" as a talisman for healing.

White often demonstrated this "Big Bible" as he visited Adventist Colleges promoting his grandmother as a prophet. On these occasions he advertised that he was coming and offered students the opportunity to see how long they could hold the Bible outstretched in the manner of the young prophetess. During his visit to Walla Walla College (an Adventist higher education institution), few people, even young men working in the forests of the Northwest, could hold it outstretched more than two minutes.

Before White's visit a clever student at Walla Walla went to the woodshop and fashioned a wedge to fit under his right arm inside his suit and designed it so that when he lifted his arm the wedge would snap into the position and lock into place. After the audience had their opportunity,

---

[5] The legend was promoted by Elder J. N. Loughborough in his book (*The Great Second Advent Movement*) written 45 years later. The story has never been verified and was not told by either Ellen or James White. The White Estate continues to repeat this legend without documentation.

this student came up to try his own outstretched hand. The wedge under his coat snapped into place and he held the Bible for five minutes, then ten minutes. The enthralled audience began clapping. At twelve minutes White became suspicious. He felt under the student's arm, found the locked wedge, and halted the demonstration. When the faculty discovered that Benny Armstrong (not his real name) had sullied the reputation of the prophetess, they expelled him from the college. He went to another Adventist college and eventually finished medicine at the College of Medical Evangelists (now Loma Linda University Medical School). [6]

Tom took a leave of absence at Campion Academy near the end of October 1940 when Ruth was approaching death. She coughed constantly, could not digest her food, and became steadily weaker. Seeing the end in sight, she summoned each family member to her bedside and whispered goodbye. Ruth gave each one an individual message of hope and the assurance of meeting on the other side. After everyone left, she asked Tom to get in bed with her and hold her tight, "Don't let me go." Tom talked to her about the promises of heaven and promised to take care of the children. He held her tight until her breathing stopped and felt the worst pain he had ever known. Ruth passed away at 9:40 A.M. on Sunday.

Tom held her a little longer. A wonderful spouse had been taken from him. He then went downstairs and told the waiting family that Ruth had passed away. Almost immediately Ruth's father jumped forward and lost his temper. Ruth was his favorite, perhaps the most talented of his children. Unbelievably, in the course of his outrage he blamed Tom for the death of Ruth and son Lloyd joined in the accusation.

How could the father and son possibly blame Tom for the death of Ruth? It was because Tom had dissipated the vital forces of Ruth after only two years of marriage. She was in good health before marriage, and now, two years later, she was dead. Nothing was left of her vital force to sustain her. This bizarre force notion was taught by John Harvey Kellogg, the renowned physician of Battle Creek Sanitarium, and voiced by Ellen White, the trusted prophetess of the Adventist church. In his famous book *Plain Facts for the Old and Young*, Kellogg stated that "The reproductive act is the most exhaustive of all vital acts," and went on to discuss the loss

---

[6] Account told to the author by Alice Gregg, Librarian at Loma Linda University. She was a student at Walla Walla College when this event occurred in the 1940s.

of vital force through excessive sexual activity.[7] Ellen White conveyed her views about intercourse between married couples with the language of phrenology:

> *It is not pure, holy love which leads the wife to gratify the animal propensities of her husband at the expense of health and life. If she possesses true love and wisdom, she will seek to divert his mind from the gratification of lustful passions to high and spiritual themes by dwelling upon interesting spiritual subjects. It may be necessary to humbly and affectionately urge, even at the risk of his displeasure, that she cannot debase her body by yielding to sexual excess. She should, in a tender, kind manner, remind him that God has*

---

[7] In the early part of the twentieth century, John Harvey Kellogg gained a reputation as a physician, nutritionist, and sex adviser. The foods that Kellogg created (including the now-famous corn flakes) were designed to promote health. His brother Will participated in the invention of breakfast cereals and went on to become a wealthy man. The two brothers disagreed over how to market and produce their cereals.

Famous Americans from all over, including Henry Ford, Lowell Thomas, George Bernard Shaw, Howard Taft and Tomas Edison, visited the Battle Creek Sanitarium. Kellogg opened nearly fifty "branches" from California to the Rockies and Midwest and all the way to New Zealand, Australia, Egypt. Japan, India, South Africa and Palestine. Ellen White worried about worldly influences and businesses resulting from the rising power of Battle Creek Sanitariums. In 1902 the Sanitarium in Battle Creek burned down and Ellen White claimed to have seen an angel with a fiery sword. Then, mysteriously, ten months later the Review and Herald building also burned down. It seemed that someone was trying to destroy the Adventist empire in Battle Creek. Ellen White, along with the General Conference president A. G. Daniels, opposed the headstrong John Harvey. Mrs. White reminded him that God had given him success as a physician. Unable to control the doctor, she claimed that Satan had taken over his life. "I have spent hours agonizing with God over this matter. We need to get ready. It is not God's plan for our people to crowd into Battle Creek."

John Harvey Kellogg thought sex was the ultimate abomination and remained celibate himself even in marriage. He thought masturbation, the worst sin imaginable, led to leprosy, tuberculosis, heart disease, epilepsy, dimness of vision, insanity, idiocy, and death. He also preached that masturbation led to bashfulness in some people, unnatural boldness in others, a fondness for spicy foods, round shoulders, and acne. Among 84 books, his *Plain Facts for the Old and Young* was the most popular, selling an estimated half-million copies. It was sold door-to-door by canvassers.

the first and highest claim upon her entire being, and that she
cannot disregard this claim, for she will be held accountable
in the great day of God. [8]

This exchange in the house where Ruth died effectively terminated all goodwill between the Cowins and the Willeys.

Elder J. M. Howell presided over Ruth's funeral in the Oakdale Methodist church. "Everything that human wisdom and kindness could do," he said, "was done to relieve her suffering in the attempt to bring her back to health, but each month witnessed a gradual decline in strength. She earnestly pled with God to give her life and strength with which to care for her family but was resigned to His will and faced whatever future He might see fit to grant her with true Christian fortitude. Her last act was to call the several members of her family together and give each a parting admonition, asking each to meet her in the glad resurrection morning. A letter written sometime before her death but sealed until after she should die, gave instructions in regard to the training and care of her children." [9]

Friends and neighbors around the farm brought food and encouragement to the Cowins during the funeral. Afterwards, Tom picked up the two children in Lincoln and took the train to Balfour, North Dakota where he stayed for a few weeks with his sister Genevieve and Elvin Rasmussen. The Rasmussen's sought to adopt the two children, but because Tom's sister was not Seventh-day Adventist, a stipulation in Ruth letter, the Cowins objected to this, and so they went back to Darrell and Dee Cowin in Lincoln. Eventually, they were raised separately.

The violence at the moment of Ruth's death in Lincoln over a supposed loss of vital force could have been the subject of a novel by Sinclair Lewis. As noted earlier, the grotesque accusation left a lasting impression on some of the family.

The Death of Frank Cowin

Frank Cowin, Ruth's father, was born in January 1877 in a pioneer's log cabin on the John Cowin homestead. There he would farm and raise

---

[8] Ellen G. White, *Adventist Home*, 124-126.
[9] *The Oakdale Sentinel,* November 3, 1940.

a family. He passed away on November 21, 1940, at the age of sixty three. Sadly, he had hung himself from the windmill put up by his father on the farm to pump water. [10]

During the two weeks after burying his daughter Ruth, Frank felt only despair and depression, and, of course, he blamed the death of Ruth on Tom. Known to be unstable mentally, he did not return to his home in Oakdale, but instead went to live with his brother William who promised to watch over him. During a moment of not being watched he slipped away and committed suicide. Children walking on the road to school saw his body hanging on the windmill and told their teacher. It was removed by the owner of a furniture store in Neigh and the sheriff.

Frank's death ruined the farm because in 1934 he had taken a second mortgage under the Emergency Farm Mortgage Act of 1933 for $1,000 while the Federal Land Bank of Omaha held the first mortgage for $6,000.[11] Eventually the farm was sold to a bidder for $5,983.

---

[10] Ibid. November 21, 1940.

[11] In the District Court of Antelope County, Nebraska: "The Federal Land Bank of Omaha, vs. Roas Cowin and others," May 14, 1941.

THE APPEAL OF THE
SECOND COMING
CHAPTER TWENTY-FOUR

The life of homestead farm families in the 19th century US Midwest was very difficult. Their success and very survival depended on things they could not control, like the weather, the sale price for their produce, and accidents that could injure and kill. They had no insurance for protection from disasters and limited access to medical care. Their workdays were long and arduous, requiring strong physical effort with little relief from work routines. Only strong and determined people could succeed and survive in such difficult conditions.

Religion provided stability and hope for these people. They believed in a supernatural God who gave them principles to live by, principles like honesty and care for family and neighbors. Their religion linked together a small community that shared similar beliefs and provided mutual support. Their religion taught them to reduce the physical work of humans and animals to a minimum one day a week. Perhaps most important, they believed in a future heaven where they would not have to worry about food to eat or physical safety. Christ was soon to return to Earth to take believers to heaven, the living along with the resurrected dead believers. That belief sustained them in winter blizzards, plagues of grasshoppers, and severe illnesses.

People acquire their religious notions and beliefs from their parents. This was true of father. He was raised a Seventh-day Adventist because his mother and father held to that faith.

I had many wonderful discussions about religion with my father. His spiritual "world" was not clear as to how "sinful man" got to heaven. The faith that he knew and practiced doubted salvation through Christ's saving grace alone because obedience to God's law and conformity with God's will was also required. Reaching a celestial heaven depended on sustaining good works while on earth, converting people to the faith, paying tithe, and never killing another person. If you lived thusly, you might bear the seal of God's approval on your forehead after passing through an investigative judgment.

Repentance worked for most sins — if forgiveness was necessary, but some sins were said to be unpardonable. The closing of probation hung over the sinner's head, after which no more sins would be forgiven, and you never knew when your probation was going to close. In modern times, this God of the Old Testament had stopped speaking directly to his people. The New Testament proclaimed that God had created man in His image, but sin had tarnished that image. Christ then came to earth and lived a fully human (but also fully God-like) life. To understand this, one had to interpret the Bible properly and listen to the preachers and teachers who had been indoctrinated in the message.

Near the end of his life my dad came to see Adventism as a complex religious system that advanced a lot of fantasy, imagination, and manipulation. The observance of Saturday as the Sabbath, loyalty to other parts of God's law, salvation essentially by works, the fear of God's judgment, the idea that Christ could return as a thief in the night, all seemed to him to be an outright swindle. Adventist doctrines were bundled together as a package and driven in part by a woman prophetess who incited fear of the end. As God's chosen people, Adventists would be persecuted — hunted down and forced to flee their homes by Sunday keeping Protestants and Catholics. A time of trouble like the world has never known would have to be endured before the Second Coming.

My father thought that only a defective salvation story could limit the redeemed to 144,000. Nor could God have swept nearly all mankind and the animals out of existence by drowning them in a flood, as recounted in the story of Noah. After much study, my father dismissed the whole notion of a world-wide flood that happened four thousand years ago.

The idea of a devil named Satan lurking behind the scenes to tempt loyal believers preoccupied and troubled my father. This devil had rebelled against God in heaven and been banished to the earth. He saw his mistake and pled with God to forgive him, but God did not offer a second chance.

Father's religious beliefs, inherited from the family that persisted through droughts, grasshoppers, and Billy's death, thus didn't measure up for him at the end of his life. A factor that probably influenced this decision was the silence of God when he and his young wife Ruth pled for her healing.

Ruth, on the other hand, found solace in her beliefs until her last breath. From the day in early January 1940 that she first felt something wrong in her body, until her passing, was about 10 months. Those months brought progressively increasing discomfort to Ruth, starting with pain and swelling in her neck and shoulder. The cancer treatments added more pain, constipation, and inability to keep food down. The focus of her thoughts during this difficult period was on her "babies," Tommy Joe and Marcia, separated from her and each living with a different family member. On August 11, Ruth wrote to her friend Lura:

> I have been down again with the old trouble and another batch of [radiation] treatments. I am just getting so I feel pretty good again. I know, however, that there is still some of it [cancer] in my system and as long as there is, I know what to expect. I am not a bit discouraged, though. The Lord knows best.

On September 27, Ruth wrote to the Willeys:

> I wish I could tell you I'm feeling just <u>grand</u> and will be with you soon. But I can't say that, not yet, and it just about breaks my heart. I am so tired and sore and breathless. . . I'm tired of trying to figure it out. God will take care of tomorrow, but in our human way, we try to fix it all ourselves. I lay awake at night and worry about having the babies, or what will happen to them when I am gone, until I am quite sick at heart, and it gives me such a feeling of sadness I can hardly keep from weeping. I should trust the Heavenly Father's goodness to care for them, but sometimes it is hard, for His ways are past understanding.

Ruth reached her 24th birthday on October 3. Exactly one month later on the morning of November 3, she passed quietly to her rest. She had trusted God a long way and looked forward to the promised life without pain and sorrow in heaven.

POSTSCRIPT BY JOE'S WIFE BARBARA

As the author's wife of 40 years and a primary care physician, I dedicated my heart, soul, and medical expertise to help Joe extend the waning days of his life. I want to share with his readers my personal experience of the harsh struggles he endured to complete his book before the death he knew was imminent. Joe's efforts to finish the writing showed his determination and they are a testament to the blossoming of the human spirit when watered generously by the love of family and friends.

In what Joe referred to as his "first potting", he was a celebrated neuroscientist, authoring 40 papers published in peer-reviewed journals such as *Neurology*. In his "second potting" he created a new kind of service business known as Employee Leasing. To support this business, he wrote 13 books and traveled the world explaining the benefits of this new kind of service.

In Joe's "last potting" he turned to creative writing, specializing in religion and church history. He went about this with the same intensity displayed in his earlier careers and routinely researched and wrote for eight to ten hours a day. During this phase he also began to write about his family history. To enrich this history with true stories and factual details, he traveled to Nebraska, Iowa, and North Dakota, scouring small-town libraries and newspaper archives. Joe dedicated four years of research and writing to this family history project before his failing health started to limit his writing capabilities.

Joe's "slug paced" slide toward death started six years earlier when he was admitted to the cardiac ward with a struggling heart. Arriving two hours later, I was alarmed to see on the monitor that his blood pressure was a frightening 40/0! I rushed for a nurse to ask what treatment he was given to support his sagging circulation. Based on my five years of experience in an Emergency Department, I had to struggle to display a relatively calm exterior to mask my inner panic! I knew that such a low reading could not sustain his life for any extended period. The nurse arrived in a flurry with a vial in hand which she swiftly plunged into his intravenous line. "What have you tried," I asked? "We have given him two other vasopressor agents with no results," she replied. It took about ten minutes, but his blood pressure finally began to climb, eventually reaching 70/40. This provided enough blood flow to nourish his brain and some other parts of his body, but too little for his kidneys. They had already been receiving an inadequate blood supply for the past several years as his heart gradually deteriorated and this episode ended their functioning completely. Thereafter, continuing life for Joe would mean ongoing artificial kidney function.

Doctors first put Joe on hemodialysis. This worked for a few months, but his subnormal blood pressure of 70/40 repeatedly set off the machine's alarm, frightening the staff. Finally, the nephrology team kicked him out of the unit. The only alternative remaining to prolong his life was home peritoneal dialysis. This form of dialysis uses the fatty, vessel-laden covering of the intestines and inside the abdomen (the peritoneum) as a filter where an exchange of fluids can clear waste from his body. Joe had a tube coming out of his abdomen that he connected to his computer-controlled dialysis machine every night for a twelve-hour treatment. During that period, his machine cycled four 5-liter bags of fluid through his abdomen.

With his dialysis treatments, Joe did not have enough energy to write for the next three years. The treatments extended his life, but his condition steadily deteriorated with more frequent shortness of breath and inability to walk much farther than the bathroom. I consulted with his doctor and we decided that it was best to put him on hospice care in October, 2017. It appeared that his life expectancy was about six months.

In December of that year, Joe and I attended a friend's funeral at the La Sierra University Church. With every known acquaintance of the deceased talking at length (their allotted two minutes stretching to ten), the service lasted for more than three hours. Sitting there, Joe and I decided that we did not want our families to endure an experience like that. In addition, I am not fond of funerals because when I was eighteen, my father was killed in a private plane crash just two months after five other close relatives perished in a similar accident.

As an alternative to a funeral, we hit upon the idea of celebrating Joe's life while he was still alive and could appreciate the impact he made on others. Joe was excited about this idea, so with the help of our two sons, I organized a celebration event in January, 2018, at the beautiful Mission

Inn in Riverside, California. One hundred thirty of Joe's family and friends ate and mingled together to honor and celebrate him. Three prominent executives came from across the US to describe the great influence Joe had in the business community. Joe was able to hear many of his friends relate personal expressions of his contributions to their lives.

Key events in our lives can awaken feelings deep within and change our direction. The celebration of life did just that for Joe. Several days after the event, he came to me and announced that he now felt the energy to finish his book. Before the celebration, he had been at death's door, but now he returned to his habit of going to his office daily to write, now for a shorter period of three to four hours. An internal force was driving him to get his story on paper completed. Writing about his family and their ancestral journey, Joe believed that he could better understand his own life passages as he too wrestled with similar spiritual and emotional issues. His book was also an expression of love and appreciation for his family and for their traditions and ideas that were the roots of his own beliefs.

On October 16, 2018, Joe came home and announced that he had finished his book, with the caveat that it still needed some polishing and editing. A week later, as Joe lay in bed, I noticed that he had a slightly twisted smile and garbled speech as he tried to tell me what he wanted to eat. Recognizing that he was having a stroke, I reached for his hands and received a weak left grip. I tried to test the strength in his legs, but he had minimal movement. It was as if he was glued to the bed, devoid of the strength to even turn from side to side. Joe then blurted out "I'm not going back to the hospital." "Joe, I will take care of you," I assured him. I promised to be by his side, twenty-four hours a day, seven days a week. With the help of friends, family, hospice care, and the nephrology team, I was determined to follow through on my commitment.

Periodically, we worked at getting Joe out of bed to improve his core strength, but it took two of us with a sling and a hoist to lift him from his bed into a wheelchair and a little later, back into his bed again. He could only tolerate about fifteen minutes of sitting, or rather slumping, because his low blood pressure (70/40) provided little reserve strength.

Polishing his book drained too much energy from Joe and after three months, he was unable to continue the work. He was sure he was going to get better and never expressed to me any feeling that he might not recover.

Two months before his death, I asked him, "Joe, if you want to go, I could disconnect the machine." Without hesitation, he said. "No. That would be giving up!"

Joe's nephrology team made weekly visits to check on his status and make any needed adjustments to his dialysis treatment. They observed that he was losing a lot of weight and reluctantly informed me that I should not continue his treatments if he did not eat. We tried giving him marijuana cookies, protein milkshakes, and all his favorite foods to increase his appetite, but with little success.

Six months to the day after his stroke, the dialysis machine was turned off. Joe had not eaten more than two tablespoons of food in five days and that simply was not enough to sustain him. Lapsing into a coma, he was motionless except for an infrequent breath. While sitting at his bedside, I reached over to hold his one good hand and was both shocked and pleasantly surprised by the strong grip he offered in return. To me, it was a signal of his love and devotion, a last valued touch.

Then there was a final stillness and he was gone forever. Gone from a body racked with uremia from five-years of end-stage renal disease. Gone from a fibrillating heart that had sent a stray clot to his brain, leaving him unable to roll over in bed by himself or use half of his body. Joe had endured so many losses of the flesh, but his spirit was strong to the end.

Throughout his whole downward slide, Joe showed the same indomitable spirit that his homesteading forefathers had demonstrated time after time when their bumper crop of wheat was destroyed by hailstorms, prairie fires, or hordes of locusts. They endured deaths and other losses, turning to their religion and their God to sustain them as they anticipated the second coming of their Savior. They knew that heaven was a long way to go.

Joe, the author of this book, died on April 23, 2019.

As a final note, I would like to share what Joe's sister said about him during his Celebration of Life as it captures many qualities of Joe that I also love and appreciate about him:

> *Joe and I developed a bond and closeness from our very beginning that has lasted all our lives. Our mother died shortly after I was born and I always looked up to my brother, the one original family link remaining.*

Joe, even as a young boy, seemed to understand that his responses to people had creative power. He reacted with a safeness and likability that made him loved, very popular, and a favorite with everyone. I love this about him; his sense of humor, shared freely even in serious discussions, disarmed a person of any contentious direction and instead, lightened and warmed you with fondness.

Joe was gifted with ambition, dreams, intelligence, athleticism, handsomeness, determination, and vision, making the way for his success in whatever he chose to do. He seemed loaded with lucky endings, even if it took a while to get there. I asked him how that came about. His answer was, "I turn over more stones."

Lightning Source UK Ltd.
Milton Keynes UK
UKHW010214081020
371205UK00006B/81